The Norway Campaign
and the
Rise of Churchill
1940

Dedicated to the memory of my father Harold Dix
who was sent with the North Western Expeditionary Force
to Norway in 1940
and thankfully returned safe and sound.
It is also respectfully dedicated to
the memory of all those who did not return.

Lieutenant Colonel H.A.G. Dix
Royal Army Ordnance Corps

The Norway Campaign and the
Rise of Churchill
1940

Anthony Dix

Pen & Sword
MILITARY

First published in Great Britain in 2014
and republished in this format in 2022 by
PEN AND SWORD MILITARY
an imprint of
Pen and Sword Books Ltd
Yorkshire – Philadelphia

Copyright © Anthony Dix, 2014, 2022

ISBN 978 1 39902 270 5

The right of Anthony Dix to be identified as the author of this work has been
asserted by him in accordance with the Copyright, Designs and Patents Act 1988.

A CIP record for this book is available from the British Library.

Typeset in Times by CHIC GRAPHICS
Printed and bound in the UK by CPI Group (UK) Ltd, Croydon, CR0 4YY

Pen & Sword Books Limited incorporates the imprints of After the Battle,
Atlas, Archaeology, Aviation, Discovery, Family History, Fiction, History,
Maritime, Military, Military Classics, Politics, Select, Transport, True Crime,
Air World, Frontline Publishing, Leo Cooper, Remember When, Seaforth
Publishing, The Praetorian Press, Wharncliffe Local History, Wharncliffe
Transport, Wharncliffe True Crime and White Owl.

For a complete list of Pen & Sword titles please contact

PEN & SWORD BOOKS LIMITED
47 Church Street, Barnsley, South Yorkshire, S70 2AS, England
E-mail: enquiries@pen-and-sword.co.uk
Website: www.pen-and-sword.co.uk
or
PEN AND SWORD BOOKS
1950 Lawrence Rd, Havertown, PA 19083, USA
E-mail: Uspen-and-sword@casematepublishers.com
Website: www.penandswordbooks.com

Contents

Maps

Fig. 1. Map of Scandinavia.

Fig. 2. The Finnish Campaign, 1939/40.

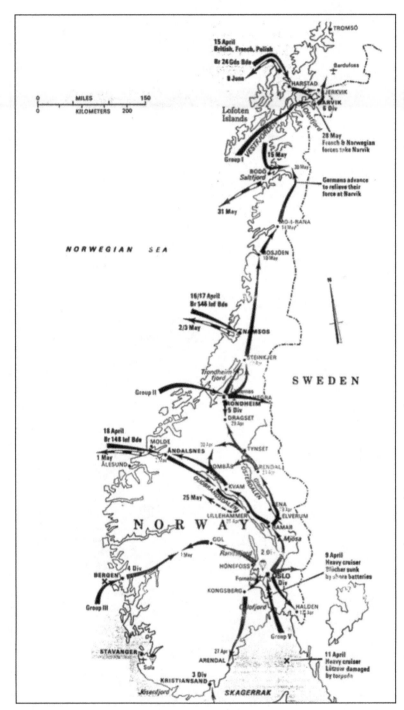

Fig. 3. General Map of Invasion.

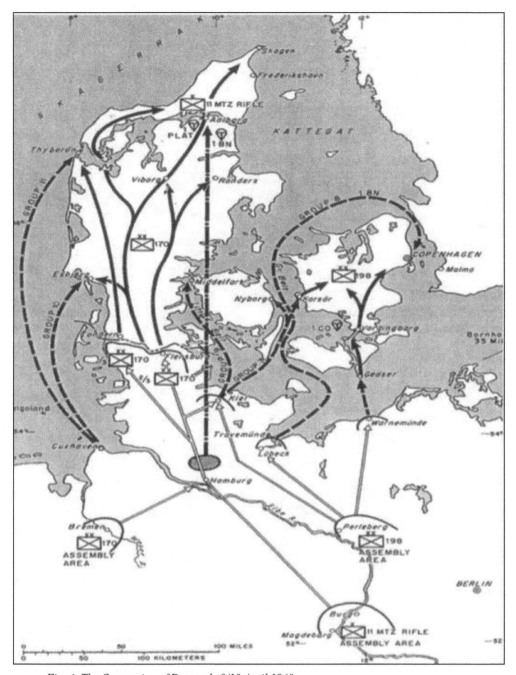

Fig. 4. The Occupation of Denmark, 9/10 April 1940.

Fig. 5. The Western Front.

Photographs

The author gratefully acknowledges the sources listed of the following photographs.

1. Chamberlain's War Cabinet 1939. *Imperial War Museum*
2. First Cruiser Squadron off Norwegian Coast. *National Museum Royal Navy*
3. HM destroyer *Bedouin* in Narvik Fjord. *National Museum Royal Navy*
4. HM destroyer *Eskimo* after bows blown off. Narvik Fjord. *National Museum Royal Navy*
5. General Ruge appointed Norwegian commander. *Imperial War Museum*
6. Norwegian ski troops in action. *Imperial War Museum*
7. German troops taking cover in Valdres uplands. *Imperial War Museum*
8. The Gudbrandsdahl at Kvam. *Epsom Print Centre*
9. British troops search ruins of Namsos for survivors. *Imperial War Museum*
10. View of burning ship through port hole. Namsos Fjord. *National Museum Royal Navy*
11. Troops of 24th (Guards) Brigade land at Harstad. *South Wales Borderers Regt. Museum*
12. British anti-aircraft battery at Harstad. Puffers in background *Imperial War Museum*
13. The French Foreign Legion at Bjerkvik with Hotchkiss tank. *Imperial War Museum*
14. The final prize – Narvik (Luftwaffe photo). *Imperial War Museum*
15. HMS *Glorious* in happier times. *National Museum Royal Navy*
16. French and Polish troops on their way back to Britain. *National Museum Royal Navy*

Acknowledgements

First and foremost my heartfelt thanks are due to my daughter Bettina who is responsible for producing the drafts of this short history. She has put in many hours correcting the text for which I am duly grateful and I could never have typed out the first drafts without her patient guidance. I would also thank my wife Ellen for checking the final manuscript and for consistent support over the years.

My thanks are also due to numerous individuals who have helped along the way such as Commander Neil Murray RN, the staff at the Imperial War Museum, the Museum of the Royal Navy, the curators of the War Museum in Oslo and Narvik and various booksellers such as Jason of Camden Lock Books who were able to obtain out of print texts for me. I would also like to thank Ann Douglas for advising me on publishing and Susan Smyth and the staff at the Print Centre [Epsom Ltd] for their consistently high standards. I would like to thank most sincerely my publishers, Pen and Sword Books, in particular Matt Jones and my editor, Irene Moore.

I would also like to thank the following publishers who have graciously given permission to print short extracts from the following publications:

Aschhoug Oslo, *Field Diary*, General O. Ruge
A P A Publications, *Insight Guides to Denmark, Norway, Sweden and Finland*
The Crowood Press, *Norway 1940 The Forgotten Fiasco*, J. Kynoch
Her Majesty's Stationery Office,
    Rise and Fall of the German Air Force, Air Ministry
    Grand Strategy, J. Butler
    The Campaign in Norway, T.K. Derry
    House of Commons Debates, Hansard
    British Intelligence, F.H. Hinsley
    Economic Blockade, W. Medlicott
    The War at Sea, S. Roskill
    The Royal Air Force 1939/45, Richards & Saunders
    British Foreign Policy, L. Woodward
    Britain & Norway in the Second World War, P. Salmon
Hodder & Stoughton, *Engage the Enemy More Closely*, C. Barnett
Harper Collins, *Norway 1940*, F. Kersaudy
Methuen, *The Norway Campaign*, J. Moulton
Orion Publishing, *Norway 1940*, B. Ash
    Downing Street Diaries, J. Colville
    Diaries of Sir A. Cadogan, D. Dilks

Oxford University Press, *Norway and the War 1939/40*, M. Curtis
Pen & Sword, *The Carrier Glorious*, J. Winton
Regimental Trustees
 The South Wales Borderers, J. Adams
 The Irish Guards, J. Fitzgerald
 The Scots Guards 1919-1955, D. Erskine
 The Doomed Expedition, J. Adams
Time Warner Books, *Hitler's Naval War*, C. Bekker
Chief of Military History US Army, *The German Theatre of Operations*, E.F.
 Ziemke
Yale University Press, *Five Days in London 1940*, J. Lucaks

A more comprehensive bibliography of books which I have found invaluable is listed at the end of this publication. In many cases the copyright has expired and the authors have long since shuffled off this mortal coil. I would nevertheless like to express my deepest gratitude to all those who have gone before and who have shed light on this important subject.

Anthony Dix

Introduction

A personal note

Setting out to write a book is like setting out on an adventure. You don't quite know where it is going to lead, and there are events along the way which had not previously crossed your mind. One of my passions is reading, my special interest being European history. I am an unrepentant romantic and am still inspired by battles and heroes, I would rather read an account of the Crusades than a study of the incidence of the Black Death in a medieval English village. My family background may have had something to do with it. My grandfather, a professional soldier, had been blinded in the second battle of Ypres and my boyhood was filled with stories of snakes and monkeys in India and life in the trenches. Each one of us is the product of a unique generation. In my case I first became conscious of contemporary events in 1939. I used to read the *Picture Post* avidly each week and there were usually pictures of Hitler and Stalin invariably smiling. With the streets full of men in uniform the war was an all-embracing subject. In 1940 things really started to change. First my father was sent on the Norway expedition, from which thankfully he returned, and this was followed by the drama of the Battle of Britain glimpses of which I saw.

In a long life I have made several attempts at authorship and at an early age concluded that I had little creative talent. I am better suited to the plodding nature of trying to write history. My first serious attempt was a biography of Franz Joseph, the penultimate Austro-Hungarian Emperor, whom I became interested in while working as a trainee in a bank in Vienna in the Fifties. It was too slipshod and poorly researched to reach publication but it did make me realize that I had made two strategic errors. First, it is more judicious to pick a subject of short duration such as The Battle of Britain rather than the life of a man like the Emperor Franz Joseph who was called to the throne in 1848 and reigned until 1916. Secondly, it was all very well being able to speak day-to-day German but to try and read through academic texts in High German, printed in Gothic script is an entirely different kettle of fish. Some years later I derived some satisfaction from the reception of a pamphlet entitled 'Britain's Forgotten Army' on the subject of the size of the prison population, written for the Social Democrats. More recently, a short account of a voyage round Britain in my small yacht has given pleasure to a number of my friends.

I had been considering the subject of Norway for a long time. When I finally embarked upon the project I had no idea that I should still be working on it ten years later. One of the best motives for writing a book is to have an emotional or personal interest. My father had been a London stockbroker before the war and he and all his five partners volunteered on the first day of the war. He was soon commissioned in the Ordnance Corps and shipped off to Harstad. Although non-combatant, the Second World War was the first major conflict in which there was no front line. On his safe return he did not speak about it much but there is little doubt that he had experienced being heavily bombed. Even as a small boy I noticed that he returned a quieter and more reserved person.

The more that I have looked into the subject, the more I have considered Norway to be worthwhile. First of all it was not a wild venture from either the German or the Allied point of view. Hitler's invasion of Norway was part of an integral plan for his offensive in the West. Second it is part of the essential fabric of the first ten months of the war. The Winter War in Finland and the shattering denouement in France were all part of it. I became fascinated by the effect that the debacle in Norway had on domestic politics which led to Winston Churchill's rise to power. As regards essential background information, I would advise readers to look at the appendices at the end of the book first.

A note on sources
If you mention the campaign in Norway to even an average well-read person, as often as not they will give you a puzzled look. Nevertheless there is a huge amount of material available. I started out by looking at some original source material in the Public Records Office and have made use of Hansard's reports of Parliamentary debates. Original sources have been so well mined that it is more a question of cutting down on the material available than trying to discover something new. This work is therefore almost entirely derived from secondary sources.

Professional historians have rightly seized upon the subject as it is crucial to an understanding of the first year of the war. Moreover extensive research has been done not only in Britain, Norway and Germany but also in France and the United States. For example a French professor, Francois Kersaudy, the author of one of the best single volume texts *Norway 1940* writes in English and speaks Norwegian. Here I have been at a disadvantage as I speak no Norwegian despite visiting the country and meeting many friendly and hospitable people. This has disbarred me from reading such essential books as General Ruge's *Field Diary*.

The Norwegians have now produced a monumental official history of the war which will remain a closed book to me. Geirr Haarr, a professional historian, has just produced two volumes *The German Invasion of Norway* and *The Battle of Norway 1940*, published by Pen & Sword. These must now be regarded as the definitive work. The flow of publications on the subject shows no sign of drying up.

I have not sought to interview individuals who took part in the campaign. Even when I set out to write this short account they were a diminishing band of old men. In earlier years one has met a number of people who were involved and they invariably came up with an anecdote or two. My father used to recall that he was sitting in an air raid shelter in Harstad when he realized that the RNVR officer opposite, also white with fear, was a fellow he had worked with in the Stock Exchange. The latter told him that the following night the officers on his destroyer were having a guest night; 'would he care to come?' During dinner the destroyer, which kept under way, was bombed and all hell broke loose upstairs. Those officers, not called away to action stations, appeared to be unconcerned and continued to sip their port, while discussing the prospects for the season's salmon fishing in Scotland. All my father wanted to do, he said, was to put his head under the table.

Since this book is written for the English reader, as regards sources, pride of place must be given to Professor Derry's *Official History of the Campaign in Norway* published by HMSO. He was professor of Scandinavian studies at London University and a fluent Norwegian speaker. As far as the war at sea is concerned there were other Allied ships involved but the massive preponderance was British. The best single volume is that written by Captain Macintyre simply entitled *Narvik*. I have found Correlli Barnett's *Engage the Enemy More Closely* useful, but it is about the war at sea generally. If I had to give a prize for the best general read, I would award it to Professor Kersaudy; he more than anyone else inspired me to study the political crisis in April/May 1940. A most fascinating book on Churchill's rise to power is *Five days in London, May 1940* by John Lukacs published in 1999.

Most of the books written by Free French and Polish soldiers have been translated into English and I have made some use of these. I am aware that some of my countrymen actually enjoy fighting and have since learned that some Frenchmen and Poles positively revelled in it. The largest number of Allied casualties were British which is one reason for using mainly English sources. Another reason is that I am writing primarily for the British public who are, so to speak, interested in what our boys did.

In general I find battles difficult to explain and even harder to make interesting. Colonel Jack Adams in *The Doomed Expedition* published in 1989 not only makes battles come alive, but he actually took part in some of them. Years ago a veteran of the campaign in Burma said to me: 'You can always tell a book written by someone who was not actually there.' I have therefore made extensive use of Regimental histories. Finally I loved the earthy comments of Jo Kynoch in his book *Norway 1940*. The sub title is *The Forgotten Fiasco*. Let us make sure that the campaign is never forgotten.

Anthony Dix
Epsom 2012

About the Author

Anthony Dix was born in Surrey in 1930 and educated at Tonbridge School. National Service took him to Nyasaland where he served with the King's African Rifles. In 1956 he was called to the bar as a member of Lincoln's Inn and in later life took the University of London B.Sc [Econ] as an external student. In 1964 he contested the South Kensington constituency for the Liberal Party and in 1974 fought Bridlington for Labour. For three years he was a Labour councillor on Merton Borough Council. He served for a number of years on the Board of Visitors of Wandsworth Prison and also as a Justice of the Peace on the Wimbledon Bench. He earned a living as a stockbroker for over fifty years. For many years he and his wife and three daughters lived in Wimbledon before he and his wife retired to Epsom.

The author in his yacht leaving Scapa Flow, the Orkney Islands, 2010.

Chapter 1

Disarmament, pacifism, rearmament and appeasement

The die was cast in 1931. In effect this was the start of nine years of Conservative rule in which events relevant to the drama of 1940 occurred and of which the Norwegian adventure formed a part. It was also the period in which most of the public figures in Britain involved came to prominence [see Appendix I]. The Wall Street Crash had occurred in October 1929 and the next eighteen months saw the western world slide into a recession with cumulative effect causing awesome unemployment figures. As a result of the financial crisis, in the summer of 1931 Ramsay MacDonald, Prime Minister of a minority Labour government, was induced to form a National government with Tory support. Within months there was a general election. The Conservatives played the patriotic card. Had we not just had two years of Labour government? What was needed was a National coalition with a Tory majority and in October 1931 this is exactly what happened.

The coalition returned 472 members which included the former Lloyd George National Liberals led by the distinguished advocate Sir John Simon. The remnants of Asquith's Liberals remained outside the coalition. The election also devastated the rump of the Labour Party which remained outside the coalition. Only thirteen Labour members flying the National colours were returned, nevertheless their leader MacDonald was again invited to form a government with Stanley Baldwin, the leader of the Conservative Party as his right-hand man. Neville Chamberlain was appointed Chancellor of the Exchequer and it was to him that Baldwin was to increasingly turn.

The year was also that in which Winston Churchill broke irrevocably with Baldwin, an event which Anthony Eden described as one of the greatest political tragedies of the Thirties. The specific issue was the India Bill. It was based on Sir John Simon's comprehensive report advocating Home Rule for India. Opposition to the Bill was led by Winston Churchill. To him the British Empire was sacred and India was the jewel in the imperial crown. By the time that the

1

Bill had reached the committee stage, Churchill had made sixty-eight speeches opposing it. Its eventual passage was a triumph for Samuel Hoare, the Secretary of State for India. It was a disaster for Churchill and the first and last time that he had thrown himself into the arms of the Tory right wing. He even managed to antagonize Leo Amery.

In considering defence expenditure in the inter-war years it is essential to distinguish between disarmament, pacifism and rearmament. In 1918 Britain had much the largest navy in the world. By the end of the Great War Haig's sixty divisions, battle hardened and well equipped, were regarded by the Germans as their most formidable adversary. It is all very well criticising governments in the Twenties for cutting down on defence expenditure, but Britain was also deeply in debt to the United States and effectively bankrupt.

The choice for Britain was simple. We could afford to maintain a large navy or a large army, but not both. In peacetime Britain had traditionally maintained a large navy and a small professional army. There was thus a return to this policy. Two reports produced in the Twenties by Sir Eric Geddes in 1922 had called for massive reductions in the Army and Navy estimates, the notorious Geddes Axe. Even Churchill's record was not entirely lily-white. One of his last acts as Chancellor of the Exchequer in the Baldwin government had been to reaffirm what was known as the Ten Year Rule under which defence planning was based on the assumption that no major war would threaten within ten years.

A new situation was created by expenditure required for the air force. A new and devastating factor in any future war would be the destruction of cities from the air. Thus if the army became the Cinderella of the armed forces it was only because of the priority given to the other two services. As it turned out Britain was hard put to keep pace with the other two naval powers Japan and the United States. As compared with the miserable performance of France, Britain did succeed in building up a small but credible air force.

A key theme in setting up the League of Nations under the Treaty of Versailles had been disarmament but despite good intentions the Disarmament Conference in 1927 failed because France demanded that security should precede disarmament. A further disarmament conference failed in 1932 because Germany, which had been admitted to the League of Nations in 1926, now demanded the same equality in armaments which she had achieved in almost all other fields.

The last disarmament conference was called in January 1933 after Adolf Hitler came to power. He asked beguilingly, that the other European powers should reduce their armaments to Germany's level, or that she should be allowed to rearm on the same basis as the other powers. The French refused to reduce their army and the British refused to reduce their navy. In October 1933 the Germans gave notice of their withdrawal from the conference and intended resignation from the League of Nations. This marked the end of collective security as worked out under the Locarno Pact of 1925 when Germany and France had entered into a pact of non-aggression and the Franco-German border was defined and guaranteed by Britain and Germany.

In the inter-war years there was a strong pacifist movement throughout Europe. This was expressed in a flood of literature of an anti-war tenor, for example Vera Brittain's *Testament of Youth*. There was also the steady march of socialist parties in all European countries, all renouncing war to a greater or lesser extent. In 1933 the Oxford Union passed a motion 'that this House will in no circumstances fight for King and Country'. This was widely reported in the international press most significantly in France, the United States and Germany. There was fortunately, beyond the pampered confines of Oxford colleges, a more numerous and robust breed of young man. For example Geoff Armstrong, then serving an apprenticeship in his family printing firm recalls that 'when we heard about it we said to hell with Oxford' – or words to that effect.

Churchill had begun his warnings of the danger of disarmament as early as May 1932. In February 1934 he gave Parliament a lurid account of what an air attack on London might mean. Replying for the National government, Baldwin pledged 'that in air strength, this country shall no longer be in a position inferior to any country within striking distance of these shores.' In July 1934 the government announced a programme that within five years the RAF would be increased to forty-one squadrons of first line strength. Both the Liberals and Labour opposed the measure. In June 1935 MacDonald was succeeded by Stanley Baldwin. Ironically almost the last act of MacDonald, the apostle of peace, was to publish a White Paper stating that Britain must put its defences in order. Additional expenditure on the armaments of the three Defence Services could no longer be safely postponed.

The only serious crisis with which Baldwin had to deal was over Abyssinia. Having repulsed the Italians at the turn of the century, Abyssinia was one of the few independent states in Africa. In seeking to add this jewel to its imperial crown, Italy was only acting as most European nations, and Britain in particular, had acted throughout the nineteenth century. By the Thirties, however attitudes towards imperialism had altered. It was thought that the imposition of economic sanctions would deter Mussolini, but the French were lukewarm about antagonizing the Italians and Britain too was keen on pursuing a general policy of friendship towards Italy. In Paris a backstairs deal was struck between Sir Samuel Hoare and the French Prime Minister, Pierre Laval, whereby it was agreed that neither Britain nor France would intervene. The political reaction in Britain was much sharper than Baldwin had anticipated. In a debate in the House, Clement Attlee, the Labour leader made it an issue of 'the honour of this country'. The government won the debate but Baldwin's reputation was never quite the same and he only saved himself by sacrificing Sam Hoare. In his place Anthony Eden was appointed Foreign Secretary. In May 1936 Mussolini announced the incorporation of Abyssinia into the Italian empire.

It is ironic that both Franklin D. Roosevelt and Adolf Hitler should have come to power in 1933 with effectively a new deal for their respective countries, but whereas Roosevelt had massive popular support, Hitler at first had to devote himself to consolidating his position. He proceeded to suspend all other political parties and shortly had his political rivals within the National Socialist party, murdered on 'the night of the long knives'. His larger ambitions included the complete reversal of the terms of the Treaty of Versailles and the return of Germany's colonies together with an ill-defined expansion of Germany in Eastern Europe. In order to realize these larger aims he proceeded pragmatically taking any opportunity that presented itself.

There is little doubt that Hitler took note of the impotence of The League of Nations over Abyssinia. In March 1936 German troops marched into the demilitarized zone of the Rhineland. The German general staff expected the French to respond militarily; nothing happened. Hitler then started the blandishments, with which the world was to become so familiar, along the lines 'we have no further territorial demands to make in Europe'. Several consequences flowed from the remilitarization of the Rhineland as far as Britain was concerned. First the government, owing much to Chamberlain's insistence, brought forward a White Paper outlining further expansion of the armed forces. One of the failures of the Baldwin government in the defence field had been the failure to set up a thoroughgoing Ministry of Supply. When he appointed a mediocrity, Sir Thomas Inskip as Minister for the co-ordination of defence, they were saying in the Parliamentary lobbies that it was the most bizarre appointment since Caligula made his horse a Proconsul. The second consequence was that the Labour Party, hitherto opposed to rearmament, began a series of agonizing internal debates.

It was the outbreak of the Spanish Civil War in July 1936 which transformed the attitude of liberals in general and many socialists. General Franco had led a revolt against the Republican government, which enjoyed the support of socialists, anarchists, and communists. Passions ran high. Volunteers from all over Europe and beyond flocked to join the socialist International Brigades. Benito Mussolini sent several divisions of the Italian army to support Franco. The Germans sent the Condor Legion, a thinly disguised unit of the Luftwaffe. In Britain there was a sea change with the left becoming the war party while the Conservatives, in the main, preferred to pursue a policy of non-intervention. Russia actively aided the Republicans and Leon Blum's *Front Populaire*, composed of socialists and communists was broadly sympathetic to the

Republicans. It was the lack of preparation by France for what could so easily have developed into a general European war that held her back from intervention.

In May 1937, following his adroit handling of the Abdication Crisis, Baldwin had handed over to Neville Chamberlain, his natural successor. The latter differed from Baldwin in that he was much more pro-active particularly in foreign policy. He genuinely believed that the way to preserve peace in Europe was to talk personally with the dictators. Appeasement was widely believed to be the best policy. Chamberlain tended to rule through an inner coterie consisting of Lord Halifax, Sir John Simon, Chancellor of the Exchequer, and Sam Hoare, back as Home Secretary. Anthony Eden continued as Foreign Secretary but was not part of the magic circle.

If anybody doubts the ability of civil servants to influence statesmen, they should study the case of Sir Horace Wilson, who enjoyed the title of Chief Industrial Advisor to the government. He had first attracted Chamberlain's attention at the Ottawa Trade Conference in 1932. He has been described as hard working, self-controlled, never rushed, quick to master documents, always ready to play for safety, and to find the soothing formula which each party would accept. Chamberlain used to go for a walk with him in St James's Park. There is little doubt that his views on foreign policy strongly influenced the Prime Minister.

Another key civil servant was Sir Alexander Cadogan. Chamberlain had removed Sir Robert Vansittart, permanent head of the Foreign Office, who was anti-German and pro-French and appointed Cadogan in his place. Fortunately for us the latter kept a diary, so we have a fairly clear idea where he stood on most issues. Like so many servants, he was not above criticizing his political masters. He once described Kingsley Wood as a 'mutton head'.

The first casualty of Chamberlain's personal diplomacy was Anthony Eden who had been criticized in the German press. The previous November Chamberlain had sent Halifax on an unofficial visit to Berlin, rather than his Foreign Secretary. When the Abyssinian crisis broke Chamberlain thought it best to become reconciled with Italy and behind Eden's back entered into talks with Count Grandi, the Italian ambassador. The main point at issue was the withdrawal of Italian troops from Spain which Eden thought should have been a precondition for talks. Chamberlain's cavalier treatment of his Foreign Secretary, resulted in Eden's sensational resignation. Shortly afterwards, Chamberlain appointed Lord Halifax whose support for appeasement was, contrary to popular belief, by no means unreserved. R.A. Butler was appointed as his number two and the two men, although never close, worked well together. The appeasement label was to dog Butler all his life, despite his frantic efforts later, when Churchill had come to power, which even extended to doctoring his diary.

In March 1938 the all-German state of Austria was invaded by a token force of German troops and Adolf Hitler, the local boy made good, drove into Vienna to a tumultuous welcome from eighty per cent of the population. Looking at the map it was obvious that Hitler would seek to incorporate Czechoslovakia into the Reich. Europe did not have long to wait. In September 1938 Hitler demanded that the Sudetenland, the northern part of Czechoslovakia inhabited by three million Germans, should be ceded to Germany. It was then that Chamberlain took the initiative and telegraphed Hitler offering to fly out to southern Germany and visit him at Berchtesgaden. This took the wind out of Hitler's sails who remarked to a subordinate 'but I cannot let that old man come all this way to see me, I will go to London'. In the event Hitler was dissuaded and Chamberlain paid him a visit at Berchtesgaden and later at Godesberg on the Rhine.

This led to the final meeting in Munich when Chamberlain was accompanied by Sir Horace Wilson. They met Hitler together with Daladier, the French Prime Minister, and Mussolini. The latter famously remarked that the English contingent gave the impression of being 'the tired sons of successful businessmen'. At Munich, without so much as bringing the Czechs into the meeting, Hitler got all he had asked for. After the meeting Chamberlain produced a document which both men signed by which they resolved to pursue the consultative method in future: 'symbolic of the desire of our two peoples never to go to war with one another again.' This was the infamous scrap of paper that Chamberlain waived at reporters at Heston Airport on his return.

From 3/6 October 1938 the Commons debated the Munich agreement. Attlee said it was one of Britain's greatest diplomatic defeats... 'a gallant and democratic people had been betrayed and handed over to a ruthless despotism'. Churchill warned the House, 'this is the first foretaste of a bitter cup which will be proffered to us year by year, unless by a supreme recovery of moral health and martial vigour we arise again and take our stand for freedom as in olden time'. A vast majority of Conservative MPs supported the Prime Minister with enthusiasm; the rest of the nation breathed a sigh of relief. The only heavyweight minister to resign was Duff Cooper, the First Lord of the Admiralty and previously the Secretary of State for War.

Historians will debate until the end of time whether Chamberlain, backed by Halifax, Hoare and Simon was right to give appeasement a try. Chamberlain genuinely believed at the time that it might work. Had we not eliminated one option after another, he asked. Collective Security and the League of Nations? Let us not be tied to a corpse. Alliances? Let us not forget 1914 [when Europe was divided into two armed camps]. Isolation? An empty dream. The opposition policy of arms for Republican Spain, sanctions against Japan, standing up to dictators? War then on three fronts and war before we are ready. Chamberlain certainly did not agree to the Munich terms for the sole purpose of giving Britain another year in which to rearm. As it turned out this was the one tangible benefit to emerge and Britain continued to rearm with vigour.

The policy of appeasement came to an abrupt halt when the Germans overran the rest of Czechoslovakia in March 1939. Even so the possibility of appeasement lingered on as a remote option even during the first winter of the war. For Chamberlain, the annexation of Czechoslovakia was a personal and political blow from which he never really recovered. Chamberlain was a man of puritanical commercial principles, who believed that once you had given your word, to break it was not only a breach of trust but also a mortal sin. Nevertheless, there was no real challenge to his leadership within the party and the opposition from Labour and the Liberals counted for little.

Probably the best organized opposition group within the Tory Party was the Eden group or as the Tory whips dubbed them 'the glamour boys' on account of Anthony Eden's good looks and sartorial elegance. There were about thirty of them including Alfred Duff Cooper, Leo Amery and Harold Macmillan. No Conservative newspaper supported them and Tory Central Office made life distinctly uncomfortable for them in their constituencies. A significant cross party group of dissidents in the winter of 1939/40 was to develop under the leadership of Clement Davies, later leader of the Liberal Party. It was made up of Liberal MPs such as Sir Archibald Sinclair, some National Liberals and Labour MPs such as Attlee and Arthur Greenwood. Churchill did not belong to any specific group, rather he stood like a lonely rock, his political views promulgated through newspaper articles, broadcasts and books besides his unrivalled oratory in the House of Commons.

Churchill's political following was nurtured through endless dinner parties in London. The nearest he came to having a political group of his own was the 'Other Luncheon Club', frequented by the likes of Violet Bonham Carter, daughter of Herbert Asquith, the Liberal Prime Minister in 1914, who despite her brilliant oratory and dominant position in the old Liberal Party, never succeeded in getting a seat in Parliament. Another member of the Other Club was Bob Boothby, a rumbustious young Tory MP with a voice not dissimilar in tone from that of Churchill. Loyally supported by his wife Clementine, the Churchills held court at Chartwell. Anybody who might be of use to him was invited. General Ironside, the future Chief of the Imperial Staff and an old Boer War acquaintance recalls how one weekend he and Churchill sat up drinking whisky until five in the morning. Harold Macmillan was staying at Chartwell when the Abyssinian crisis broke. Churchill was immediately galvanized into action, calling for maps, putting through telephone calls and demanding information as to the precise position of Britain's Mediterranean fleet. Macmillan recalls: 'I shall always have a picture of that spring day and the sense of power and energy, the great flow of action which came from Churchill although he then held no public office. He alone seemed to be in command when everyone else was dazed and hesitating.'

Let us return to the situation in Central Europe. Hitler was deeply imbued with the world as he had known it as a young man. Czechoslovakia had been created out of the former provinces of Bohemia, Moravia and Slovenia, all part of the Austro-Hungarian Empire and all part of the ancient German Reich. Hitler had now reincorporated these three provinces once again into his Third Reich. The ancient kingdom of Poland had never been part of the Reich, but in the late eighteenth century had been partitioned between Prussia, Russia and Austro-Hungary.

When Poland was recreated as an independent state under the Treaty of Versailles a corridor between East and West Prussia was allotted to Poland in order to give her an outlet to the sea at Danzig. This ancient free city, like so many Eastern European cities, had been built up by German merchants and settlers. In 1939 Danzig even had a mayor who was a Nazi sympathizer. It could hardly have come as a surprise to informed opinion in the West when, in March 1939 Joachim von Ribbentrop, by now German Foreign Minister, placed demands before the Polish ambassador for the cession of Danzig to Germany and amendments to the Polish corridor. On 31 March Chamberlain announced to the House that in the event of any action which threatened Polish independence, 'His Majesty's Government would feel themselves bound at once to lend the Polish government all support in their power.' While this would be perfectly clear to an Englishman, a German might well have interpreted it as meaning that the British could always wriggle out of it, if it came to the crunch. Most significantly, the French joined in this guarantee.

Unlike a totalitarian regime, in Britain matters of importance have to be debated in Parliament. This may well have encouraged the German leader to think that he could get away with it once more. In the debate that followed in April Lloyd George said, 'I cannot understand why before committing ourselves...we did not secure beforehand the adhesion of Russia...we have undertaken a frightful gamble'. The gamble became all too evident when in 1939, Ribbentrop announced a Russo-German agreement providing for a mutual non-aggression pact for ten years and that neither country would join a third party in war against the other. This monumental act of appeasement by the Russians was to cost them dear eighteen months later, although after Hitler's fulminations against Bolshevism, they took steps to rearm with vigour.

On 1 September German troops crossed the Polish frontier. On 3 September Britain declared war on Germany. On the same day the Cabinet was reorganized to include a smaller War Cabinet. An offer was made to the Labour Party to form a coalition, but they refused to serve under Chamberlain, nevertheless the latter retained the confidence of the majority of his party for the time being. The War Cabinet consisted of Sir Samuel Hoare as Privy Seal, Sir John Simon, Chancellor of the Exchequer and Lord Halifax as Foreign Secretary. It included the three service ministers. Sir Kingsley Wood remained Secretary of State for Air. Leslie Hore-Belisha who had been at the War Office for eighteen months and had displayed considerable courage in introducing conscription in peacetime, remained, but was replaced by Oliver Stanley in January 1940.

The most significant appointment was Winston Churchill as First Lord of the Admiralty. It was a deft move on Chamberlain's part; Churchill would have been far too dangerous a critic to leave out. Why not appoint him to the Admiralty which he had administered with such vigour and imagination between 1913 and 1915? Churchill for his part was delighted to have a specific ministry in which he could demonstrate his very considerable administrative talents. Before the war he had been seen by many in the London political elite as an adventurer, and in the Conservative Party as a turncoat. Many recalled his leaving the Tory Party at the start of his parliamentary career and then ratting on the Liberals in the Twenties. At best he was regarded as a delightful rogue, but lacking in political judgment! At worst he was seen as unscrupulous, unreliable and ambitious. Such powerful figures as Queen Elizabeth, the late Queen Mother, regarded him as brash and, it is said, disliked him. To the considerable pacifist element in the Labour and Liberal parties he was regarded as a warmonger.

Lord Hankey was appointed as Minister without Portfolio on account of the unrivalled knowledge that he had gained as Secretary to Lloyd George's War Cabinet. As late as May 1940 he could write to Sam Hoare saying, 'God help the country which commits its existence to the hands of a dictator [a shrewd assessment of Churchill] whose past achievements [no doubt he had Gallipoli in mind] even though inspired by a certain amount of imagination, have never achieved success'. He was to serve in the same capacity with distinction throughout the war and along with many others lived to modify his view of Churchill.

The War Cabinet also included Lord Chatfield, an erudite Admiral of the Fleet who served as chairman of the Military Co-Ordination Committee, which stood between the War Cabinet and the all-important Chiefs of Staff Committee. The Military Co-ordinating Committee consisted of the three Chiefs of Staff and the three service Ministers: Kingsley Wood, Hore-Belisha and Churchill. As the senior minister, Churchill would often take the chair if Lord Chatfield were absent. The latter resigned in March 1940 and was not replaced. The system had never been wholly satisfactory. As Churchill was later to write, 'The committee's deliberations consisted of a copious flow of polite conversation leading to a tactful report'. A slightly different view was expressed by

Chamberlain: 'Churchill in his enthusiasms put more intense pressure on his advisers than he realised and reduced them to silent acquiescence.'

There were other problems. There was a failure to integrate the three services at the executive level. All three services were governed by a body which included civilians. The army was governed by the Army Council. It included Hore-Belisha, able, but like so many politicians, worrying what tomorrow's newspapers would say, also the elderly General Ironside, Chief of the Imperial General Staff who, while one of the youngest generals in the First World War, was one of the oldest in the Second. The Air Council included Kingsley Wood, the most able of the Service Ministers and Air Marshall Sir Cyril Newall whose record is beyond reproach. The First Sea Lord, Admiral Sir Dudley Pound's phlegmatic character exactly complemented his master's mercurial temperament.

This then completes a brief review of the crew with which the creaking ship of state sailed off into battle. The government in 1939 was not an entirely happy ship. Anthony Eden had been brought in as Secretary of State for the Dominions, a relatively minor post. Duff Cooper and Harold Macmillan remained out of office. Generally speaking the appeasers remained in power. With the exception of Churchill none of the leading men had ever heard a shot fired in anger let alone fired one themselves.

Chapter 2

Churchill at the Admiralty

A main theme of this short account of the Norwegian campaign is that, however inadequate the British land expedition may have been, the campaign at sea was a major one and on the whole successful for the Royal Navy. A feature of the Second World War was that the Navy had to move into top gear from day one. Winston Churchill, the First Lord of the Admiralty, did not spare himself. Within hours of his appointment he moved into a flat at the Admiralty and besides his arduous Cabinet duties he embarked on a rigorous administrative routine which included visits to ships, dockyards and naval bases all over the country. He worked seven days a week and barely paused for breath over Christmas 1939.

In the autumn of 1939, Churchill had to reinstate the convoy system which had been developed in the First World War. Surface raiders had to be constantly borne in mind, but much the most serious threat was from U-boats. The Germans scored two spectacular successes in the first few months of the war. The aircraft carrier *Courageous* was sunk in the Bristol Channel by a U-boat and even more spectacular, a U-boat penetrated the Home Fleet's main anchorage in Scapa Flow in the Orkney Islands and sank the battleship *Royal Oak*. Within months the Germans had launched the first of their secret weapons, the magnetic mine, laid at night by destroyers in British waters. This seriously disrupted coastal traffic until an antidote known as degaussing was developed. It was therefore with relief that the public were treated to a taste of success when two light cruisers and one heavy cruiser attacked the German pocket battleship *Graf Spee* in the South Atlantic inflicting sufficient damage to cause her to take refuge in Montevideo and later to scuttle herself.

One of the first tasks which the Admiralty had to address was the reinstatement of the blockade of enemy ports which had proved to a large extent effective between 1914 and 1918 despite the continuation of German imports through Holland and the Scandinavian countries. No blockade is ever going to be total. Closing the Dover Strait was simple, but closing the North Sea well-nigh impossible. Owing to the demands placed upon the Royal Navy, part of the blockade line from the Orkneys and Faroes to the Norwegian Coast was patrolled by armed merchantmen. The hazardous nature of these patrols is illustrated by what happened to the *Rawalpindi*, an armed merchantmen commanded by Lieutenant Commander Kennedy (the father of Ludovic Kennedy). On 23 November two fast modern battleships the *Scharnhorst* and her sister ship the *Gneisenau* suddenly appeared out of the blue. In accordance with naval tradition it was unthinkable that Kennedy should strike his colours and the *Rawalpindi* was shortly blown out of the water.

Between 1917 and 1918, the British and the Americans had constructed an expensive barrage of mines across the North Sea from the Orkneys to a point just south of Bergen. It was decided to revive this plan, but it still left a gap at the Norwegian end. An examination of an atlas shows that almost from the southerly tip of Norway right up to the North Cape, there is a continuous string of islands within Norwegian territorial waters. This inshore passage known as the Leads constituted a perfect rat run for merchant ships coming in from the Atlantic and bound for German ports, and also unofficially for U-boats.

As early as 19 September 1939 Churchill wrote a note to the First Sea Lord, Admiral Pound saying, 'I brought to the notice of the Cabinet the importance of stopping the Norwegian transport of Swedish ore from Narvik. I suggested that we laid a minefield across the three mile limit'. The Norwegian government had agreed to a similar arrangement in September 1918, but by then of course, Germany had been palpably beaten. Quite how sympathetic they would be at the beginning of the Second World War would remain doubtful. The problem of German imports of Swedish iron ore may be briefly summarised. Germany had few other sources of iron ore besides some domestic production. This remained the position until she overran the French ore fields in Lorraine in 1940. It was estimated that Germany would need to import nine million tons of ore from Sweden during the first year of the war.

The reason why Churchill's more general plan for a mining barrage across the North Sea was not pursued by the War Cabinet between 19 September and 19 November was that Britain was engaged in negotiating the all important agreement for chartering Norwegian mercantile tonnage and also a trade agreement with Sweden. On 19 November Churchill again propounded the idea of a northern barrage, which would have taken six months to complete and on 30 November this was agreed. What led to a change of policy was the new situation created by the outbreak of the Russo-Finnish War.

The more delicate question of mining the Leads remained an item of controversy. Halifax pointed out that any invasion of territorial waters would lead to German retaliation. Churchill thought that this would be beneficial in that it would open up the war. The Cabinet therefore asked the Chiefs of Staff to report on such military factors that would be involved in stopping the ore by either a naval force in Vestfjord, the approach to Narvik, or alternatively by mining part of the Leads, i.e. in Norwegian territorial waters.

Admiralty intelligence had learned that the Norwegian government was considering convoying ships of all nationalities within their own territorial waters. Churchill suggested to Halifax that in view of the risk of a clash between our patrol vessels and Norwegian escorting vessels it would be better to revert to the mine laying idea. Lord Halifax was ideally suited to the Foreign Office, a department well versed in the art of vacillation. The Foreign Office doubted the legality of the minefields which would affect the ships of all nationalities. Britain might be involved in a serious incident if the Norwegians started to sweep the mines and we tried to stop them. How might that have affected the loyalty of the Norwegian crews of the ships which Britain had so painstakingly chartered? On 16 December, Halifax asked the Cabinet to postpone its decision until the Chiefs of Staff had completed their report and as usual the Cabinet sided with Halifax.

The main Swedish iron ore deposits are in the Gällivare area of northern Sweden whence the ore is sent by rail down the Baltic coast to Lulea. In the five winter months rail deliveries continue to add to the stockpile at Lulea when the port is closed by ice. In winter ore continues to be sent on the single-track line through the mountains to the port of Narvik on the Atlantic coast which is open all the year round. Thus rail capacity was the governing factor in the amount shipped. There is also a smaller field at Grangesberg about 100 miles north of Stockholm, producing some five million tons of ore a year from the port of Oxelösund.

Later in December, the Joint Chiefs of Staff produced a more detailed report based on the conclusions reached by the Ministry of Economic Warfare. These conclusions were: first, that if exports from Narvik only were stopped, Germany could still obtain between nine to ten million tons of iron ore annually through the Baltic ports. Secondly, if the entire export of the northern field were stopped, Germany would be confined to the Grangesberg deposits which could only give her five million tons per annum. The ministry concluded that such a closure 'might well bring Germany to a standstill and would in any case have a profound effect on the duration of the war'.

Churchill had been quick to grasp the possibilities opened up by the Russian attack on Finland. On 30 November he reintroduced the idea of mining Norwegian territorial waters and forcing the ore ships out into the open sea where they could be sunk. His hand had been strengthened when naval intelligence reported that between 27 and 30 November three German ore ships had arrived in Narvik and four more had been sighted. Hitherto Lord Halifax had opposed this policy on the grounds that it would have meant carrying the war into neutral waters. Churchill therefore altered his proposal to capturing enemy ships under the blockade system rather than sinking them.

There remained Neville Chamberlain's worry about what the neutral countries, especially the USA, would think. Churchill had anticipated this and asked Joe Kennedy, the American ambassador and father of JFK, to ascertain what President Roosevelt's attitude might be. Roosevelt was facing a presidential election and it was a paramount political necessity to assure the public that 'no American boy would be sent to die on the European battlefields'. Churchill was happy therefore to be able to report to the Cabinet that the President's reactions were more favourable than he had hoped.

Churchill's hand was further strengthened on 15 December when he reported to the Cabinet that one Greek and two British vessels had been sunk by German U-boats within the three-mile limit. He again urged that minefields should be laid in selected parts of Norwegian territorial waters and he now suggested that in addition four or five destroyers should have authority to arrest all ore ships within Norwegian territorial waters. On 16 December, the indefatigable First Lord drew up yet another memorandum opening with a typical Churchillian fanfare. 'The effectual stoppage of Norwegian ore ranks as a major offensive... no other measure is open to us for many months to come which gives so good a chance of abridging the waste and destruction of the conflict...the ore from Lulea [on the Gulf of Bothnia] is already stopped by the ice...the ore from Narvik must be stopped by laying a series of small minefields. The ore from Oxelösund, the main ice-free port on the Baltic, south of Stockholm must also be prevented from leaving by methods which will be neither diplomatic nor military.'

Churchill's memorandum concluded by saying 'small nations must not tie our hands when we are fighting for their rights and freedom'. The Foreign Office agreed that we could not fight the war on the basis of allowing Germany to break all the laws while we tried to keep them. The memorandum was considered by the Cabinet on 22 December, but nothing was decided. The Chiefs of Staff were however instructed to consider the military implications of future commitments on Scandinavian soil. They were authorised to plan for landing a force at Narvik for the sake of Finland, and also to consider the military consequences of a German occupation of southern Norway.

Chapter 3

Scandinavian Neutrality

During the First World War there had been some debate among the Scandinavian countries as to whether or not they should join in. Their sympathies were in the main with the liberal democracies of England, France and the United States. In the event, Denmark, Norway and Sweden prudently decided to stay neutral. This does not mean to say that they were not affected by the war. All three suffered from shortages due to the British blockade. The Norwegians in particular, but also the other Scandinavian countries, lost ships on charter to the Allies, especially after 1917 when the Germans embarked on a policy of unrestricted U-boat warfare. On the outbreak of the Second World War, the Scandinavian countries decided to pursue the same policy of neutrality.

A complicating factor in 1939 was the fear of Bolshevik expansionism. When the Russians attacked Finland, the question arose, should the other Scandinavian countries go to the aid of Finland? Were they in a position to do so? All Scandinavian countries had supported The League of Nations and the concept of collective security. Before the war Denmark, Norway and Sweden had Social Democrat governments which had pursued policies of expenditure on social welfare but had been parsimonious towards defence. This applied less to Sweden and Finland which maintained credible armies.

In considering the capacity of the Scandinavian countries to defend themselves, the limiting factors were population and resources. The total population of Scandinavia in 1939 amounted to about 17 million people. Norway is about the size of Britain in area, but in 1939 she had a population of little more than 3 million. Much of the population is concentrated in the Oslo area and the relatively fertile farming area of south eastern Norway. The rest of the population is spread thinly along the fjords in small self-contained communities. In 1939 Sweden had a population under 7 million. Like Norway the population is largely concentrated in the south. In both countries much of the north is virtually uninhabitable. Denmark, although flat and universally cultivated, is much smaller in area and in 1939 supported a population of 3.5 million. Likewise in 1939 Finland's population only amounted to 3.6 million.

By 1939 all Scandinavian countries had industrialized up to a point. The Danish economy remained strongly agricultural. The Norwegian domestic economy was substantially supplemented by earnings from the fourth largest mercantile marine in the world. Fishing was not only a major industry but many of the inhabitants of the small farms clinging to the narrow shores of the fjords supplemented their earnings by fishing. Ship building and ship repair services are a natural corollary to ship-owning. One of the most remarkable developments in the inter-war years was the construction of the Norsk Hydro project in central Norway harnessing massive resources of hydro-electric power. Offshore oil had not then been discovered.

Both Norway and Sweden export base metals and in the case of Sweden, the biggest export is iron ore. Sweden, which accounts for nearly half of all the population of Scandinavia, had a more sophisticated economy, including such international corporations as Ericson, the telecommunication company, and some of the finest engineering companies in Europe. The Bofors anti-aircraft gun was adopted by the Royal Navy. Finland also had a small engineering industry. The common building material in Norway, Finland, and Sweden is timber which made the towns in Norway particularly vulnerable to incendiary attack from the air. Finland's main export today is still timber.

A crucial factor in the Europe of 1939/40 was the will to fight, something that the British did not wholly rediscover until Churchill came to power in 1940. With the exception of the Finns, the Scandinavians had not been involved in war since 1864. Despite a pan-Scandinavian movement in the nineteenth century, Sweden (which then included Norway) had failed to come to the assistance of Denmark when attacked by Bismarck's Prussia over claims to the Duchy of Schleswig Holstein. The pusillanimity of the Swedish government on that occasion had deeply shocked many Scandinavians, including Ibsen, the Norwegian playwright. On the other hand the Scandinavians had been wise not to intervene in the Great War of 1914-18. They would not have made much difference and they might have suffered a great deal. After 1918 there was a general revulsion against war in Europe and this was reflected in the political composition of the various Scandinavian governments.

In Denmark a general belief in disarmament prevailed and from 1929 to 1940 there was a coalition government of social liberals and social democrats. In April 1940 Denmark had only 14,000 men under arms, and two thirds of these were reservists. The Allies appreciated that Denmark fell within the German sphere of influence owing to her common border and the indefensible nature of her flat terrain. In the spring of 1939, Denmark was the only Scandinavian country to sign a non-aggression pact with Germany.

In the sixteenth and seventeenth centuries Sweden had a vigorous aristocracy and glorious military tradition. At the same time she developed a tradition of constitutional government and the rule of law. In the inter-war years the far right was hardly a factor. The government was drawn from the majority coalition of Social Democrats and Agrarians. Nevertheless a rearmament programme had been initiated in 1936 and by 1939 Sweden had 400,000 men under arms or in the reserve. This undoubtedly was a factor which the Germans took into account when considering action in Scandinavia. It did not alter the fact that the Swedish armed forces were desperately short of artillery and anti-tank guns but which Sweden had the capacity to produce. Sweden did have some 700 tanks and 250 aircraft of varying quality.

After gaining her independence in 1905, Norway's armed forces had been oriented against Sweden, but in the Twenties for all practical purposes she had disarmed. In 1935 a minority social-democrat government came to power following the general world slump of 1929/32. The main government priorities were economic recovery together with social justice. It was assumed that just as Norway had remained neutral in the First World War she should be able to remain neutral in the Second. Only reluctantly did the government agree to increase the war budget as a deterrent to any would be aggressor [Germany or Russia]. The latter was known to covet an ice-free port in Norway. In September 1939 there was the suggestion of forming a National government, as had been done in Sweden, but Johan Nygaardsvold, then Prime Minister, turned it down.

Norway's army was based on conscription. The peacetime establishment consisted of six divisions, some 56,000 men in all, but this figure would be doubled on mobilisation by reservists. Deficiencies in equipment were similar to those of Sweden: tanks, anti-tank guns and anti-aircraft guns. There was a tiny navy consisting of four modern escort destroyers, two large but ancient coastal defence vessels, three small destroyers from the Great War era and about fifty smaller vessels. There was an embryo air force of sixteen modern aircraft and about forty outdated machines.

It was realised from the outset that the Scandinavians as neutrals were entitled to trade with Germany and that there was little that the Allies could do to prevent them. Thus Swedish exports to Germany, mainly of iron ore, were to remain a delicate question up until 1945. Generally speaking the Norwegians favoured the liberal democracies of Britain and France. This was reinforced by the balance of trade. In peacetime about thirty per cent of Norway's imports had been supplied by Allied countries as against only seventeen per cent from Germany. Moreover Allied countries took thirty-five per cent of Norway's exports as compared with fourteen per cent exported to Germany.

The real prize was not wood pulp or fish but Norway's mercantile marine. As seafarers, the spirit of the Vikings lived on. Whaling in the bleak southern oceans was virtually a Norwegian monopoly. Before the war Norway had the fourth largest merchant fleet in the world. From the outset the British government sought to charter as many Norwegian ships as possible. As early as 5 September 1939 Sir Cecil Dormer, the British Ambassador in Oslo, had opened discussions with Dr Koht the Norwegian Minister for Foreign Affairs, with a view to securing a War Trade Agreement. Halvdan Koht, an internationally known historian, had dominated Norwegian foreign policy since 'labour' came to power in 1935. In common with other social democrats he abhorred Nazism, but in common with many other Scandinavians he tended to regard all great powers as culpable. Traditionally Norwegians thought that they were relatively free from the danger of attack by Germany because of Britain's naval superiority. This conviction began to wane as Britain's resolve was called in question after Munich and the subsequent occupation of Prague. On the other hand they knew that they had to deal with the British because of Britain's ability to enforce the blockade.

The Norwegians drove a hard bargain. The Norwegian Ship Owners' Association demanded high rates of charter, which they got and insisted on high war-risk insurance, as well they might. Agreement was finally reached and initialled on 11 November. For the duration of the war the British secured 700,000 tons of tramp tonnage and, of even greater strategic value, 1,500,000 tons of ocean going tankers. About a third of the Norwegian tanker fleet was made up of modern ships with up-to-date diesel engines. The Norwegians used the shipping agreement as a bargaining counter insisting that ratification of the agreement by the Norwegian Parliament would be necessary. This was not reached until well into the New Year. It was an open secret that at the same time the Norwegians were negotiating a war trade agreement with the Germans.

Chapter 4

The Winter War

In August 1939 the Germans brought off one of their most brilliant diplomatic coups. The Russo-German Agreement negotiated between Ribbentrop and Molotov, among other things, assigned Finland to the Soviet sphere. The Finns had a profound distrust of the Russians believing that at some stage they would seek revenge for their defeat in 1919 when the Finns had won their independence. In principle the Finns thought that any concession granted to the Russians would only turn out to be the thin edge of the wedge. At the same time the Soviet government was profoundly suspicious of Nazi Germany. Hitler had so often condemned Bolshevism that the Russians assumed that at some point they would attack them, as indeed turned out to be the case. The Russians also correctly predicted that Finland, which had some claims in central Karelia, would become an ally of Germany. In the nineteenth century eastern Karelia had been the more backward part of the Duchy of Finland but became more important to the Russians when the Tsarist government had completed a railway line through eastern Karelia from St Petersburg to Murmansk.

It was with a view to defending the northern flank of the Soviet Union that Molotov, the foreign minister had requested the Finnish government to send a delegation to Moscow. Between 12 October and 9 November 1939 there were three rounds of talks between Stalin and Molotov on one side, and the Finnish delegation on the other. Stalin's main points were 'we must be able to bar the entrance to the Gulf of Finland' and 'we cannot move Leningrad so we must move the border'.

More specifically the Russian demands were four in number:

• the Finnish border on the Karelian Isthmus between Lake Ladoga and the Baltic should be moved some 70 kilometres back from Leningrad.
• with a view to safeguarding Leningrad from seaborne attack, certain islands in the Gulf of Finland should be ceded to Russia.
• that Hanko, the naval base at the entrance to the Gulf of Finland should be leased to the Russians for thirty years.

• that Petsamo on a fjord on the Arctic shore of northern Finland should be ceded to Russia in order to provide a shield for the nearby Russian naval base at Murmansk. With its egress to the North Atlantic, Murmansk was Russia's only major port which remained ice free all the year round.

Despite the apparently sweeping nature of these demands, it is possible to empathise with the Russians. In the event the parties were not far from reaching a compromise. The Russians were even prepared to cede part of central Karelia north of Lake Ladoga as a quid pro quo for Petsamo. The Finns were ready to accede to most of Russia's demands. They were ready to give up Petsamo. They were prepared to cede certain islands. They were even willing to offer the Russian navy alternative dockyard facilities, but they were not prepared to yield Hanko. At the end of November the Finnish delegation returned to Helsinki.

The Germans were genuinely surprised when hostilities broke out. Many influential Germans were outraged. Reichsmarschall Hermann Goering wanted to send military aid to the Finns but Hitler would do nothing that might jeopardize the Russo-German agreement. Public opinion in France, Britain and America was equally shocked. The Scandinavians could see that the war was not one which the Finns could win on their own. What weighed with the Swedish and Norwegian governments was that if they became embroiled in the war, a victorious Red Army might not stop at the Finnish border but might push on to the ore fields in northern Sweden and a warm-water port on the Atlantic which they had always coveted. On December 5 they put out a statement to the effect that neither Norway nor Sweden would go to the aid of the Finns. In fairness to the Scandinavians and the Swedes in particular, considerable numbers of individuals crossed the border to fight for the Finns.

The League of Nations had long since been seen to be impotent. Nevertheless on 14 December the Secretary General asked members to give all possible material and humanitarian assistance to the Finns. The British representative, who happened to be R.A. Butler, supported the motion and promised all help short of war. The British government even authorised the despatch of fighters and bombers. At the same time HM Government was careful not to disturb the trading agreement with Russia. They needed our machine tools and we needed their timber.

The odds stacked against the Finns were horrendous. The Finnish army was only able to field ten divisions in all. Most equipment was short. The Finnish artillery was inadequate. Each division had only thirty-six pre-1913 guns. There were shortages of automatic weapons, although they had some of the modern 9mm Suomi submachine gun which could fire up to 900 rounds a minute. There were shortages of mortars, shells and short-wave radios. They had few tanks and no air force. The Finns had retained a reasonably large defence force of

300,000 men and it was highly trained. There was a volunteer militia of 100,000 and a woman's force of 100,000 Lotte Svard. Above all the Finns were fighting for their homes and freedom from Bolshevism and domination by Russia.

Marshal Gustaf Mannerheim, the legendary Tsarist cavalry general who had led the struggle for independence in 1919, emerged from retirement at the age of 72 to take command. The Finns had over a month in which to mobilize and Mannerheim deployed his forces as follows:

• Nine independent battalions covered the eastern frontier from Petsamo in the far north for 650 miles of bleak sparsely inhabited tundra down to Ilomantsi.
• Two divisions covered the more inhabitable farmland for 60 miles between Ilomantsi down to the shore of Lake Ladoga in eastern Karelia.
• The 10th Division formed a reserve on the Gulf of Bothnia.
• Seven Divisions of about 14,000 men each were stationed where the main fighting was anticipated on the Karelian Isthmus between Lake Ladoga and the Gulf of Finland.

The Finns had built a line across the Karelian Isthmus similar, but not as elaborate as, the Maginot Line. It ran for 88 miles and consisted of 66 strong points each of which consisted of two or more pill boxes or bunkers designed to cover all roads or open ground with machine-gun fire. There were also minefields and interconnected trenches.

By the end of November there were opposite the Finns no less than four Russian army groups:

• The 7th Army on the Karelian Isthmus consisted of 10 Infantry divisions and 6 tank brigades totalling 240,000 men, 1,500 tanks and 900 guns and supported by 300 planes. The 7th Army was commanded by General Meretskov.
• The 8th Army consisted of 150,000 men, 545 tanks supported by 520 guns and 200 planes. The strategy was logical. The 8th Army was to attack along the north shore of Lake Ladoga and take the defenders of the Mannerheim line in the rear.
• The 9th Army consisted of five divisions amounting to 95,000 men supported by 275 tanks and 360 guns. The strategy was that the 9th Army should drive through central Finland to the Swedish border at the head of the Gulf of Bothnia.
• The 14th Army consisted of three infantry divisions amounting to 55,000 men supported by 165 tanks and 220 guns. They were to first take Petsamo and then move down the Arctic Highway for 300 miles to

the town of Rovaniemi where a railway line continued down to the Swedish border. This was the only front upon which the Russians met little resistance.

See Fig. 2 The Finnish Campaign map p.ix.

The Karelian Isthmus was always going to be where the outcome of the war would be decided. At 07.00 on 30 November, without warning, 600 Russian guns opened fire. Mannerheim had hoped that his outlying pickets would hold up the Russian advance but such was the weight of the Russian offensive that within a few days Russian forces had reached the Mannerheim Line. On 17 December General Meretskov opened the main assault. Wave after wave of infantry and tanks in dense formation tried to break through on the main road to Viborg. The Finns fought like cats. Where tanks broke through, two or three men teams attacked them with 6-13lb charges of high explosive or Molotov cocktails made up with bottles of petrol. Sometimes the Finns succeeded in jamming logs between the tank tracks. They were particularly adept at attacking during the long hours of darkness and one way or another knocked out 239 tanks. The Mannerheim Line held and after four days General Meretskov called a halt. On 27 December the Isthmus offensive was called off.

To begin with the Russians made some progress round the north shore of Lake Ladoga. The Finns soon learned not to oppose them directly. The Finnish army had been trained to move about on skis, to wear white camouflage and to fight at night. Surprise was their best weapon and while they could see their enemy the Russians had difficulty seeing them against the desolate snowy landscape. They called the Finnish soldiers moving about silently on their skis 'the white death'. With inadequate winter clothing, a large number of Russian soldiers simply died of exposure. The majority of Finns were countrymen and excellent marksmen and had perfected the technique of survival. At night they would build wigwams out of fir branches and heat them with portable wood burners. Central Finland has few roads and the Russians were advancing into a trackless waste. While they were confined to the roads, the Finns with local knowledge could move across country and attack the long drawn out Russian columns on the roads at a point of their choosing. The Finns developed the technique of hit and run raids. Emboldened by success they developed a technique of cutting up the Russian columns into more vulnerable groups.

Within the confines of one chapter it is impossible to do more than select a few of the dramatic exploits of the Finns in Central Finland. On 7 December, the Russian 163rd Division had taken Suomussalmi village. Elements of the 9th Division under Colonel Hjalmar Siilasvuo cut the road behind the Russians and surrounded them. By Christmas Colonel Siilasvuo had five new battalions, two anti-tank guns and eight 76mm guns. On Christmas Eve, 163rd Division attempted to break out. Floundering through chest-high snow and snipers' bullets the Russians were forced back into their freezing holes. Three days later 163rd Division had ceased to exist. The Finns captured eleven tanks but they only took 500 prisoners.

General Vinogradov's 44th Motorised Division was ordered to relieve the 163rd Division but they arrived too late. Thus 18,000 men and 40 tanks were strung out for some 60 miles along the road and the Finns were able to cut them off. Finnish engineers then cut what was known as a snow road along the line of small lakes to the south. They set up heated shelters and provided hot food for their forward troops. Trails were then laid to concealed points of attack. The results were that by 8 January, no less than 27,500 Russian soldiers had been killed either by bullets or simply frozen to death. A huge amount of equipment and baggage was captured by the Finns.

Inevitably the inquests started. The hapless General Vinogradov, who had managed to escape the massacre, was summoned back to Moscow and shot, no doubt in order to encourage the others. Stalin summoned his generals and some of his advisers to his *dacha* outside Moscow. Over dinner with his guests well plied with alcohol, he launched into a diatribe against his generals and against Marshal Voroshilov the Commissar of Defence in particular. The latter was not the sort of man to take it lying down: 'You have only yourself to blame for this... you are the one who had some of our best generals shot', he thundered. Nikita Kruschev recorded that 'it was the only time in my life that I have ever witnessed such an outburst.' The remarkable thing was that Stalin took his old revolutionary comrade's words to heart and the veteran revolutionary General Timoshenko was placed in supreme command of the Finnish campaign.

The practical deficiencies of the Red Army were ones which the Russian leadership started to address but the process was by no means complete by the time that the Winter War was over. For example clothes and white camouflage were inadequate. Anti-frost protection for equipment and for fuel was lacking.

One of the disadvantages of a winter campaign was that aircraft, with 1940 technology only had a short day in which to operate. Neither the air attack on Finnish towns nor support for Russian ground forces were particularly effective. Despite the inadequacies of the tiny Finnish air force the Russians lost a total of 800 planes in the Winter War.

Back in London the Cabinet had approved the formation of an organization to aid Finland under the chairmanship of Leo Amery. The only significant thing that was achieved was the decision to send two parliamentarians as observers to Finland, one of whom was Harold Macmillan. This was to have far reaching political consequences several months later. Harold Macmillan arrived in Finland on 12 February and he has given us a lively account of his visit to the front and the remarkable spirit and discipline of the Finnish Army which he said reminded him of his time in The Guards during the First World War. After conversations with various members of the Finnish staff, Macmillan cabled the Prime Minister and the Foreign Secretary: 'Finnish Command admits situation grave... urgent need artillery of all calibres and appropriate ammunition and aeroplanes, both bombers and fighters. If these made available at once believe position can be held until thaw. After that our troops could operate'. He also, for reasons best known to himself, cabled Churchill: 'please ask to see my telegram'.

Local Finnish tactical victories had achieved one thing. They had the effect of persuading the Russian government that the war should be brought to an end as soon as possible. And at the end of January the Russians intimated to the Finns that they would be prepared to negotiate. Meanwhile General Timoshenko had taken over with reinforcements of nine divisions and an armoured brigade. Intensive training based on the co-operation of tanks, artillery, aircraft and infantry was introduced. On 1 February a fresh offensive was launched on the Karelian Isthmus opening with a tremendous bombardment. On 11 February the Finnish line broke. The Finns retreated to a new defensive line, but on 25 February this was breached. On 9 March Marshal Mannerheim advised his government to sue for peace. Naturally the Soviet terms were harsher than they would have been four months earlier. The Finns had to cede the whole of the Karelian Isthmus, including the north shore of Lake Ladoga and the ancient Finnish fortress of Viborg [Viipuri]. The Finns signed the treaty on 12 March and Finland had then to absorb no less than 400,000 refugees from Karelia.

An extraordinary aspect of the war was the scale of the Russian losses. No less than 200,000 men perished, many of them from exposure, compared with only 25,000 Finns. A far reaching consequence of the war was that the German leadership was encouraged into thinking that the Soviet Union could be easily defeated. Equally significant were the steps taken by the Russians to remedy the defects in training and equipment. Stalin's purges of the late Thirties had got rid of much of the dead wood in the Red Army but it had also undermined morale. After the Winter War the Red Army was thoroughly reorganized, not the least important step being the reintroduction of a more traditional hierarchy of ranks.

The Peace Treaty of 1940 was not quite the end of the story. The Finns rebuilt and expanded their army and joined the Germans after their attack on Russia in 1941. However they refused to advance beyond their 1939 frontiers. When the Germans were palpably beaten, the Russians negotiated a separate peace treaty which restored the 1940 frontier. The Russians were only too happy to secure peace on their northern flank and by a miracle remained content to tolerate an independent democratic Finland after 1945.

Chapter 5

The Allies Dither

The Supreme War Council had met in London on 19 December to discuss the Finnish question. Among those attending were the Prime Minister, the Foreign Secretary and the Minister for the Co-ordination of Defence, Admiral Chatfield. The French were represented by the Prime Minister, Edouard Daladier, the Commander-in-Chief General Gamelin and Admiral Darlan. The French General Staff had already studied plans for operations designed to cut Germany's strategic supply lines, such as disrupting traffic on the Danube, and sending an expedition to the Black Sea to disrupt oil supplies and even bombing Baku. Yet whenever any proposal which might have led to war with Russia was mooted, the British, justifiably as it turned out, always held back.

The French Prime Minister had for some time been under pressure from the press and had also been attacked for his inertia in the Chamber of Deputies. Like Chamberlain, Daladier was by temperament and background not really the man to run a war. As a radical socialist he abhorred war. As a former Minister of Defence he must bear some of the responsibility for the state of French rearmament, and as Prime Minister at the time of Munich he was irrevocably tainted with the policy of appeasement.

A direct offensive by Allied armies, which were about eighty per cent French, had so far, realistically, been ruled out. There existed a temporary convention by which neither side would start bombing each other's cities. In view of the parlous state of the French air force this was just as well from their point of view. Indeed there was muted talk, throughout the winter of 1939, of a patched-up peace.

Now there was talk of a diversion in Scandinavia. This was particularly attractive to the French. First of all any diversion away from French soil would be a relief to the French public. Secondly, just as the British relied heavily on the French army for operations on the Western Front, so the burden involving amphibious warfare would inevitably fall largely on the British. Daladier was enthusiastic about the proposal. Here was a heaven sent opportunity for the French government to win points in the eyes of the French people. General Gamelin was not so enthusiastic about dispersing his own forces and thought that any initiative in Scandinavia should be largely undertaken by the British.

At the meeting of the Supreme War Council on 19 December a pre-war report which Baron Thyssen, the German steel magnate, had produced was discussed. The baron, then living in exile in Switzerland, had concluded that any future war involving Germany would be won by the side which controlled the ore fields. As a prominent Frenchman, Admiral Auphon frankly admitted later: 'no-one really hoped to stop the Soviet army and save Finland. The idea was to use the pretext of such an operation to lay our hands on Swedish iron ore and thus deny it to the Germans'.

The Finnish War had a subtle effect on politics in London. Hitherto the Admiralty had made all the running, but now the Army became more involved. Once the decision had been taken to draw up plans for mounting an expedition to Scandinavia, the Chief of the Imperial General staff, General Edmund Ironside, sprang to prominence. Like Churchill, Ironside was continuously searching for some means of inflicting a defeat on the Germans, rather than passively waiting for them to attack on the Western Front. Most people expected the Germans to launch their offensive through Belgium, and indeed on several occasions in the winter of 1939/40 Hitler had postponed an offensive. Ironside was also convinced, as he declared privately, that eventually the Germans and the Russians would be bound to fall out. Like everybody else he had considerable sympathy for the Finns, but warned against antagonizing the Russians.

At the meeting of the War Cabinet on 22 December, Chamberlain pointed out that there were now two distinct projects: the original plan to sow mines in the Leads which only involved naval action. Now there was a major project to secure the ore mines by despatching an expeditionary force to Scandinavia. The Prime Minister said: 'Everyone is agreed that the assent of Norway and Sweden was essential to the success of the major project, but there was no doubt that the minor operation would displease the Norwegians and embarrass the Swedes; it was therefore inadvisable to risk compromising the major operation by carrying out the minor one.' Arising out of these deliberations, the Chiefs of Staff were asked to draw up more specific plans.

Christmas 1939 saw members of the cabinet dispersing to their respective country retreats, the Prime Minister to Chequers and Lord Halifax to his country seat at Garrowby in the East Riding of Yorkshire. Not so the First Lord who remained at his flat over the Admiralty. The result was that when the War Cabinet reconvened after the Christmas break it was presented with yet another memorandum in which Churchill outlined a possible timetable for the expedition. This only led to more discussion, albeit with a liberal contribution from the First Lord, the generation of more hot air and no decisions whatsoever.

One positive decision that had emerged from the meeting of the Cabinet on 22 December was that the Foreign Office was instructed to send a communication to the Scandinavian governments telling them that the Allies proposed to stop the supply of ore and to await their reaction. Since Stockholm was at that time the spy capital of Europe, the British government might just as well have given notice to the Germans as well.

It was fairly obvious that the Norwegians and the Swedes were in no position to defend their towns and cities from air attack and would be unlikely to give their consent. The Swedes were the first to reply on 4 January. They were nervous of the consequences of giving aid to Finland. King Gustav had even said that he thought that Russia would attack Sweden. The Swedes took the view that their neutrality would best serve Finnish interests. They said that if Allied assistance to Finland were given in such a way that Sweden was associated in a common action against the USSR then both Russia and Germany might take counter measures which would in any case lead to the collapse of Finland.

The Norwegians were less obdurate. On 15 January, Erik Colban, the Norwegian Minister in London left an *aide memoire* at the Foreign Office to the effect that the Norwegians would not object to the transit of materials across Norwegian territory and of technicians in a private capacity. The Hague Convention of 1907 was cited as authority for this proposition.

The report by the Chiefs of Staff which involved Lieutenant General H. Massy, the Deputy Chief of the Imperial General Staff was produced with commendable speed. It ran to twenty-one pages and was far reaching in its conclusions. After analysing the iron ore problem, the Chiefs of Staff stated among other things:

1. The only method of stopping the export of iron ore from the northern fields is by the despatch of an expedition. They recommended two brigades, specially equipped and trained to reach its objective by the end of March.
2. Both Norwegian and Swedish co-operation is essential.
3. We may be called upon to send a force to support the Swedes and Norwegians against German attack. Four to six divisions were mentioned [this was realistic, when one considers that in the event the Germans found seven divisions adequate].
4. The extra naval commitment might absorb two flotillas of destroyers as well as transports.
5. The report suggested one fighter squadron and one co-operation squadron in the north [hopelessly inadequate] and up to twelve squadrons, should it be necessary, in southern Sweden.

The Chiefs of Staff plan was based on two questionable but not unimaginative, hypotheses. To begin with they thought that our action would compel the

Germans to invade Sweden to regain control of the ore fields and that this would rule out a successful offensive by the Germans in the west. They said that Allied policy so far had been to remain on the defensive on land and in the air while our armaments were being increased. They seemed to overlook the fact that at that point in the war, the Germans still had unused capacity to arm faster than the Allies. The second hypothesis was more in the nature of a caveat: 'provided vital points elsewhere are secure'. In little more than four months the Western Front proved to be far from secure. Nevertheless the Chiefs of Staff concluded: 'the opportunity is a great one'.

The War Cabinet considered the Chief of Staff's report on 2 January. Ironside noted in his diary 'a long day... actually eight & half hours in conferences and meetings. You cannot make war like that... The Cabinet meeting to consider the Scandinavian show became a debating morning. Winston was all-out to start at once without thinking much of the consequences... I think that the main argument against this project of the First Lord's is that it may, I think it will, accelerate any contemplated German action in Scandinavia. We are not ready for this till the middle of March.'

On the subject of sending a land force to Narvik, the Prime Minister thought that we should tell the Norwegians first what was afoot and await their reply before we came to a final conclusion. According to Sir Alexander Cadogan, Permanent Secretary at the Foreign Office, on 6 January Lord Halifax had a painful meeting with Erik Colban when he delivered a memorandum in the following terms: referring to the torpedoing of two British and one Greek ship in Norwegian territorial waters it said: 'by these hostile acts, German naval forces have made Norwegian waters a theatre of war and have in practice deprived them of their neutral character. HM Government are therefore making appropriate dispositions to prevent the use of Norwegian territorial waters by German ships and trade. To achieve this purpose, it would be necessary for His Majesty's naval forces at times to enter and operate in these waters.'

A couple of days later the Norwegian Minister delivered a letter to the Foreign Office stating that the Norwegian government considered that infractions of their neutrality by one belligerent did not authorize another belligerent to violate it. More telling perhaps was a private message from King Haakon to his nephew George VI in which he asked him to use his influence with his ministers to bring them to reconsider their plan.

On 9 January the War Cabinet considered the Narvik traffic in the light of the Scandinavian reactions. Halifax then informed the Cabinet that now there was evidence that the Germans might themselves be planning the invasion of Scandinavia. Halifax thought that if they did so it would be the best thing from our point of view as we should then escape the odium of being the first to take such a step. From the military point of view this would be tantamount to handing the initiative to the enemy. It was in the course of these deliberations that the rift between Halifax and Churchill became more apparent. Churchill thought that we should take naval action immediately. He said it was questionable whether our actions would bring about a German invasion [how wrong he was on that point]. Churchill concluded by saying 'we should not allow neutrals to tie our hands while we were fighting to defend their liberty'.

A certain Swedish banker, Marcus Wallenberg, had been in London negotiating an Anglo-Swedish trade agreement, in effect acting as an unofficial go-between on behalf of the Foreign Office. He said that the Germans, who he maintained already had plans for the invasion of Scandinavia, might regard British action in Norwegian waters as a first step in an Allied plan to establish themselves in Scandinavia. Wallenberg said that if Germany attacked Sweden, the latter could not help Finland. Halifax replied that HMG had already made an offer to help Sweden if she were involved in a war with Germany. Wallenberg questioned what help the Allies could give since Sweden had no access to the Atlantic. Wallenberg emphasized that most Swedes would argue that the immediate necessity was to keep Germany quiet.

On 12 January, Halifax told the Cabinet that his conversation with Wallenberg had led him to decide against the Narvik plan. The Chiefs of Staff's view which was reported to the Cabinet was that the Narvik project would prejudice the larger project for which the active co-operation of Norway and Sweden was essential. The Prime Minister then said that he could not agree to a proposal to seize the ore fields against Norwegian and Swedish opposition. Some historians have suggested that there was a fundamental conflict between Churchill's minor project and the major project of the Chiefs of Staff headed by Ironside. All the evidence suggests that Churchill supported Ironside's plan. Where they differed was that Churchill wanted immediate action. Churchill's passion for action may have overflowed at times for on 15 January we find him writing to Halifax a half apologetic note as follows:

'Dear Edward.
My disquiet was due to the awful difficulties which our machinery of war conduct presents to positive action... just look at the arguments which have had to be surmounted in the seven weeks we have discussed the Narvik operation.
Firstly, the objectives of the Economic Departments.
Secondly, the Joint Planning Committee.
Thirdly, the Chiefs of Staff Committee.
Fourthly, don't spoil the big plan for the sake of the small, when there is really little chance of the big plan being resolutely attempted.
Fifthly, the judicial and moral objections.

Sixthly, the attitudes of neutrals, and above all the United States. But see how well the United States has responded to our demarche.

Seventhly, the Cabinet itself with its many angles of criticism.

Eighthly, when all this has been smoothed out, the French have to be consulted.

Finally, the Dominions and their consciences have to be squared,

He concluded 'Pardon me if I showed distress... one thing is absolutely certain, namely that victory will never be found by taking the line of least resistance'.

Despite the decision to postpone action in Scandinavia, the planning of the major project continued. In order to draw up plans for a campaign it seems that half the battle is to dream up a codeword. In the event the Chiefs of Staff came up with three:

1. **Avonmouth** – The original plan had provided for a landing in the Narvik area of two divisions which were to move through to the Swedish ore fields and then perhaps proceed to Finland.

2. **Stratford** – It was appreciated that Avonmouth would probably provoke the Germans into invading Southern Norway. It was therefore proposed that five infantry battalions should land in Central Norway and occupy Trondheim, Bergen and Stavanger.

3. **Plymouth** – It had become apparent that the Swedes would not co-operate for fear of an invasion of Southern Sweden and therefore the plan was modified to provide for two divisions to land at Trondheim to assist the Swedes if need be.

The Chiefs of Staff recommended that all three operations should be launched together. General Ironside was under no illusions as to the resources at his disposal. Between October 1939 and March 1940 ten regular divisions had been sent to France. Only two regular divisions remained in the UK and the territorial divisions were desperately short of equipment. On 29 January the Cabinet considered an enlarged report from the Chiefs entitled 'Intervention in Scandinavia', calling for a force to land at Narvik to occupy the ore-fields, a force to co-operate in the defence of southern Sweden and smaller bodies of troops to occupy Trondheim, Bergen and Stavanger. The deadline was considered to be 20 March when the port of Lulea would have thawed out. The Chiefs of Staff were now in favour of the operation going ahead as giving us 'the first and best chance of wresting the initiative from the Germans and shortening the war'.

The next excuse for delay arose from a counter-suggestion from General Gamelin and Admiral Darlan. They proposed sending three to four divisions to land at Petsamo, the Finnish port which had fallen into Russian hands. This led to Chamberlain, Halifax, Churchill, Oliver Stanley and Kingsley Wood trooping off to Paris on 5 February to a meeting of the Supreme War Council for yet more talks. Chamberlain emphasized that the defeat of Finland would be seen by the USA and other neutrals as a defeat for the Allies. The only decision that was taken was to make another appeal to Norway and Sweden to allow Allied forces a right of passage.

On 10 February Bjorn Prytz returned from Stockholm saying quite simply that Sweden was resolved to maintain her neutrality. In private he admitted that this was not very heroic but he put the Swedish point of view that they could not intervene because it would mean that Germany's enemies would be on Swedish soil and this would lead to a German invasion and clearly the Germans could reach Sweden on a larger scale much more quickly than the Allies. What it boiled down to was that the Swedes feared the Russians more than the Germans. Put cynically, but probably justifiably, the Swedes thought that the best solution would be a quick settlement of the war and they even offered to act as mediators. On 19 February King Gustav of Sweden made a declaration to the effect that he regarded it as his imperative duty to keep Sweden out of a war between the Great Powers. He had warned the Finnish government from the very start not to count on Sweden for military intervention, although the Swedes did try to help in just about every other way. Something was later made of King Gustav's pro-German sympathies. Be that as it may, his actions were largely dictated by realpolitik.

Any thought of the priceless military advantage of surprise could now be forgotten. The Scandinavian press were openly discussing the options open to the Allies. Ironside actually recorded in his diary on 20 February that the Swedish military attaché in London had told him that he had been informed by the French attaché in Stockholm that an Allied force intended to land at Narvik. As Ironside concluded, 'You cannot keep anything secret with so many people with a finger in the pie'. The plan as it had crystallized was that the British should supply two divisions and two strong brigades while the French should supply a brigade of Chasseurs Alpins together with two battalions of the French Foreign Legion. In addition the French would provide four Polish battalions, largely recruited from Poles living in France with General Audet in command. In Britain an expeditionary force was assembled and Major General P. Mackesy appointed to command with a major general as his chief of staff. It was even being suggested that the expedition should sail in the second half of March.

On 2 February the Russians had opened their offensive on the Mannerheim Line with redoubled vigour. Most observers thought that the Allies could not reach Finland in time to repulse the Russians. Realizing that the Russians would moderate their terms to get an agreement if they thought that the Allies were about to intervene, the Finns made larger and wilder demands on the Allies. The French made more and more extravagant promises, yet none of these could possibly have been put into practice in the time available. The Russians were as keen as anyone to see an end to the war to secure their northern flank. As early as 22 February Ivan M. Maisky, the Russian Minister in London, even told the Foreign Office the terms upon which they would make peace and he added that the Soviets had no intention of making military alliances with Germany or of giving up their neutrality or even invading Scandinavia.

On 12 March, General Ironside informed the War Cabinet that the men were already embarking. He noted in his diary that the Cabinet seemed surprised... 'they presented the picture of a bewildered flock of sheep faced by a problem they have consistently refused to consider'. That evening Lord Halifax, Admiral Chatfield, Air Marshal Sir Cyril Newall, Admiral Sir Dudley Pound, General Ironside and Major General Ismay attended Chamberlain at No. 10. General Mackesy commander of the land forces and his chief staff officer, General Kennedy were in attendance and Admiral Sir Edward Evans, who had been appointed to command the Narvik expedition, presented the whole plan. Despite the scepticism among the senior officers present as to whether the expedition would sail, Chamberlain shook hands with them all saying 'good luck if you go'. But events elsewhere had also moved on. On the same evening agreement was reached in Moscow between the Russians and the Finns. The next morning the peace agreement was signed and published to the world. The Finnish Army was to remain intact, bloodied but unbowed.

In the light of this development the War Cabinet met. Churchill still wanted to proceed to secure the ore-fields. Chamberlain thought that to do so might panic Hitler into invading Scandinavia. He therefore proposed that all units should be stood down. Ironside thought that the Narvik force should be kept in being. Chamberlain was supported by the usual phalanx: Simon, Kingsley Wood and Hoare, which carried the Cabinet. Frustrated once more, Churchill wrote a note to Halifax that evening saying: 'All has now fallen to the ground, because so cumbrous are our processes that we were too late... whether the Germans have some plan of their own which will open upon us, I cannot tell. It would seem to me astonishing if they had not'.

Chapter 6

Consequences of the Finnish Collapse

The immediate consequence of the Finnish Armistice was the fall of the French Prime Minister. There was a general feeling in Europe and the USA that one more small country had fallen victim to a totalitarian state and that the western democracies had done very little to prevent it. Nowhere was this feeling stronger than in France. Edouard Daladier had identified himself with the Finnish cause and he had failed. On 19 March Daladier resigned and two days later Paul Reynaud, by general consent a man more suited to the role of war leader, formed a new government. Reynaud nevertheless retained Daladier as minister of defence.

If the collapse of Finland proved fatal to the French Prime Minister, the outcome of the Parliamentary debate on 19 March was to leave Neville Chamberlain mortally wounded. The debate opened with several members offering the Prime Minister congratulations on having reached his 70th birthday the day before. The Prime Minister was in a buoyant mood and said that the Finns 'have preserved their honour and they have won the respect of all the world'. He went on to say, 'Any suggestion that the Allies failed in their obligation to do their utmost to assist Finland in her hour of need, is one which cannot for one moment be maintained'.

Chamberlain listed the material allocated to Finland, despite the priority of building up our own forces, and impressive it sounded:

Aeroplanes:	152 promised, 101 sent.
Guns:	223 promised, 114 sent.
Shells:	297,200 promised 185,000 sent and so on.

The Prime Minister then went on to deal with men saying that in January Marshal Mannerheim had said that he did not need men then but when the thaw came in May, he would require 30,000 trained men. The Prime Minister also revealed that it had been planned to send 100,000 men to Scandinavia starting in March. He said that in February the Finns were asked to make a public appeal to Britain and France by 5 March 'we hoped that Norway and Sweden would feel that they could not stand in the way of such an appeal'. The Finns never made this appeal in case it would turn the Germans against them. It will be recalled that German troops had saved the Finns from the Reds in 1918.

The opposition then sought to widen the debate on the general progress of the war. The hazards of disclosing details about men and equipment in time of war were fully appreciated and several members asked for the debate to take place in secret session. The decision to hold the debate in public was therefore the government's. This did not inhibit Clement Attlee, the leader of the official opposition but not usually the most eloquent of speakers, from launching a devastating attack on the war leadership. He started by saying that the real battle had not been joined. 'Hitler may continue to evade decisions in the West... people are asking, what are we going to be doing in the meanwhile?... the initiative must not be left to Herr Hitler... you cannot have a policy of wait and see... we must realize that we are meeting an enemy who has been organizing for war year after year... we cannot meet that by half measures. There is urgency. There is need for drive... I have the impression that there is too much waiting for decisions, too much waiting for Treasury permission and so on.'

Sir Archibald Sinclair, leader of the Liberals then spoke, 'The Prime Minister told us how much material was sent. How much actually arrived?' He wound up by saying, 'It is time we stopped saying: what is Hitler going to do? It is about time we asked: what is Chamberlain going to do?'

Other distinguished back benchers weighed in. Colonel Wedgwood said 'we must insist upon a change of government and get a real national effort... it is only right that the Labour front bench should be taking their full responsibility... we have got to get the working classes of this country heart and soul behind us'. Richard Law a veteran anti-appeaser said that, 'the present Cabinet is a fairly large body composed partly of harassed and over-burdened departmental Ministers... that is not the kind of body which won the last war'. He then concluded 'I am convinced that the country today is not getting the leadership, drive, determination and decision which it deserves'.

The most damning speech of all was delivered by Harold Macmillan. He later recorded that he was greatly aided by the absence (diplomatic) from the front bench of Churchill and Eden. His debating skills were fully revealed in the following passages: 'In his statement of 13 March, the Prime Minister used these words: 'the Finnish government have made repeated requests for materials and "every one of these requests has been answered and today he used the words: every request was considered as far as possible"... That is a very different picture from the one which was given to me when I was in Finland.' [Macmillan had been one of an all-party group of MPs which had visited Finland during the winter.] 'They gave me the impression of a series of appeals for larger quantities of materials, appeals which fell almost entirely, at first, on deaf ears and were sent always in too small quantities and always too late.'

Macmillan quoted a specific request made on 2 February. It was acknowledged on the 12th as follows: 'none of the weapons or munitions which your country requests can be spared from our resources. That was seven days after the government decided to make an expedition in force to rescue these people. Macmillan asked, 'Is it generally known that although 148 aeroplanes were released [the Prime Minister's figures today], only 4 left England in December, only 44 in January and only 27 in February, the rest in March? Macmillan reminded the House that the whole of this war material was sold to the Finns on an ordinary commercial basis.'

In his peroration Macmillan said 'It does I think throw a piercing light on the present machinery and method of government, the delay, the vacillation, changes of front, standing on one foot one day and on the other the next day before a decision is given... these are patently clear to anyone'. The forces in opposition to Chamberlain did not go so far as to move a motion of no confidence and on this occasion the government won the debate.

When the Supreme War Council met in London on 28 March, Chamberlain spoke for ninety minutes. It is hardly surprising that in the course of his speech, the French Minister for Air, the Foreign Secretary and also Winston Churchill were observed to have dozed off to sleep! One thing Chamberlain made abundantly clear was that Britain would not allow itself to be dragged into a war with Russia. The delegates to the Supreme War Council did finally agree a timetable that would stretch their respective staffs to the limits:

1. On 1 April Norway and Sweden would be informed that the Allies reserved the right to stop iron ore traffic.
2. On 4/5 April mines would be laid in Norwegian territorial waters.
3. On 4/5 April mines would be laid in the Rhine and other German waterways.

The British General Staff immediately realized that these actions would probably lead to a German reaction, commonly assumed to be the occupation of Southern Norway. 'Stratford', the plan to land troops at Trondheim, Bergen and Stavanger, and 'Avonmouth', the plan to land at Narvik, were reinstated. Lieutenant General Massy, the Deputy Chief of the Imperial General Staff noted on 2 April that these plans had been reconstituted without consideration of the consequences. There were to be no ski battalions, few anti-aircraft guns and the men were to be equipped as lightly as possible.

At this late stage the French government backed away from agreeing to Operation Royal Marine (the mining of German waterways) for fear of reprisals against French cities. Nevertheless on 5 April the War Cabinet agreed that operation 'Wilfred', the mining of Norwegian territorial waters should go ahead and on 6 April the four mine-laying destroyers sailed. They were escorted by the heavy battle-cruiser *Renown* and the cruiser *Birmingham* with eight destroyers under the command of Vice Admiral W. Whitworth.

On 7 April Operation R4, as it had been labelled, got under way.

- At Rosyth on the Firth of Forth the four battalions bound for Bergen and Stavanger embarked on two cruisers.
- On the Clyde the troops destined for Trondheim and Narvik boarded one transport and the cruiser *Devonshire*.
- Neither group put to sea.

Chapter 7

Weserubung

While Britain and France conducted their affairs under the scrutiny of a relatively free press and in the public arena of Parliament, the Germans conducted theirs in strict secrecy. Hitler's rule was modelled on that of his idol Frederick the Great. He used to discuss and decide policy with the minister concerned, but rarely met his ministers collectively. He had concentrated control of the armed forces in his own hands in 1938 as head of the *Oberkommando der Wehrmacht* (OKW), aided by his two chief staff officers: General Keitel, the titular head and General Jodl, who saw that decisions were put into practice. Under the control of the OKW, direction of the army was exercised by the *Oberkommando des Heeres* under the command of Field Marshal Brauchitsch. The navy was controlled by *Oberkommando der Kriegsmarine,* under Grand Admiral Raeder and *Oberkommando der Luftwaffe* under Hermann Goering.

The germ of an idea that Germany might intervene in Scandinavia goes back to a book published in 1929 by Vice Admiral Wolfgang Wegener entitled *The Sea Strategy of the World Wars*. The general thesis was that the main function of the German Navy should be to open and maintain access to ocean trade routes. This had not been achieved in the First World War when the German Navy had been confined to the North Sea ports from whence all it could do was to menace the Home Fleet. If the Norwegian coast were occupied then the line of the British blockade which ran from the Shetland Islands to Norway would have to be withdrawn to the longer and less effective line: Shetlands, Faroes, Iceland.

The British Admiralty did not come to hear about Admiral Wegener's book until Sir Robert Vansittart, the head of the Foreign Service drew their attention to it in April 1939. The question of Norwegian waters was considered thereafter by a small planning staff under Admiral Drax, one of the Navy's most able strategists. His view was that if the Norwegians would not force German merchant ships out of Norwegian territorial waters after formal British protests, then the British would be justified in entering Norwegian waters. Grand Admiral Raeder took up Admiral Wegener's idea and on 10 October 1939 laid the matter before the Führer. The Admiral emphasised the advantages to German submarines of being able to operate from bases on the Norwegian coast. Hitler was only too well aware of the iron ore problem and the vulnerability of ships conveying iron ore from Narvik to Germany.

In the middle Thirties, Hitler had told Hermann Rauschning that should war break out, one of his first moves would be the invasion of Sweden, for he could not abandon the Scandinavian countries to either Russian or British influence. However, nothing more was heard of this proposal. On 2 September 1939 Germany declared the inviolability of Norway, so long as this was not infringed by a third power. Whether or not the intervention of Vidkun Quisling had much effect on Hitler is a matter for historical debate. Nevertheless, Quisling seems to have been the catalyst that brought about the commissioning of *'Studie Nord'*.

Quisling, rather like Hitler himself, was one of those talented but somewhat unbalanced individuals, who from time to time stride across the stage of history. The son of a clergyman, he was interested in philosophical questions and had graduated from the military academy with top marks. The famous explorer Fridtjof Nansen thought highly of him as his assistant in bringing international relief to the Ukraine after the Russian Revolution. Later Quisling became so appalled at Stalin's methods that he determined to fight communism by any means possible. In 1930 he wrote a pamphlet entitled 'Russia and Ourselves', in which he accurately predicted that the Soviets would seek to acquire the Baltic States and possibly Finland and Poland. In 1933 he had started his own rightist political party 'The National Union' but he did not possess Hitler's leadership or oratorical talents, moreover conditions in Norway were quite unlike those in Germany.

After the invasion of Finland, Quisling became convinced that the Russians would invade Norway next. He therefore resolved that the power his party had failed to secure at the polls could be achieved with the help of the Germans. Through his party's contacts in Berlin he procured an introduction to Admiral Raeder and also Alfred Rosenberg, the Nazi Party's ideologue. Rosenberg was taken with the idea of solidarity between the peoples of Northern Europe. It was Rosenberg who engineered a meeting between Quisling and Hitler on 14 December.

In the course of this meeting Hitler expressed the view that such a small party as the National Union would be unlikely to be able to seize power in Norway, but he promised financial help. Hitler was interested in Quisling's view that British propaganda in Norway was intended to pave the way for some sort of intervention in Scandinavia. He told Quisling that he had always been an anglophile but should the danger of a British violation of Norwegian neutrality ever become acute, he would land in Norway with six/twelve divisions to beat the British to the post. General Jodl noted in his diary that evening: 'Führer orders investigation, with the smallest possible staff as to how the occupation of Norway could be carried out.' Thus the *Studie Nord* was born. Four days later Hitler met Quisling and said that Germany had an interest in the strict enforcement of Norwegian neutrality and that a sharp look out would be kept. The reason that Hitler did not want to be distracted by a Scandinavian diversion was that he was planning to launch his main offensive in the West in January. This, as we know, was postponed several times before May 1940.

From the start Admiral Raeder's staff under Captain, (later Admiral) Theodore Krancke made the running and the first draft of *Studie Nord* was presented to Hitler on 20 January. The next day Hitler ordered a Special Staff to be set up to draw up contingency operational plans, henceforward to be known as Operation Weserubung (the Weser exercise). On 5 February the planning staff were addressed by General Keitel in the following terms: 'Your task is to prepare an operation for the occupation of Norway...we are in possession of information indicating that the British intend to occupy the ports of the western coast of Norway in co-operation with the French. We are also informed that the British have already approached the Norwegian government...given our situation of naval inferiority it would clearly be in our interest that Norway should remain strictly neutral. The occupation of the western coast of Norway by Allied forces would be a major setback for us. We must therefore prepare an operation ourselves, on a theoretical basis at first, so that it could be rapidly implemented in case of necessity. Such an undertaking must remain absolutely secret.'

The Kriegsmarine report provided the basis for a plan which proposed the simultaneous occupation of all the main ports by naval units. The first wave of troops should be carried in warships and parachute troops should capture Oslo and Stavanger airports. At first the plan was entirely theoretical but a single event completely transformed Hitler's attitude.

After the destruction of the pocket battleship *Graf Spee* off Montevideo on 17 December 1939, an intensive search had been mounted for her 12,000 ton supply ship the *Altmark*. She was believed to be carrying a number of prisoners from various merchant ships which the *Graf Spee* had sunk. The captain of the *Altmark* thought that his best chance of getting back to the Fatherland was to lie low in the South Atlantic for a bit. He then made his way north and passing just south of Iceland he arrived off Trondheim. On 14 February the *Altmark* was sighted by the RAF.

Meanwhile a squadron comprising one cruiser and five destroyers had left Rosyth on the Firth of Forth and was sweeping up the Norwegian coast. On 16 February Admiral Sir Charles Forbes, Commander-in-Chief of the Home Fleet told Captain Philip Vian that his primary task should be to intercept the *Altmark*. But it was not until the following afternoon that two Coastal Command aircraft sighted her again. An hour later one of Vian's destroyers sighted her being escorted by two Norwegian destroyers. The *Altmark* refused to stop and entered Jossingfjord where she anchored. Captain Vian aboard the destroyer *Cossack* followed her into the fjord and demanded from one of the Norwegian escort vessels that the British prisoners should be handed over. The Norwegians replied that the *Altmark* had been searched the previous day in Bergen, was unarmed and that there were no prisoners aboard.

Captain Vian, then very correctly withdrew outside Norwegian territorial waters and cabled the Admiralty for instructions. At this point the First Lord of the Admiralty stepped in. By all accounts Churchill was in a high state of excitement. He did however communicate with the Foreign Secretary, after which he instructed Captain Vian to offer the Norwegians jointly to escort the *Altmark* back to Bergen. If this were refused he was authorized to board her. As was later pointed out, the Admiralty's signals should have been routed through the C-in-C Home Fleet but that would have meant delay. It so happened that on this occasion Churchill's intuition turned out to be absolutely justified.

Late on the evening of the 17 February Captain Vian re-entered the fjord. The Norwegian escorts stood aside. The *Altmark* tried to get away but only succeeded in running aground. The *Cossack* laid alongside and a party of sailors, armed with revolvers and naval cutlasses [still the same weapon as used in Nelson's day], stormed aboard. After a short fight in which four Germans were killed, no less than 299 prisoners were found locked away in various parts of the ship. The cry of the boarding party; 'the Navy's' here', stirred the hearts of the nation and echoed round the British and American press.

The *Altmark* was found to be armed with two anti-aircraft guns and four machine guns. If the British had adopted a cavalier attitude towards a neutral country's territorial waters, the incident proved before the bar of neutral opinion that the Germans were freely using Norwegian territorial waters for the passage of ships of war. Neither does the Norwegian record emerge as entirely lily-white. It shows that so fearful were they of antagonizing the Germans that they were prepared to turn a blind eye to the passage of such ships.

Predictably the *Altmark* incident caused Hitler to fly into a rage. It marks the point where Operation Weserubung ceased to be a mere theoretical exercise and became the basis for a plan of action. The first thing that Hitler did was to appoint a staff with a general in command. On receiving the recommendation of the elderly General Nikolaus von Falkenhorst, Hitler questioned Keitel's judgement. Falkenhorst had served as chief of staff in 1918 when General von der Goltz had commanded the expeditionary force which drove the Bolsheviks out of Finland. However when he met him, Hitler sensed that he had got the right man and immediately appointed him. Falkenhorst records in his diary that the first thing that he did was to go out and buy a copy of Baedeker's Guide to Norway.

General Falkenhorst started by reviewing the plan so far drawn up by Captain Kranke and on 28 February a select staff started work in dead secret in Berlin. At General Jodl's instance it was decided that Weserubung could be executed independently of Operation Gelb [the offensive in the West]. On 1 March Hitler issued one of his famous 'Führer Directives'. In it he set out the general requirements for the operation and authorized the start of operational planning: Weserubung Nord provided for the air and seaborne invasion of Norway. Weserubung Sud provided for the occupation of Jutland and the Island of Funen in Denmark.

On 3 March Hitler decided that the invasion of Scandinavia should take precedence over the offensive in the West. A completely new departure was the decision that General Falkenhorst should be answerable directly to the *Oberkommando der Wehrmacht* that is the ministry of war, the head of which was Hitler. This produced a howl of protest from the professional heads of the army and air force. The army objected on two grounds: firstly that they had not been brought into the planning stage earlier and secondly at the novelty of troop dispositions being made independently of the Army general staff. The latter were opposed in principle to anything that would water down Operation Gelb, the pending offensive in the West.

A further provision was that the air force units allotted to Weserubung were to be placed under the tactical control of Army Group XXI. The head of Luftwaffe, Hermann Goering lodged a strong protest. As an ex fighter ace he could not stomach units of the air force being placed under the control of a land commander. General Falkenhorst therefore staged a special presentation at Goering's summer villa 'Karinhalle'. The air component was reduced and Goering was mollified. A feature of the plan was that most of the forces allocated to the conquest of Denmark, were to move on to Norway once their objective had been accomplished.

By a Führer directive of 7 March, Hitler approved the allocation of units as follows:

Weserubung Nord. The XXI Group consisting of the 3rd Mountain Division, the 69th, the 163rd, the 196th and 181st Infantry Divisions.

Weserubung Sud. The XXXI Corps consisting of the 170th and 198th Infantry Divisions, together with 4 Motorized Rifle Brigade.

It is a mistake to suppose that Army Group XXI was an all-professional force. It was not, many troops were wartime conscripts. Out of six divisions one was specialized, the 3 Mountain Brigade which was trained for fighting in the snow.

It was commanded by a friend of Hitler's from the old Munich days and the troubles which had led to the formation of the Nazi Party. General Dietl was an expert on mountain warfare and had participated in Norwegian mountain manoeuvres before the war.

The nub of the problem for the German planners was to find a way of transporting six divisions and all the extra equipment required with speed and as much secrecy as could be maintained. Some half a million tons of shipping would be required. It was therefore decided to carry out the strategy in three stages:

1. It was decided to send on ahead the slower moving transports, loaded with equipment. These ships, some of which were to be flying neutral flags, would lie in wait in Norwegian ports.
2. The main striking force of some 8,850 men would be transported in warships.
3. Once bridgeheads had been established in the main ports, reinforcements were to be sent through Oslo, the nearest and safest port from exposure to the British Navy.

In one major respect the German plan differed from that of the Allies. The Germans proposed to employ a realistic number of aircraft. The X Air Corps based on Hamburg would support the invasion with a total of 1,212 aircraft of which about 600 were transport planes, many of which had been taken over from pre-war civil airlines. The initial aim was to seize the main airfields at Oslo and Stavanger employing paratroops for the purpose. About 100 fighter planes would dispose of the tiny Norwegian air-force. A force of about 400 bombers would support the landing, terrorize the civilian population and deal with British naval forces. The German plan was simple, comprehensive and above all bold. Despite inter-service rivalry, co-operation between the various branches of the services was remarkable as compared with that of the British armed services at that stage of the war.

See Fig. 3 General Map of Invasion p.x

Chapter 8

The Invasion Fleets

Hitler remarked to Goering on the eve of the invasion of Poland that he had always been a gambler. Grand Admiral Raeder and the entire naval staff knew what a gamble Weserubung would be. The disparity in strength between the German navy and the Royal Navy was immense [see Appendix IV]. Just as the British Army was the Cinderella, so in the German scale of priorities the Kriegsmarine came last.

At 02.00 on 7 April 1940 the battleship *Scharnhorst* and her sister ship *Gneisenau* emerged from their berths at Wilhelmshaven on the river Jade under the command of Vice Admiral Günther Lütjens, later the ill-fated commander of the *Bismarck*. They were joined at the Schillig Roads, off Wilhelmshaven, by the cruiser *Admiral Hipper* and four destroyers. A further nine of the most modern destroyers available, commanded by Commodore Friedrich Bonte, joined them from their base at Bremerhaven on the Weser. About half of the destroyers in the entire German fleet had been allocated to conveying Groups 1 and 2 bound for Narvik and Group 3 bound for Trondheim.

The timing of the German invasion of Norway depended upon several factors. There was a new moon on 7 April and the German fleet could sail under cover of darkness, but on 2 April Hitler postponed the operation until 9 April. Under the German plan, this meant that the supply ships for the furthest destinations had to set sail on 3 April. Group 6 bound for Egersund and group 5 bound for Kristiansand, both on the southern coast of Norway put out into the North Sea on 8 April. On the same day Group 4 bound for Oslo left Kiel on the Baltic.

Meanwhile the British had made their moves. An admiral exercises command from the ship on which he flies his distinctive admiral's flag, and on 4 April Admiral Sir Edward Evans hoisted his on the cruiser *Aurora* moored in the Clyde. The *Aurora,* together with another cruiser at Scapa Flow, were to escort a large transport to Narvik. By 7 April a single battalion was aboard a second transport in the Clyde bound for Trondheim. A further four battalions bound for Stavanger and Bergen together with 90 tons of stores were loaded on to four more cruisers lying in the Forth.

The Allied Supreme War Council had taken the decision to mine the Norwegian coast on 28 March. The cruiser *Birmingham* was already in the Lofoten area when intelligence was received that the Norwegians had moved four (in fact two) coastal defence vessels to Narvik. The Admiralty decided to order Vice Admiral W. Whitworth to proceed to Narvik flying his flag aboard the heavy battle-cruiser *Renown*. Weighing in at 32,000 tons and armed with six 15-inch guns she was escorted by four destroyers: *Greyhound, Glowworm, Hyperion*, and *Hero*. Each destroyer was armed with 4.7-inch guns together with torpedoes. Clearly the Admiralty had more than coastal defence vessels in mind.

The mine laying force had set sail on 5 April. It was composed of three flotillas: one was to lay dummy mines and one known as force WAK, consisting of four mine laying destroyers and four escort destroyers, which were destined to mine the Vestfjord. Reaching down from the north Norwegian shore in a great arc 70 miles long, the Lofoten Islands shield the Vestfjord from the open sea. The mining of the Vestfjord was duly carried out in the early hours of 8 April. Simultaneously the British action was communicated to the Norwegian government and as expected the Norwegians protested vigorously.

There was mounting evidence from diplomatic and intelligence reports that something was afoot but the first hard evidence that the German fleet was at sea came from the Royal Air Force. At 08.00 on 7 April Hudson reconnaissance planes sighted one cruiser and six destroyers steering north through the Skagerrak between Denmark and Norway. Owing to the practice of maintaining radio silence, the news did not reach Scapa Flow until 11.20. Meanwhile Coastal Command despatched a force of twelve Blenheim two-engine fighter bombers which attacked the German squadron, but without scoring any hits of consequence. They did however report on their return in the afternoon that the force appeared to be composed of one pocket battleship, two cruisers and ten destroyers.

At this stage there was a general assumption by Churchill, the Admiralty and Admiral Forbes at Scapa Flow in the Orkney Islands that this was an attempt by a substantial German force to break out into the Atlantic shipping lanes through the Faroes/Iceland gap. When the Director of Naval Intelligence had passed the information first received from the RAF to Admiral Forbes at Scapa Flow, he also referred to the various diplomatic and other reports of an impending invasion of Norway saying: 'all these reports are of doubtful value and may only be a further move in the war of nerves'.

It was not until 17.30 on 7 April that Forbes gave the order to the Home Fleet to raise steam. Such was the nature of massive steam turbines that it took several hours to get up the requisite pressure. It was not until 20.15 before the last ship cleared the anchorage at Scapa Flow. Flying his flag on HMS *Rodney*

(33,950 tons), armed with nine 16-inch guns, accompanied by the battleship *Valiant*, the heavy cruiser *Repulse*, two light cruisers and ten destroyers, Forbes steered north east. At the same time the 2nd Cruiser Squadron sailed from Rosyth under Vice Admiral G. Edward-Collins with two cruisers and eleven destroyers to sweep the Norwegian coast.

The weather had been deteriorating for twenty-four hours. Now a force seven near gale was blowing making it difficult for the destroyers to maintain their station. Admiral Lütjens was experiencing similar difficulties. What was not appreciated by the German soldiers packed on board the destroyers, few of whom had ever been on anything more than a days outing on the River Spree and most of whom were paralysed by seasickness, was that the weather was their greatest ally. Visibility at sea level was down to a few miles and observation from the air was shielded by cloud. If the Germans had been making for the Atlantic, Forbes may well have intercepted them. In the event the two fleets were sailing on almost parallel courses. Their tracks were about sixty miles apart with Lütjens ahead and Forbes further out in the Norwegian Sea. Given the technology available in 1940 they might just have well been hundreds of miles apart. Churchill, ever able to paint a picture in words told the Commons several days later: 'When you get out on the sea with its vast distances, its storms and mists, with night coming on and all the uncertainties that exist you cannot possibly expect the kind of conditions appropriate to consider in respect of the movements of armies, have any application to the chance and haphazard conditions of collisions by ships of war at sea.'

Just such a haphazard collision did take place on the morning of 8 April on approximately the same latitude as Trondheim. By this time Admiral Whitworth was far to the north approaching Vestfjord. On the way one of his escorting destroyers, the *Glowworm*, turned back to pick up a sailor who had been swept overboard. By chance a couple of German destroyers, which had been unable to keep up with Lütjens force, hove in sight. Without hesitation Lieutenant Commander Gerard Broadmead-Roope, in command of the *Glowworm*, pressed home the attack. The German destroyers, believing the *Glowworm* to be part of a larger force, retired towards Trondheim and a running battle ensued. The force destined for the landing at Trondheim included the German heavy cruiser *Admiral Hipper* (14,000 tons) armed with eight 8-inch guns. In order to synchronize the landings at various points on the Norwegian coast, this force was marking time. The *Hipper* immediately answered the German destroyer's call for assistance. In the poor visibility it was not long before the *Glowworm* found herself facing almost certain destruction. She could neither outgun nor outrun the cruiser. The *Admiral Hipper* opened fire with accuracy. The *Glowworm* soon caught fire, but not before she had fired several torpedoes at the cruiser all of which missed. The destroyer then put down a smoke screen and the Germans assumed that she was trying to escape. On emerging through the smoke, the *Admiral Hipper* beheld the *Glowworm* steering straight for her at full speed. The German captain subsequently claimed that he turned with the intention of ramming the *Glowworm* but as he later admitted, had he done so, the *Admiral Hipper* might well have done herself more damage than she in fact suffered.

The *Glowworm* was too nimble for the cruiser and struck the larger vessel just below the bow. Sliding down the side of the cruiser, the *Glowworm* ripped away no less than 120ft of the *Admiral Hipper's* armoured belt. Shortly afterwards the *Glowworm* rolled over and sank. In those latitudes men in the water do not last long, but the Germans were able to rescue some of them. Ironically, Broadmead-Roope reached the *Admiral Hipper's* ladder but while climbing up he lost his grip and fell back into the heavy swell, never to be seen again. He was posthumously awarded the Victoria Cross, the first such award of the Second World War.

While Forbes continued to press northward, Whitworth was ordered to cut off the northbound German force. This meant steering away from the Norwegian coast. By the greatest of ironies, the Admiralty sent a signal to the mine-laying force and its escorting destroyers in Vestfjord: 'destroyers should report to Admiral Whitworth in order to strengthen his hand'. This left Vestfjord open to the German troop-carrying destroyers bound for Narvik.

On the morning of 8 April the Polish submarine *Orzel* was cruising off Lilliesand at the southern tip of Norway. She was part of Admiral Horton's submarine flotilla patrolling the Kategat and Skagerrack when she surfaced to challenge a large steamer the *Rio de Janeiro* heading north. This was readily identified as a pre-war German liner and in compliance with the Geneva Convention time had to be given to the crews of non-combatant ships to take to the boats. Once the niceties of the convention had been complied with (almost the last time that they were), a single torpedo sufficed to send her to the bottom. Shortly after a Norwegian destroyer and some fishing boats arrived and took the survivors aboard. Many were German soldiers in uniform who stated candidly that they were on their way to Bergen to protect Norway from the British. This was known to the Admiralty in the early afternoon, was published to the world by Reuters at 20.30, but not reported to the C-in-C Home Fleet until 22.55. This raises a number of questions: why didn't the Admiralty act more decisively and earlier? The Admiralty merely sent a message to Forbes saying that the intelligence sent the previous day, classed as of doubtful value might after all have been true. Why did not the Norwegians mobilize immediately?

The same afternoon at 14.30 a sea-plane from Forbe's force reported a battleship, with cruisers and two destroyers about eighty miles ahead and steering west. In order to synchronize the landings, it was in fact the *Admiral Hipper* and the ships destined for Trondheim, marking time. Forbes accordingly steered north-west to intercept them. The *Admiral Hipper* shortly turned east for Trondheim. Also in the afternoon British submarines off the Skaw (the northern tip of Denmark) reported enemy warships sailing north. This news was relayed to Forbes. By the evening, in a rising gale, having missed the Trondheim force, Forbes turned south. Earlier he had sent the battle-cruiser HMS *Repulse*, the cruiser *Penelope* and some destroyers, first to help the *Glowworm* and then to proceed north to reinforce Whitworth. He was now convinced that he was dealing with an invasion of Norway and hoped to make a rendezvouz with Vice Admiral Edward-Collins's 2nd Cruiser squadron and to intercept the other German warships reported to be off the southern Norwegian coast.

Part of the German plan was that once Admiral Lütjens had dropped off the force destined for Narvik, the *Scharnhorst* and the *Gneisenau* should steer north, then out into the Atlantic in order to create a diversion. By this time Whitworth had been ordered back to cover the approach to Narvik and he therefore altered course to the south-east. Luck then swung in favour of the British. At 03.37 on 9 April, when in the far north it is already getting light, Admiral Whitworth's flag ship HMS *Renown* was off the southern tip of the Lofoten islands. According to her log, the *Renown* spotted two battleships with the unmistakeable rising sheer of the bows favoured by German naval designers, hard against the dawn light, six minutes before they spotted her. Turning to intercept them, the *Renown* opened fire first at a range of 15,000 yards (about 8.5 miles). Any degree of accuracy at that range, with ships pitching and rolling in a near gale, must have been problematic. Nevertheless, early on the *Renown* disabled the *Gneisenau*'s main gunnery control system and later knocked out a forward gun turret. The *Scharnhorst* immediately moved to lay smoke and to place herself between her sister ship and the enemy. The two modern battleships perhaps missed an opportunity to avenge the sinking of the *Graf Spee* by eliminating the elderly British battle-cruiser, for despite her heavier guns, her lighter armour was more vulnerable. But they were under strict orders to lure the Home Fleet out into the Atlantic and in any case the damage to the *Gneisenau* settled the matter. In the ensuing chase, HMS *Renown* was compelled by the steep seas to reduce speed in order to fight her forward guns, whereas the Germans could draw away at full speed while firing their aft guns. In the rough seas, sleet and squalls the German ships were soon lost to sight.

Early on the following day, April 9, the Norwegian Prime Minister, Dr Koht telephoned Sir Cecil Dormer, the British Ambassador, informing him that four large German warships were proceeding up Oslofjord, five ships were approaching Bergen and at least one Stavanger. The news reached the Foreign Office at 03.45 and was immediately relayed to the War Cabinet Office and the duty officers at the Admiralty, the War Office, and the Air Ministry. At 05.00 the Admiralty signalled Forbes with the news.

Having failed to intercept the invasion force, there remained the question of the *Scharnhorst* and the *Gneisenau*, so Forbes once more turned north. In fact the two German ships had sailed far out into the Norwegian Sea then turned south and passing just east of the Faroes, they sailed between the Orkney and the Shetland Islands, reaching Willemshaven on 12 April, their mission accomplished.

On several occasions the Admiralty had intervened when it might have been better if they had not, for example ordering Whitworth's destroyers to leave the entrance to Vestfjord unguarded. Indifferent intelligence and delays in transmitting intelligence from the RAF did not help. Even Churchill admitted: 'Looking back, I consider the Admiralty kept too close a control on the Commander in Chief.'

Chapter 9

Is it Christmas?

Indications that something was afoot had begun to gather momentum from December 1939. At the turn of the year a number of Secret Intelligence (MI6) Reports asserted that German forces were assembling and carrying out combined operations exercises in the Baltic involving the army, navy, and air force. In February, the military attaché in Stockholm had relayed the view of a Romanian diplomat that Germany was preparing to occupy the Swedish ore-fields together with one or more naval and several air bases in Southern Norway. With the accumulation of straws in the wind, why were these and later reports not made better use of? There had been no delay in bringing these reports to the notice of the Chiefs of Staff. On three occasions before 3 February, the Chiefs of Staff resumé had included items drafted by Military Intelligence summarizing the SIS reports but qualifying them. The last report dismissed the idea that the reports justified the view that a German expeditionary force was being prepared.

Obsession with an *idée fixe* is not confined to the profession of arms. Military intelligence had concluded in December that Germany would need twenty-five to thirty divisions for an invasion of Norway and Sweden. Intelligence reports that there were only six divisions in the northern coastal region were correct. This was all that Weserubung would require, but military intelligence had drawn the conclusion that they were not adequate for the invasion of Norway and Sweden.

In the spring the pace began to quicken, and on 26 March telegrams were received from Stockholm as follows: The air attaché reported that it was the view of the Swedish naval staff that Germany was ready to seize Norwegian ports and air-fields. The naval attaché reported that there was a concentration of fast merchant vessels at Kiel, the main German naval base on the Baltic, and that fifty merchant vessels had passed through the Kiel Canal into the Baltic. On 2 April the naval attaché in Oslo reported that there were troop concentrations on the Baltic coast at Rostock. There was a further report from the Swedish government of German troops concentrating on the Baltic at Stettin and Swinemunde.

49

In so far as British Intelligence took these reports seriously, it was assumed that the objective would be southern Norway. Nobody dreamed that Narvik might be an objective. Were the Norwegians any better informed than the British? On 5 April the Norwegian Legation in Berlin had cabled Oslo: 'Rumours of occupation of points on the south coast of Norway'. From 1000 on 8 April messages had flooded in from Denmark of a large number of ships, many of them flying neutral flags steaming north through the Great Belt, the islands lying west of Copenhagen and through the Kattegat between Denmark and Sweden.

As recounted, at midday on 8 April the Polish submarine *Orzel* had sunk the *Rio de Janiero* with German troops in uniform aboard. On receiving this news the Norwegian government failed to order mobilization. The Norwegians first got wind of Group 5 approaching Oslofjord shortly before midnight. At 00.30 on 9 April, the order was given by the Norwegian Admiralty to douse all lights. In Oslo the air-raid sirens sounded and the city was blacked out. The two island fortresses of Rauoy and Bolarne laid a beam of light across the fjord and the *Blucher* a brand new heavy cruiser, which had not even completed its sea trials became held in the searchlights. The Norwegians opened fire briefly with 15cm guns [approx. 6-inch] but no damage was done. The three large German vessels sailed on at 18 knots, the *Blucher* in the lead, followed by the renamed *Lutzow*, formerly the pocket battleship *Deutschland*, and the older light cruiser *Emden*.

The first action took place when a German torpedo-boat the *Albatross* was challenged by the *Pol III*, a Norwegian patrol vessel, at the entrance to the fjord. It was only a matter of minutes before the patrol boat was blown to bits. The next objective was the small naval base at Horton on the western bank of the fjord. Detachments of infantry were transferred to R-Boats [small motor minesweepers]. Again the Norwegians put up a fight. The mine-layer *Olaf Trygvason*, with 12cm guns [4.5-inch] sank the R17 and damaged the R21.

The capital was to be secured by General Engelbrecht commanding 163rd Division. This called for a landing at first light and Rear Admiral Oskar Kummetz proceeded up the fjord. A few miles south of Oslo there are the Drobak narrows with Fort Oscarsborg on an island on the western side of the main stream and the Kaholm Island on the eastern side. Besides light artillery, Kaholm was equipped with three 28cm [11-inch] guns, ironically supplied in 1905 by Krupp, the German armaments manufacturer. In the half light of dawn, the ships stood out, but the batteries were obscured. At 05.20 Colonel Eriksen, the 65-year-old battery commander on Kaholm, ordered the first salvo. A shell from the antiquated guns, fired at a range of 600 yards, stuck the superstructure of the *Blucher* and another set the aircraft hangar on fire. At the same time the 15cm batteries on the eastern shore opened up and the cruisers steering mechanism was damaged. Although known to German intelligence, there was a submerged battery of torpedoes at Kaholm and within minutes two 45cm torpedoes struck the *Blucher*. The engine room became flooded and the turbines stopped.

At 05.50 a radio message from the *Blucher* handed command of operations over to Captain Thiele on the *Lutzow*. When the *Blucher* was first attacked the *Lutzow* and the *Emden* had gone astern in order to move out into the fjord. Captain Thiele knew that he could disembark the 400 mountain troops on his ship and the troops aboard the *Emden* further to seaward on the eastern shore. Meanwhile the fires aboard the *Blucher* became increasingly out of control and at 06.30 the unhappy ship, by then upstream from the forts, was shaken by a huge explosion as one of the magazines blew up. As she settled on her side the order to abandon ship was given. There were not enough life jackets to go round nevertheless some of the sailors were seen to give up their own life jackets to young soldiers. About 400 metres of ice cold water had to be traversed and 320 men lost their lives including members of the Gestapo and some of General Engelbrecht's staff. The General himself was temporarily held as a prisoner by the Norwegians. Fortunately for him, the Commander-in-Chief General von Falkenhorst had remained at his HQ in Hamburg.

It was not until the afternoon of 9 April that a combined attack by troops, warships and aircraft overwhelmed the fort at Drobak. Kaholm held out until the following morning. Part of the plan to take Oslo had involved paratroops landing at Fornebu airport some miles south west of the capital but they had been delayed by fog. It was these airborne troops who were the first to march into Oslo which had been declared an 'open city', six hours behind schedule. The delay had momentous consequences. At 01.30 King Haakon had been woken with the words 'Your Majesty, we are at war', to which he had very properly replied 'with whom?' At about the same time members of the government gathered at the foreign ministry on the Victoriaterrasse. They had been informed that foreign warships were sailing up Oslofjord and there were reports of further foreign warships off Bergen and Stavanger. Dr Halvedan Khot, the foreign minister, rang up the British minister in Oslo, Sir Cecil Dormer, who was in bed, and told him the news. At the same time, the minister of defence ordered a mobilization. This did not involve more than four brigades, while the remainder were to be called up by post.

Meanwhile, Dr Kurt Brauer, the German minister in Oslo had been up all night. By 04.30 it was fully light but there was no sign of the German squadron which he was expecting. News of the fighting had come in so he called on the foreign ministry with a carefully prepared memorandum which he presented to Dr Khot. It ran to nineteen pages and stated among other things that the sole aim of German military operations was to protect Germany's northern flank from the occupation of bases by Anglo-French forces. It went on to say that in taking this action the German government was serving the interests of Norway. It was, nevertheless, made icy clear that Germany expected the Norwegian government and people to offer no resistance, adding that any resistance would be ruthlessly broken.

Dr Koht recalled in his memoirs that it appeared absolutely impossible to surrender his country to German domination. 'I knew too much about Nazi methods to wish them to prevail in Norway...I recalled vividly Hitler's broken pledges to Austria, Czechoslovakia and Poland'. Naturally he referred the matter to the other members of the government and within the hour he was able to rejoin Dr Brauer with a unanimous rejection. At 05.30 Carl Hambro, President of the Storting, the Norwegian Parliament, arrived at the foreign ministry. He and King Haakon in their resolution were to emerge as the heroes of the hour. Hambro immediately gave orders for a special train to be ready by 07.00 hours to take ministers and such members of parliament who were prepared to go, to leave for Hamar, about 80 miles north of Oslo. Both the King and the Crown Prince agreed to join the train

That afternoon the Norwegian deputies met in the Festival Hall in Hamar and a lengthy debate took place. The Prime Minister Johan Nygaardsvold although by nature defeatist, agreed that the Labour government should remain in office, but should include representatives of the right, the Agrarian party and the Liberal left. The Prime Minister and the leader of the left Liberals were in favour of treating with the Germans but Trygve Lie, later to become so well known in the United Nations, disagreed vehemently. Both the king and the crown prince advocated a determined resistance. Their hand was strengthened when the Finance Minister, Oscar Torp announced that he had been able to evacuate the whole of Norway's gold reserves. At 19.30 they were advised to take the train to a safer destination, the small town of Elverum where the weary deputies met and wound up their deliberations by singing the Norwegian national anthem.

The late arrival of German troops and the flight of the government left a power vacuum in Oslo. It was at this point that Rosenburg's henchman in Oslo persuaded Vidkun Quisling to throw his hat into the ring. With approval from Berlin, Quisling broadcast to the nation in a speech which effectively sealed his own death warrant five years later. 'Fellow Norwegians, by laying mines in Norwegian territorial waters, England has violated the neutrality of Norway...the German government has offered their assistance with solemn assurances that national independence would be respected...the Nygaardsvold government has fled and a National government has grasped the reins of power, headed by [who do you think?] Vidkun Quisling.'

The light cruiser *Karlsruhe* approached Kristiansand in southern Norway at 04.00 on 9 April but had to wait several hours for the thick fog to clear. Captain

Rieve decided to put the troops ashore by patrol vessels near to the shore batteries. Two attempts were made to force a passage, but each time the shore batteries opened fire. The Norwegian battery commander then received a message that British and French warships were approaching. The German patrol vessels were flying the French flag and were permitted to land. By midday the town was in German hands. In the evening the *Karlsruhe* was able to put to sea for the homebound voyage but within the hour was attacked by a British submarine, the *Truant* [action described later].

The three major ports on the west coast, Stavanger, the most southerly, Bergen, the former Hanseatic League entrepot and Trondheim the ancient capital and cathedral city, are all situated an hour's steaming distance from the open sea. Just as lookouts in days gone by had given warning of marauding Viking parties so much the same purpose was served by the respective shore batteries. The landings at these ports did not go entirely to plan and might have gone considerably worse if the Norwegians had been better organized.

One of the main prizes at Stavanger was Sola airfield some eight miles to the south west of the city. The first the Norwegians knew of it was when six Messerschmidt 110 fighter bombers attacked the airfield and destroyed two Norwegian aircraft on the ground. Ten Ju52 transport planes then flew in carrying 120 paratroops who proceeded to capture the airfield. This was followed by 180 aircraft which flew in carrying the 69th Division designated to occupy not only the Sola airfield but also Stavanger and the nearby seaplane base. It was the first time in history that an airborne force had captured a major military objective.

A larger force commanded by Rear Admiral Hubert Schmundt was sent to Bergen, Norway's most important port. There were already several German ships lying at anchor in the fjord flying neutral flags. The light cruisers *Koln* and her sister ship *Konigsberg* together with an elderly cruiser, the *Bremse* carrying 1,900 troops of the 69 Division approached with doused lights. The *Koln* then signalled 'HMS *Cairo* proceeding to Bergen for a short visit'. She was allowed to pass the outer forts, but a searchlight on the island of Kvarven picked her out. Within a short space of time the batteries on the island opened fire hitting the *Konigsberg* three times and also damaging the *Bremse* and one of the German destroyers, the *Karl Peters*. The German flotilla sailed on. Two German trawlers supported by fast patrol vessels disembarked 2,000 troops. The forts were overpowered and the troops soon made themselves masters of the city.

Some 30 miles north-west of Trondheim, the approach from the sea into Trondheim Fjord is at its narrowest, about two miles. The main forts are at Brettingen and Hysnes. The German commander decided that boldness was required and the heavy cruiser *Admiral Hipper* and four destroyers steamed down the narrows at 25 knots. The guns on the Brettingen fort opened fire without doing much damage, but the first two salvoes from the German ships destroyed the electric cables leading to the forts and the searchlights were extinguished. At 07.00 troops landed at Trondheim and the city offered no resistance. That was not quite the end of the story. One German destroyer was left behind to land troops and deal with the forts. At Hysnes, the Norwegians opened fire damaging the destroyer so badly that she had to be beached and the brave defenders of the fort did not surrender until the afternoon. Vaernes airfield, some 16 miles east of Trondheim, which was essential to the German plan for bringing in reinforcements by air, held out until midday the following day.

In the far north the Germans benefited from an almost incredible stroke of good fortune. Following the *Glowworm* incident the Admiralty thought that the Germans were attempting a breakout in force into the Atlantic shipping lanes. The Admiralty ordered the four mine-laying destroyers and their four destroyer escorts in the Vestfjord to join Admiral Whitworth off the southern tip of the Lofotens. Thus on the night of 8/9 April, Commodore Bonte, commander of the German destroyer flotilla bound for Narvik, was able to sail up the Vestfjord and into the Ofotfjord undetected. On board were Major General Eduard Dietl and three battalions from the Mountain Division. At 03.00 they passed the Tranoy pilot station at the entrance to the Ofotfjord. At 04.10 they passed the island of Baroy. Both the British and the Germans thought that there were coastal batteries; there were in fact none. There were however two small patrol vessels and they were able to sound the alarm.

Coming up to Narvik, Bonte instructed some of his destroyers to proceed beyond Narvik to Herjangsfjord. At the head of the fjord was Elvegaard a small military depot which soon fell to a German landing party without a fight. With the *Wilhelm Heidkamp*, the *Arnim*, and the *Thiele* the commodore approached Narvik. At the entrance to the harbour they were challenged by the *Eidsvoll*. Although built in 1900, the *Eidsvoll*'s armament was not inconsiderable: two 21cm guns (8.2-inch) and six 15cm guns (5.92-inch). As the German flagship approached the harbour through the mist, the *Eidsvoll* fired a shot across her bows and ordered her to heave to. Commodore Bonte signalled 'am sending boat with officer'. The German was received on the bridge of the *Eidsvoll* where he read out a prepared statement demanding surrender. The Norwegian captain, Odd Willoch, replied that his honour would never allow him to do that. It seems that the Germans gave the Norwegians a fair chance to surrender but they did not give them a fair chance should they decide to fight. As the pinnace was returning to the *Heidkamp* the German officer moved out of the line of fire and fired a red star shell. Thereupon the *Heidkamp* fired two torpedoes. Within seconds the *Eidsvoll* broke in two and sank. There were only eight Norwegian survivors.

The remaining Norwegian naval vessel, the *Norge* was inside the harbour breakwater. The first German destroyer to enter the Harbour was the *Arnim*. The *Norge* turned her guns on the destroyer but the Germans were quicker with their more modern guns and followed up their salvo with two torpedoes. Both struck home and the *Norge* rolled over and sank. Only 96 Norwegian sailors survived out of 201. This concludes the catalogue of heroic but hopeless self-sacrifice of a few resolute and courageous coastal battery commanders, naval officers and their men, on that first day, by which the honour of Norway was redeemed. The rest of Norway was asleep.

Narvik was a thriving town of some 10,000 people whose prosperity was based on the terminal of the railway line running from the Swedish iron ore fields. For several days the *Jan Wellem* had been lying in the harbour flying a huge Nazi flag, laden with fuel for the German destroyers. It seems that the Germans did not storm ashore with guns blazing, but disembarked on the quay in an orderly manner. Narvik had a garrison of about 400 men commanded by an elderly major named Sundlo who was later accused of being a Nazi sympathizer. He concluded that discretion was the better part of valour and surrendered the town without a shot being fired. In the confusion half the garrison refused to obey the order and marched away on the inland road. In the middle of the morning Mayor Broch and members of the town council proceeded to the German headquarters in the Royal Hotel. General Dietl then told Broch that Major Sundlo had been sensible to surrender the town to him as he made it clear that otherwise he would have blown the town to bits. At his trial after the war Major Sundlo was acquitted of high treason but he was sent to prison.

Theodor Broch, the youthful and talented mayor of Narvik describes what it was like on that first morning in his unforgettable memoir *The Mountains Wait*. His home was a comfortable villa situated some way above the harbour. He and his wife were woken by the first explosion which they thought came from the railway. They quickly realised that the further explosions came from the harbour and their small daughter rushed into the room saying, 'Is it Christmas?'

Chapter 10

The Rape of Denmark

On 9 April, while German warships were steaming up Oslofjord and approaching other Norwegian ports, what might be described as the rape of Denmark took place between 05.15 and lunchtime. Denmark is virtually indefensible against a great power. It is only 240 miles from the German border to the northern tip of Jutland and the distance from Copenhagen to the North Sea is about the same. The country consists of the mainland Jutland peninsula and two large islands. Funen is separated from Jutland by a narrow band of water known as the Little Belt and Zealand is separated from Funen by a somewhat wider passage known as the Great Belt. Copenhagen on the eastern shore of Zealand looks across the Sund which separates Denmark from Sweden.

In August 1939 the German foreign ministry had informed the Danes that Germany would respect the country's integrity adding ominously 'in so far as Denmark maintains strict neutrality, but that Germany would not tolerate breaches of neutrality by third parties'. It must have been fairly obvious that if Germany wished to launch an attack on Sweden or southern Norway, Denmark would have to be involved. Captain Krancke's original plan envisaged employing diplomatic means only. It was thought that the threat of occupying northern Jutland would be enough to induce the Danes to grant the Germans the use of airfields in north Jutland.

When General Falkenhorst was appointed commander of Weserubung his staff reviewed the Krancke plan and proposed that the whole of Jutland should be occupied. On 28 February, Falkenhorst reported to the Chief of Staff of Combined Services at OKW, General Keitel, and asked that a provisional corps headquarters and two divisions should be allotted to the Danish operation. On 1 March Hitler issued a Führer directive authorizing an actual operational plan which would be known as Weserubung Sud and that it should provide for the occupation of Jutland and the island of Funen. Landings were also to be made on Zealand which could be expanded should the Danes resist.

The XXXI Corps headquarters was set up in Hamburg and the 170th Division assembled at Bremen. The 198th Division and 11 Motorized Rifle

Brigade assembled south east of Hamburg. On 7 April 11 Motorized Brigade and the 170th Infantry Division moved up to the Danish border and bivouacked on the Schleswig/Flensburg Road. The 198th Division, which was to be transported by sea, moved up to three ports on the Baltic: Kiel, Lübeck and Warnemünde. Operations by land went almost without a hitch. At precisely 05.15 on 9 April the 11 Motorized Rifle Brigade and the 170th Division moved across the border. Small special units had been sent ahead to secure vital bridges. Some resistance was put up by a few units of the Danish army but these were quickly dealt with and by 08.00 all fighting had ceased.

One of the features of Operation Weserubung was the flexibility which enabled a unit from one division to be temporarily assigned to another division. Thus a parachute platoon and a battalion of infantry from the 69th infantry division were transported by air to capture the airfield at Aalborg at the northern end of Jutland. The 69th Division had been earmarked for Norway and it was the intention to transfer it on to Norway as soon as the mission had been accomplished. By the late afternoon of the same day elements from 11 Motorized Rifle Brigade had reached the airfield at Aalborg. This meant that almost immediately the airfield could be used to support operations in Norway. A further bonus was that the railway from the south to Aalborg in the north was taken over intact and put to good use by the Germans on the same day.

Operations against the islands were a bit more complicated as ships had to sail many hours before zero hour in order to arrive at dawn. Two groups No. 10 and No. 11 set sail for the two ports of Esbjerg and Thyborn on the North Sea coast, where small bodies of troops encountered no opposition. Funen is linked by a rail bridge with the mainland at Middlefart where Group 9 consisting of a merchant ship and several smaller craft landed an infantry battalion at 06.30 in order to secure the bridge.

The main prize was Copenhagen, the political centre of the country, and it was decided to carry out a three-pronged operation. A battalion crossed over from Warnemünde on the North German coast on two train ferries and advanced across one of the small islands to land in south Zealand. With the aid of a parachute company a bridgehead was established by 07.30. Group 7 consisting of the staff of 198th Division together with a battalion of infantry embarked at the Baltic naval base at Kiel. They were bound for the two ferry ports; from Nyborg on Funen to Korsor on Zealand. While a torpedo boat and two minesweepers secured Nyborg, the main force embarked on an old battleship, the *Schleswig Holstein* and two merchant ships were destined for Korsor. The formation passed through the Great Belt in the early hours of the morning but the *Schleswig Holstein* ran aground and had to be abandoned. The landings were not opposed and the rest of the troops landed safely. By 13.00 forward units had crossed Zealand and entered Copenhagen.

The Germans had decided to approach Copenhagen as diplomatically as possible. Hitler had originally wanted a representative force only to land in the capital, but was advised that the Citadel [Kastellet] ought to be taken by force if necessary. On 7 April Major General Kurt Himer, the Chief if Staff to XXXI Corps, had arrived in Copenhagen in civilian clothes accompanied by a legation secretary from the Foreign Ministry. He was able to establish a telephone link with XXXI Corps headquarters in Hamburg and reported on the state of the harbour and the Citadel. He also contacted the German Minister, von Renthe-Fink and told him what was going on. Earlier a major attached to the invasion force had arrived in the city and been shown over the Citadel by a Danish sergeant!

Group 8 consisted of an infantry battalion which embarked at Travemünde on the motor ship *Hansestadt Danzig* escorted by an ice breaker, which wasn't necessary, accompanied by two picket boats bound for Copenhagen. Although searchlights illuminated the ships apparently the shore batteries could not open fire. The official reason given later was that there was grease in the barrels. The landing was accomplished without incident. Meanwhile the Danish Ministerial Council had been hastily convened and Renthe-Fink invited the government to capitulate. Their decision was hastened by General Himer's ultimatum that if they did not immediately comply, Copenhagen would be bombed. At 10.00 negotiations regarding the demobilization of the Danish armed forces were entered into.

In order to prevent the king from escaping, General Himer requested an audience. In point of fact the terms which the Danes were offered were remarkably lenient. Denmark was to continue to be governed by the Danish government and the Germans would merely make use of military installations. This arrangement lasted up to the end of August 1943 when increasing Danish resistance led to increasing German repression until the Danish government decided that it could no longer continue to comply with German demands and also remain a government representing the Danish people. The occupying forces then took over the government of the country like any other occupied country with all the paraphernalia of repression which that implied.

See Fig. 4 The Occupation of Denmark p.xi.

Chapter 11

The First and Second Battles of Narvik

When, on 8 April, Admiral Whitworth received a report of a substantial German warship to the south of him steering westwards, he decided to take his ships west to block what might be an attempt by German warships to break out into the Atlantic shipping lanes. As we have seen it was the *Admiral Hipper* marking time off Trondheim. Soon after dark, however, he received a message from the Admiralty: 'Most immediate concentrate on preventing any German force proceeding to Narvik.' Unfortunately the seas were so bad that he could only proceed slowly for the Vestfjord and thus it was that he came to fall in with the *Scharnhorst* and the *Gneisenau* as already recounted. While Whitworth gave chase, the atrocious weather made it impossible for his destroyers to keep up. He therefore ordered the 2nd Destroyer Flotilla to make for the Vestfjord while he turned westward in case the German battleships should attempt to break back.

During the morning of 9 April Admiral Forbes sent a message to the commander of the 2nd Destroyer Flotilla, Captain Warburton-Lee as follows: 'send some destroyers up to Narvik to make certain that no enemy troops land'. At midday the Admiralty signalled Warburton-Lee as follows: 'Press reports state one German ship has arrived Narvik and landed a small force. Proceed Narvik and sink or capture enemy ship. It is your discretion to land forces if you think you can recapture Narvik.' Thus Forbes had gone over the head of Whitworth and the Admiralty had gone over the head of Forbes and Whitworth. It must be remembered that unlike the War Office, the Admiralty is also an operational headquarters. A complicating factor was that Winston Churchill's flat, in his capacity as First Lord of the Admiralty was at the top of the Admiralty building and he kept dropping into operational headquarters.

At 16.00 the 2nd Destroyer Flotilla arrived off the pilot station on the Island of Tranoy which lies at the entrance to Ofotfjord on the southern side. An officer went ashore and the pilot station reported that six warships and one submarine had passed up the fjord. The reality was that visibility was so bad that in fact

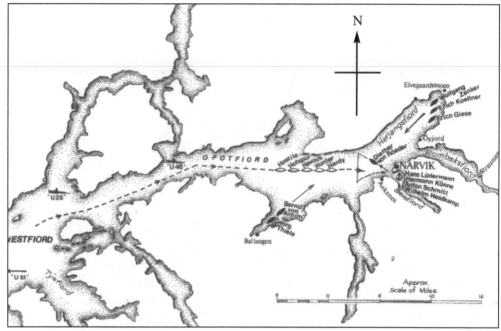

Fig. 6. 1st Naval Battle of Narvik

ten large German destroyers had sailed up the fjord. Warburton-Lee signalled the Admiralty: 'Intend attacking at dawn high water.' The point of this was that at high water his ships would have been able to float over mines laid in the narrow part of the fjord, if there were any. In point of fact there were none.

On receiving Warburton-Lee's signal, the Admiralty replied: 'Attack at dawn, all good luck'. Later they qualified it saying 'Norwegian coast defence ships *Eidsvoll* and *Norge* may be in Norwegian hands, you alone can judge whether in these circumstances attack should be made. We shall support whatever decision you take.' The onus of decision was thus placed on Warburton-Lee's shoulders, but he really had little choice. The gaze from one eye which had looked down from hundreds of steel engravings since boyhood had penetrated deeply into the subconscious of every officer in His Majesty's Navy. There could be no doubt in Warburton-Lee's mind where his duty lay.

With the benefit of hindsight Admiral Whitworth often mused afterwards that he should have ordered Warburton-Lee to wait until the reinforcement of the cruiser *Penelope* and destroyers had come up from the south. The matter had, however largely been taken out of his hands by the Admiralty so he decided not to intervene. He himself had to remain at sea marking the possible return of the *Scharnhorst* and *Gneisenau*.

On the face of it and with the benefit of hindsight, it would have paid Commodore Bonte to have set sail for home with at least some of his ships after delivering General Dietl and his troops. Logistics however suggest that the decision was not so simple. The flotilla was short of fuel. There should have been two tankers at Narvik awaiting his arrival. There was in fact only one, the *Jan Wellem*. Refuelling was a slow business. Each destroyer required five or six hundred tons of fuel and only two destroyers at a time could lie alongside the tanker. Moreover Commodore Bonte had been lulled into a false sense of security by a report from U5, a U-boat in the Vestfjord, that a flotilla of destroyers had been seen sailing westward. It was in fact Warburton-Lee's flotilla.

Commodore Bonte's flotilla was dispersed as follows:

Narvik Bay	*Wilhelm Heidkamp*
	Hans Lüdemann
	Hermann Künne
	Anton Schmitt
Herjangsfjord	*Wolfgang Zenker*
	Erich Koellner
	Erich Giese
Balangenfjord	*Bernd von Armin*
	Georg Thiele
On Patrol	*Diether von Roeder*

Just past midnight on 10 April, the British destroyers *Hunter, Havock, Hotspur* and *Hostile*, led by the *Hardy* were feeling their way up the Ofotfjord. Sailing almost blind in a snowstorm, the German destroyer on patrol missed them. In clear weather such features as the Anvil of the Gods, make for stunning views in these parts. On that night visibility was down to 500 yards and as they made their way up the fjord, the leading destroyer almost ran into a cliff.

At 04.30 just as it was getting light, the 2nd Flotilla arrived off Narvik, completely undetected. Narvik is not a harbour with breakwaters. One comes on a virtually landlocked bay on the south side of the Ofotfjord as one rounds the promontory upon which the town is built. Only the massive iron ore jetty sticks out into the bay. The first destroyer into the bay was HMS *Hardy* followed by the *Havock* and the *Hotspur*. Seeing the *Heidkamp* dead ahead, the *Hardy* fired two torpedoes. One torpedo hit the aft magazine of the *Heidkamp* and she blew up causing serious loss of life including that of Commodore Bonte. Two torpedoes were then fired at the *Schmitt* which broke in half.

In all there were five German destroyers at anchor or secured to the buoys in the bay. At first the German crews thought it was an air raid as they tumbled out of their bunks and rushed to action stations. They got their guns into action with commendable speed, but not before a British salvo hit the *Roeder* causing serious fires which temporarily disabled her. The two German destroyers alongside the tanker *Jan Wellem* managed to slip their cables, but suffered some damage. Two British destroyers had remained in the outer fjord on guard but joined in with the other three as they shelled the various merchant ships. Fortunately a torpedo which had been fired at the *North Cornwall* missed. There were a number of British merchant seamen imprisoned below decks. In all a total of six merchant ships were sunk but by a miracle – for the Germans – the *Jan Wellem* escaped.

By this time the 2nd Destroyer Flotilla was running low on torpedoes so Warburton-Lee decided to head for the open sea. He might have got clean away, had not the fortunes of war turned against him. The three German destroyers in Herjangsfjord some five miles further inland were not aware of what was going on until they received a message at 05.15. The *Zenker*, the *Giese* and the *Koellner* were each armed with five 5-inch guns as compared with the *Hardy* class of destroyer armed with four 4.7-inch guns. This belied the fact that the more modern German guns hurled a shell almost twice the weight of the British shells. Towards 06.00 as they approached in poor visibility, Warburton-Lee thought that one of them was a cruiser. This prompted him into signalling Forbes 'am withdrawing to westward at 30 knots'.

The *Thiele* and the *Von Arnim* now emerged almost dead ahead from the anchorage in the Ballangenfjord where they had lain concealed by the fog. A sharp fight developed and what proved to be Warburton-Lee's last signal 'Keep on engaging the enemy' bears an uncanny similarity with Nelson's last signal 'Engage the enemy more closely'. Within minutes a shell hit the *Hardy*'s bridge and every man on it was either killed or wounded. Warburton-Lee himself lay mortally wounded while his ship was careering down the fjord with nobody in control.

It was at this point that the ship's secretary, Paymaster Lieutenant G. Stanning took charge, despite a leg wound. Normally the paymaster lieutenant's job is an administrative one and he is not trained to fight a ship, still less command one. Dragging his lifeless leg he made his way to the wheel. The helmsman was dead and he took the wheel until relieved by an able seaman. A further German salvo cut the *Hardy*'s steam pipes and she began to lose way. Thereupon Stanning, taking the initiative gave the order to beach the vessel on the southern shore of the fjord, a decision which undoubtedly saved the lives of many of those aboard.

As the *Hardy* sheered away to port, HMS *Hunter* which was next in line drew the enemy's fire. She was soon set on fire and crippled. Astern of the *Hunter* was the *Hotspur* whose captain gave the order to swerve in order to avoid the stricken *Hunter*. At that moment a shell burst below the *Hotspur's* bridge cutting the controls from wheel to steering gear and the telephone link with the engine room. Captain Layman on the *Hotspur* watched helplessly as his ship ploughed into the *Hunter*. By a miracle Captain Layman managed to disengage his vessel from the *Hunter* which then sank. Although the Germans shortly rescued those of the crew that got clear, such were the icy waters in the fjord that only fifty survived. The remaining two British destroyers, the *Havoc* and the *Hostile* gave covering fire to the *Hotspur* as she made good her escape.

The three German destroyers which had emerged from the Herjangsfjord were so short of fuel that they had to call off the chase. The two vessels which had emerged from Ballangenfjord had suffered considerable damage as they had sailed past the British in order to join their compatriots. The *Thiele* had two guns put out of action, was on fire and had one magazine flooded. The *Arnim* had been hit five times and had one boiler room put out of action.

After breaking off the action, the three remaining British destroyers were making their way down Ofotfjord when a large merchant ship hove in sight coming up the fjord. A shot from the *Havock* hit her in the bows and set her on fire. The crew was then seen to be abandoning ship post haste. Once the boats were clear, two further rounds of high explosive were fired into her. The *Rauenfels*, a German supply ship as she turned out to be, blew up with an almighty explosion leaving little doubt that her main cargo had been ammunition.

So ended the first battle of Narvik. It would be difficult to record all the acts of bravery and self-sacrifice on both the British and the German ships, but the story of the survivors of the *Hardy*, based on Captain Macintyre's account is moving.

When ordered to abandon ship 400 yards of icy water had to be traversed to reach the southern shore. All the boats and rafts had been smashed and the able bodied in their cork buoyancy jackets had to tow the wounded. When at last Warburton-Lee was persuaded to leave his ship he was strapped to a stretcher and taken ashore, but died on the beach. He was subsequently awarded posthumously, the Victoria Cross.

The Germans continued to shell the *Hardy* and both the Chief Stoker and the doctor were wounded. They both got to the shore and the doctor despite his own shattered arm continued to tend the stoker on the beach until the latter died in the afternoon. Meanwhile the survivors made their way a short distance to some cottages where the inhabitants took them in, dried their clothes and revived them with hot soup. A Norwegian girl then set off on skis to fetch a doctor. When the doctor arrived he was able to tell them that there were no Germans further down the fjord at Ballangen. He telephoned for an ambulance and by midday the seriously wounded had been collected and taken to the cottage hospital. The rest of them, including the walking wounded set off on a gruelling 15-mile trek over the snowy roads to Ballangen cheered on with refreshments by the cottagers as they went. Three days later the survivors were able to signal to the destroyer HMS *Ivanhoe* which duly took them off.

The position of Captain Bey, who had succeeded to command of the German destroyers was an unenviable one. His three relatively undamaged destroyers were taking on fuel. The *Roeder* was so seriously damaged that she had to be berthed alongside the jetty, unfit for any serious action except harbour defence. That night Bey did attempt to break out with two destroyers, but on sighting British warships in Vestfjord, his nerve failed and he returned to Narvik. On the night of 11 April while manoeuvring in harbour, two of his undamaged destroyers ran aground. Unfortunately almost anything that you are likely to hit in Norway is likely to be a rock and not a sandbank. One destroyer damaged its propellers and the other was so badly damaged that there was no question of returning to Germany.

On the British side a diversion was caused by the news of a large tanker at Bodo, fifty miles south, with several transports. Admiral Whitworth decided to detach the destroyers HMS *Eskimo* and *Kimberley* to escort the cruiser *Penelope* south. A few miles short of Bodo the cruiser struck a rock and had to be towed back to a safe anchorage. Meanwhile the Admiralty ordered the Commander-in-Chief, Admiral Forbes to prepare to attack Narvik where it was still believed that there were two enemy cruisers. By this time the admiral was coming up from the south reinforced by the aircraft carrier HMS *Furious*. On the morning of 12 April Forbes made rendezvous with Whitworth and his two battle cruisers. He then decided to make an air attack on enemy forces in Ofotfjord.

The first squadron of Swordfish aircraft set off at 16.00 and from the start deficiencies in equipment and training became apparent. No previous reconnaissance had been made. The charts issued to the aerial navigators were photostat copies of Admiralty charts which do not show either the contours or heights of the land. Narvik itself is surrounded by mountain peaks varying between 1,000 and 3,000ft. The Swordfish was a biplane designed to carry torpedoes and was not suited to any sort of dive bombing. In low cloud with snow squalls at times obscuring the sea, the gallant young air crews set off on the 150 mile round trip to Narvik. As luck would have it, the weather cleared over the target and the aircraft released their bombs from between 400 and 1,200ft in a hail of shot and shell from the destroyers. No hits were registered. A second squadron left an hour later, by which time the weather had closed in and they did not even find the target. Happily all aircraft returned safely to the

Furious, making a landing at night which none of the pilots had attempted before.

The main plan of attack was that Whitworth should transfer his flag to perhaps the most famous British battleship of the twentieth century. Incidentally this was not sufficient to prevent HMS *Warspite* being sent to the breakers after the war by a philistine Board of Admiralty. It was rather like using a sledgehammer to crack a nut, moreover there would be some risk of attack by submarines in the restricted waters of the fjord. She was therefore escorted by five of the latest Tribal class of destroyer.

At 07.00 on 13 April Whitworth's squadron set off in order to traverse the 100 mile passage to Narvik. Captain Bey knew that they were on their way thanks to the ability of the Germans to read British signals. What they divined from this information did not have a favourable effect on German morale. Captain Bey might have done better to have concentrated all his destroyers near the narrows where they could have used their torpedoes to greater effect. In the event he did not give the order to raise steam until the *Koellner* on patrol sighted the British force as it approached the narrows at the entrance to the Ofotfjord.

At this point the *Warspite* launched a Swordfish adapted as a seaplane. Proceeding up the fjord Lieutenant Commander Brown, the navigator and Petty Officer Price did sterling work. Turning into Herjangsfjord above Narvik, looking for enemy destroyers, they spotted a German U-boat, U64 on the surface. Putting his machine into the simulation of a dive, for which it was not designed the pilot managed to release two 350lb anti-submarine bombs. One of the bombs found its mark and U64 was sent to the bottom. On the way back to the *Warspite*, the navigator noted that the *Koellner* was lurking in a bay just east of the narrow part of the fjord. Thus as the *Eskimo* and the *Bedouin* rounded the point, their guns were already trained on the bay and the *Koellner* was only able to fire one salvo before she was disabled. She was then finished off by the *Warspite*.

The next part of the battle was confused due to poor visibility which was down to about seven miles. The leading British destroyers were about three miles ahead of the battleship. About six miles west of Narvik three German destroyers, the only ones able to raise steam in time, joined the *Künne* which had been on patrol. A general action was joined with destroyers on both sides weaving from side to side to avoid the tracks of the other side's torpedoes. Another attack by ten Swordfish from the aircraft carrier *Furious* proved that, as yet, air attacks against warships under way were not very effective. Two aircraft were lost.

By 13.50 the *Zenker*, the *Arnim*, and the *Künne* had expended most of their ammunition so Captain Bey ordered them to retire. The first two retreated up Rombaksfjord just north of Narvik but HMS *Eskimo* chased the *Künne* up

Herjangsfjord. Her captain beached his ship which enabled the crew to escape ashore, before a torpedo from the *Eskimo* finished her off. The battle was not all one sided. HMS *Punjabi* had fallen victim to an accurate bombardment of 5-inch shells and fires were raging forward, amidships and aft. With her engines failing due to burst pipes, and many casualties, her captain pulled her out of the action. Nevertheless within the hour she was able to report for duty, although her speed was down to 15 knots due to a gaping hole in her bows.

The *Roeder* alongside the jetty in the harbour inflicted such damage on HMS *Cossack* that the latter's steering gear was put out of action and she ran aground on the south side of the fjord. It took twelve hours to refloat the *Cossack* under constant sniping from the Germans on the shore. Once the *Roeder* had been silenced by HMS *Warspite*, the destroyer *Foxhound* nosed gingerly towards her. It then became apparent that the crew members were rapidly disembarking so the *Foxhound* stopped short. Shortly afterwards two enormous explosions blew the *Roeder* apart. The only German destroyer left in the harbour was the *Giese*. She had had difficulty in raising steam but now she emerged to face five British destroyers. *'C'était magnifique mais ce n'est pas la guerre'* as a French general had said on observing the Charge of the Light Brigade.

The *Eskimo* then spotted the German destroyers moving up the Rombaksfjord above Narvik and she gave chase followed by the *Hero*, the *Bedouin* and the *Icarus*. Five miles above Narvik the fjord narrows down to about 500 yards before widening again. Only one ship at a time could pass. Fortunately aerial reconnaissance from the *Warspite* was able to report that two German destroyers, the *Zenker* and the *Arnim*, had gone to the head of the fjord and were disembarking their crews before, as soon became apparent, scuttling. The *Ludemann* and the *Thiele* however had turned at bay and loosed off their remaining torpedoes. The *Thiele*, by then damaged and on fire, with her captain wounded and the rest of the crew on the bridge killed, ran his ship at full speed on to the rocks where she capsized and sank.

The *Eskimo* just managed to evade the last of the three torpedoes from the *Ludemann* and the captains of the *Forester* and the *Hero* were only able to avoid them by going full steam astern but one of the second salvo of four torpedoes fired from the *Thiele* struck the *Eskimo* under the forecastle. She did not sink but as her captain steered his ship astern his anchor and cables which were hanging over the side became stuck fast on the shelving shore. The *Hero*, the *Icarus* and the *Kimberley* proceeded to the head of the fjord just in time to see the *Zenker* as she rolled over, slid off the rocks and sank. The *Ludemann* was aground with her engine room flooded and apparently deserted. She was finished off with a torpedo. Thus all ten German destroyers had been accounted for.

Chapter 12

The Royal Navy Encounters the Luftwaffe

When the Churchill government took office in 1940, the decision to build a bigger and better air force than the Germans had enormous strategic consequences, but it took defeat in Norway and at Dunkirk to convince the politicians. The Royal Navy, it might be said, got the message in one week starting on 9 April 1940. As for combined operations, the concept at that stage of the war was little more than a gleam in the eye of a few staff officers. There was no overall command of the air force and the other two services.

In the Narvik theatre, His Majesty's ships were safe from enemy air attack for the first week or so. The same cannot be said for Central or Southern Norway. Because of commitments in France and to the defence of Britain it was not possible to allocate more than a few squadrons to the Norwegian theatre. By comparison the Germans were in a position to allocate a whole air force division as part of their plan. The 12th Air Force Division at its peak strength in May 1940 numbered 360 bombers, fifty dive bombers and sixty long-range reconnaissance planes.

The key airfield in Central Norway was at Sola, eight miles south east of Stavanger. It provides an example of the amazing capability of the Germans. Within just two days that is by 11 April they were able to send out bombing missions from the airfield. In the first few days they were also able to make use of the airport at Kristiansand in Southern Norway. The airfields on the Danish mainland particularly at Aalborg on the Jutland peninsula gave Germany air command over the Skagerrak.

The workhorse of the Norwegian campaign was the two-engine Heinkel III carrying eight 55lb bombs. It had a range of 270 miles and from Stavanger could reach Aandalsnes, the southernmost point at which the British would land, but not as far as Trondheim. As was to emerge in the Battle of Britain some months later, the Heinkel was slow, but this was not a factor in Norway where there was virtually no fighter opposition. A more formidable bomber was the two-engine Junkers 88 with a payload comparable to the HE III, a speed of 300mph and a range of 615 miles. From Stavanger the JU88 could fly as far north as Bodo but not as far as Narvik. It could even fly as far as the Scottish coast. By the end of April the Germans had put Trondheim airfield into full commission which enabled them to reach Narvik and Harstad.

The great success story for the German air force in the Norwegian campaign was the Junkers 52, the slow inelegant transport plane with an engine in either wing and one in the nose. Never before had air transport been of strategic significance in a war. It was the JU52 which flew six companies of airborne troops into Oslo that enabled the Germans to take a city of a quarter of a million people before lunchtime without a single shot being fired. It was the JU52 that dropped 120 paratroops, which was enough to capture Stavanger aerodrome. In the first two weeks of the Norwegian campaign, the JU52 flew 3,018 sorties carrying 29,280 personnel, over a quarter of a million gallons of fuel and 2,376 tons of supplies. It came as a considerable surprise to the Allies to learn of the speed and the extent to which the Germans were able to fly in supplies to Oslo and troops and supplies from Oslo to Trondheim.

The most feared German aircraft by ships was the Stuka dive bomber JU57. Dive bombing was relatively accurate moreover the psychological effect of these vulture-like machines, with their peculiar W-shaped wings and fixed landing wheels projecting forwards like talons was particularly daunting to soldiers and sailors alike as they screamed down out of the sky. On the other hand the Stuka was small; it only had a crew of two; it had a payload of one 1,000lb bomb and a range of only 165 miles. This meant that from Stavanger the Stuka could not reach the port of Aandalsnes or Trondheim, but it could cover Bergen and of course 165 miles out to sea. It was slow and once Britain reached something like parity in the air, the Stuka proved particularly vulnerable to fighters.

The Norwegian air arm was a negligible factor in 1940 although later in the war the Norwegian government in exile built up a small but creditable air force. In 1940 there were only thirty seaplanes attached to coastal stations. There were eighteen scouting aircraft but only six fighters which were under army command. Two of the latter were destroyed on the ground when six Messerschmidt 110 twin-engine fighter bombers flew into the airfield at Sola near Stavanger.

By 1918, the Royal Navy had its own air arm, the Royal Naval Air Service but this was taken away and it only got a fleet air arm back in 1938. In this respect the British were behind the American and the Japanese navies. Of cardinal importance was the construction of aircraft carriers. Before the advent of American mass production methods it took several years to build an aircraft carrier. Britain had entered the war with only seven carriers in service. One of these was sunk by a U-boat in 1939. On 7 April the Home Fleet had set sail from Scapa Flow with no carriers at all. HMS *Furious* was undergoing repairs and the *Ark Royal* and the *Glorious* were in the Mediterranean. Incidentally the German navy did not have any aircraft carriers at all.

As far as air offensive weapons were concerned, official naval thinking favoured the airborne torpedo as the best means of sinking larger ships. This turned out to be correct as borne out by the air attack on the Italian fleet in Taranto Harbour in 1940 and the even more spectacular sinking of the HMS *Repulse* and *The Prince of Wales* off the coast of Malaya in December 1941. The aircraft with which the Royal Navy was equipped for this purpose was the Fairey Marine Swordfish a single-engine biplane which could only do 196 miles per hour. Nevertheless the Swordfish was robust and reliable and could carry either a torpedo or 2,000lbs of bombs. The Navy had asked for a dive bomber but what they got was the Blackburn Skua, a single-engine two-seater designed to act as a carrier-borne fighter and also a dive bomber. In the event it was not very satisfactory in either role and was withdrawn in 1941. The Navy also had the excellent biplane the Sea Gladiator.

Two branches of the Royal Air Force were mainly involved in the Norwegian Campaign: Coastal Command and Bomber Command. The latter regarded the Norwegian theatre as a side show. The official policy was that Bomber Command should concentrate on bombing German industry. They were not as yet empowered to bomb German cities in case it brought about reprisals. In fact the only two bomber squadrons serving with Coastal Command were withdrawn by the Air Ministry on 13 April. Apart from the small but significant contribution later by Fighter Command in Northern Norway, distance precluded the use of fighter aircraft based in Britain. On the other hand the reconnaissance carried out by the RAF was invaluable. The two sturdy work horses as far as the Norwegian campaign was concerned were the Wellington bomber and the lighter Blenheim fighter bomber. Neither aircraft could reach further than Bergen if operating from eastern England or Trondheim if operating from Eastern Scotland or the Shetlands.

As far as the defence of ships against air attack was concerned, conventional thinking held that anti-aircraft guns would be sufficient. Despite being able to put up a furious barrage of shot and shell, the Navy soon found out that this argument was flawed. In the first place there was always the chance that a determined bomber would get through and secondly some of the guns in use were far from ideal. Capital ships had high-angle guns but the fire control systems were found to be wanting. Destroyers were armed with two pounder pom pom guns which were clumsy and destroyers were not armed with the heavy machine guns necessary for dealing with Stukas. All this was to change after the Norwegian campaign.

It is time to turn back to the movements of the main body of the Home Fleet on 9 April. The evening before Admiral Forbes had reached the same latitude as Trondheim. Having missed the German force he knew to be ahead, he turned south. At 06.20 on the morning of the 9 April he made rendezvous with Admiral Layton's 18th Cruiser Squadron consisting of the cruisers *Manchester* and *Southampton* and seven destroyers patrolling the Norwegian coast. Confirmation of the occupation of the Norwegian ports had come in and the Admiralty ordered an attack on enemy warships and transports believed to be at Bergen and Trondheim. At 11.30 Forbes detached two extra cruisers to Layton's squadron and ordered him to proceed to Bergen. At 14.00 the RAF, which had flown several reconnaissance missions, reported that there were two cruisers at Bergen. Layton was not sure whether the enemy controlled the shore batteries and, when resolution might have paid off, the Admiralty thought that an attack through the inland fjords would be too hazardous and their lordships therefore called off the attack.

At midday Admiral Forbes had once more turned north. Since early morning long range enemy reconnaissance planes had been shadowing the Home Fleet and in the early afternoon bombing attacks began. The planes bombed from some height and despite some near misses it showed that ships travelling at speed with plenty of sea room were not easy to hit. At least in one respect conventional assumptions did turn out to be correct. One 1,100lb bomb actually hit the flagship, HMS *Rodney*, but such was the strength of the armoured deck that it did little more than superficial damage.

Admiral Layton's force, struggling to catch up with the main body of the Home Fleet in heavy seas, was more strongly attacked, and the cruisers *Southampton* and *Glasgow* suffered some damage from near misses. More serious was the fate of the destroyer *Gurkha*. In the blinding spray she had slowed down in order to work her anti-aircraft guns to greater effect. The German bombers picked on her and she received several direct hits which left her stopped and sinking. Luckily for all those aboard, the cruiser *Aurora* came upon her by chance and was able to come alongside and take the crew off.

This was a portentous first: a warship sunk from the air. The doctrine that anti-aircraft fire would prove adequate protection for ships from attack from the air, had been seriously called in question. In the rough seas experienced, the accuracy of anti-aircraft fire had been shown to be largely ineffective. Even more alarming was that in the course of one afternoon several cruisers had used up forty per cent of their anti-aircraft ammunition.

Bomber Command cannot be accused of having been idle but neither of the two main attacks was successful. On the evening of 9 April a force of twelve Wellingtons and twelve Hampden twin-engine bombers were sent against Bergen. Reconnaissance had shown that there were two modern cruisers the

Koln [Cologne] and the *Konigsberg* lying at anchor in the harbour, together with an older cruiser, the *Bremse*. Despite the gallantry with which the pilots pressed home their attack, including flying low enough to machine gun their targets, no hits were scored. One aircraft was lost.

The immediate consequence of this raid was that the *Koln* weighed anchor and set off for home. Intercepted signals told her that the British were patrolling the entrance to the fjords. She therefore hid away in the Maurangerfjord until the afternoon of 10 April when she was able to make good her escape. A further raid by the RAF on Kristiansand at the southern tip of Norway on 12 April was a disaster. Twelve slow Hampden bombers attacked shipping in daylight without scoring any hits. By this time German fighters were operational in Southern Norway and half the unescorted bombers were shot down.

Ironically the moment of truth for the Royal Navy was brought about by a British initiative. Two squadrons of Blackburn Skuas were stationed at Hatson in the Orkney Islands under Coastal Command. On 9 April a senior observer, Lieutenant Commander Hare had been seconded to Coastal Command at Lossiemouth near Inverness from whence he had been out on a reconnaissance mission over Bergen. He had seen the three German cruisers at anchor and on the way back he communicated this information to the Home Fleet. On landing back at Lossiemouth he was bundled into a waiting plane which took him back to his home station at Hatson.

Captain Partridge, commanding Hatson was given permission to take off for Bergen at first light on 10 April. The round trip was at the limit of the Skua's fuel supply and called for accurate navigation. This Lieutenant Commander Hare was able to provide. As luck would have it the weather cleared over the target but there was no sign of the cruisers at anchor. The *Koln* had gone but then the *Konigsberg* was sighted alongside one of the jetties. The Germans were caught unawares and each Skua was able to release its 500lb bomb at the bottom of the steepest dive of which the Skua was capable. The essential point was that a cruiser did not have the thickness of armour on either deck or hull to be found on a battleship. The *Konigsberg* took three direct hits and barely had the aircraft gone over the horizon than she rolled over and sank. The lesson for all to see was that a substantial warship could be sunk from the air. Only one Skua was lost.

If we could do this to one of theirs what might they not do to one of ours? The question was answered a week later. On 16 April the cruiser *Suffolk* commanded by Captain Durnford was ordered to bombard the important airfield at Sola near Stavanger. The cruiser was armed with eight 8-inch guns and eight 4-inch high angle anti-aircraft guns. She also carried two Walrus amphibious spotter planes. The *Suffolk* was escorted by four destroyers. The plan was to attack at dawn and the bombardment duly opened at 05.13. An RAF Hudson was supposed to drop marker flares on the airfield but warning rockets and enemy ack ack fire prevented their identification. The Walrus spotter planes were more successful despite faulty short wave wireless communication. The attack was successful up to a point with considerable damage done to buildings and a petrol dump was set ablaze.

Shortly after 06.00 the squadron began to withdraw seawards at 30 knots. Captain Durnford on the *Suffolk* had been ordered to steam north. Then at 08.25 the first enemy bombers appeared. A fighter escort had been sent out by the RAF but failed to find the Durnford force. Such was the intensity of the attacks that although no hits were scored, Durnford decided to stand out to sea. For almost seven hours the *Suffolk* was under continuous attack. Out of thirty-three individual sorties twenty-one were by high-level bombers which the cruiser's high angle guns were able to keep at bay. No hits were scored until 10.37 when a dive bomber put a heavy bomb into the *Suffolk*.

The bomb penetrated the upper deck near the after gun turret and actually burst in a storeroom close to the engine room. The explosion inflicted heavy damage and casualties in the engine room. The blast also ignited a cordite charge in the gun turret. In all, thirty-three officers and men were killed and thirty-eight wounded. As fires raged, the magazine in the after gun turret had to be flooded and the speed of the *Suffolk* was reduced to eighteen knots. The flooding put the steering out of action temporarily and Durnford's only means of steering was by varying the speed of the ships twin screws. It was not until the early afternoon that the first friendly fighters appeared. The following day the *Suffolk* limped into Scapa Flow her decks awash.

It was the sinking of the *Konigsberg* that had convinced Admiral Forbes and the Admiralty that anything south of Bergen would better be left to HM Submarines. Meanwhile the main body of the Home Fleet had turned west to make a rendezvous with the battleship *Warspite* and the aircraft carrier *Furious*. The Fleet then turned north east with a view to making an air attack against ships at Trondheim. At 04.00 on 11 April eighteen Swordfish biplanes took off from HMS *Furious*. Each was armed with a torpedo. Although the Swordfish was to prove itself in November 1940 in the attack on the Italian fleet in Taranto, on this occasion the attack was a failure. The heavy cruiser *Admiral Hipper*, which had been sighted at anchor the night before was nowhere to be seen. She had slipped away during the night and passed perilously close to the Home Fleet. Two destroyers were at anchor in the shallow water. This meant that some of the torpedoes hit the bottom and exploded before establishing equilibrium on a set course. No hits were scored.

Forbes resumed his course north until by 13 April he was cruising off the Lofoten Islands. The *Warspite* and destroyers were then detached to proceed to Narvik as recounted. There remained the question of the *Scharnhorst* and the

Gneisenau. After 9 April the two German battleships had sailed far out into the Atlantic to create a diversion. Then turning south they passed just east of the Faroe Islands. Sailing past the Orkney Islands, they made rendezvous with the *Admiral Hipper* from Trondheim reaching Wilhelmshaven on 12 April. Once this intelligence was received by Admiral Forbes, there was little point in the Home Fleet remaining on the Norwegian coast. The Narvik/Lofoten area is some 800 miles from Scapa Flow, that is to say two days steaming time. Thus it was that Forbes, an admiral upon whom fortune had not smiled, although some units under his command had enjoyed very considerable success, returned to base at Scapa Flow on 15 April.

Chapter 13

Submarine Warfare

The question that springs to mind is that, assuming the Germans foresaw that some of their naval units were likely to be roped in and destroyed on the Norwegian coast, what measures did they take? The answer is threefold. In the first place, all important ships were under orders to proceed back to Germany as soon as possible. Secondly they relied upon their submarines putting up a better performance than they did, through no fault of their own as it turned out. Thirdly they hoped that the German air force would be able to give effective air cover over central and southern Norway which turned out to be correct.

In one major respect fortune smiled on the British. The story of the failure of German U-boats in Norway almost beggars belief. As with the Royal Navy, the submarine arm was a minor branch of the service. A career naval officer would hope to command a destroyer then a cruiser and finally a battleship. From 1935 onwards the German U-boat service was commanded by a man of quite exceptional talent. Since 1934 Karl Doenitz had trained and built up the U-boat service displaying outstanding skill and leadership. Churchill wrote that he was the most formidable foe with which the Royal Navy had to contend since Admiral De Ruyter had sailed up the Medway and burnt the British fleet while at anchor. In 1939 he was a mere captain but was quickly promoted to admiral and later became grand admiral in succession to Admiral Raeder. In 1945 after Hitler's death he became Reich Chancellor charged with opening the capitulation negotiations.

In March 1940 the number of U-boats at sea was lower than at any point since 1939. Nevertheless U-boats had been very active, not only in attacking Allied convoys in the Atlantic, but also sowing magnetic mines in British estuaries at night. When the ebullient First Lord of the Admiralty claimed that we were winning the war against the U-boat, he was referring to the fact that fourteen U-boats had been sunk since the outbreak of hostilities. This was indeed a high percentage of the fifty-seven U-boats operational at the beginning of the war. Against this one must weigh the fact that U-boats had sunk 199 merchant ships grossing 701,985 tons, one aircraft carrier, the *Courageous* and one battleship, the *Royal Oak*.

Doenitz was not officially informed about Operation Weserubung until 5 March when he was charged with protecting German vessels during the actual invasion and also covering likely landing places in anticipation of Allied counterstrokes. In view of the length of the Norwegian coast he decided that it would be more flexible to keep his boats in open water rather than the tortuous waters of the fjords.

In all he had at his disposal 29 seaworthy U-boats which he allocated as follows: to cover German landing places he allocated four boats to Narvik, two to Trondheim, five to Bergen and two to Stavanger. In order to intervene should the British decide to invade he stationed six boats north east of the Shetlands, three small boats east of the Orkney Islands, four boats east and west of the Pentland Firth, the perilous seas off the northern tip of Scotland, and three boats off the Naze, the southernmost tip of Norway.

From the German point of view one of the most disturbing features of the war at sea in the first six or so months was the consistent reports of the high proportion of torpedoes which were reported as faulty. An example is provided by one of the most spectacular feats of the Second World War. On the night of 13/14 October 1939, U-47 commanded by Lieutenant Günther Prien infiltrated the Home Fleet's main anchorage at Scapa Flow. He had scraped his submarine through a narrow passage separating two islands but thankfully most of the Home Fleet was out at sea. There were only two ships at anchor one being the *Royal Oak*, an elderly battleship. Prien fired four torpedoes but only one exploded somewhere near the anchor chain. Those aboard the *Royal Oak* did not even know that they were under attack. In order to reload Prien had to bring his submarine to the surface in the middle of the Scapa Flow anchorage. He then fired two more torpedoes at the battleship which sent her to the bottom along with 833 British sailors. The question that arose for the Germans was: why, out of six torpedoes had only three exploded? Reports of torpedo failure continued to mount during the winter. A sample of the reports made to Admiral Doenitz headquarters after the Allied intervention in Norway are revealing:

April 11	U-48 Three torpedoes fired at the cruiser *Cumberland*, one missed, one failed to explode until the end of its run. Three torpedoes fired at the cruiser *York*, all exploded prematurely.
April 12	U-51 Two torpedoes fired, one exploded at the end of its safety run, the other after 30 seconds.
April 15	U-48 Torpedo failures against the *Warspite*.
April 16	U-47 commanded by Lieutenant Commander Prien reported from Vaagsfjord north of Ofotfjord on which Narvik stands, that three large transport vessels were lying at anchor in Bygdenfjord and that troops were being disembarked in

| | fishing vessels. At 22.42 he fired four torpedoes. Shortest range 750m, longest range 1500m. Depth setting just over four metres. No results. |
| April 19 | U-47 Prien sighted the *Warspite* and fired two torpedoes at a range of only 900m. Only one of them exploded at the end of its run. This was enough to alert the destroyer escorts who hunted U-47 with depth charges for two hours. |

In the final analysis U-boat Command found that four attacks had been made on the *Warspite*, fourteen attacks on cruisers, ten on destroyers and ten on transports. The net result had been one transport sunk. As Prien remarked later on 'you might just as well have sent us into battle with dummy rifles'. In the light of this Doenitz decided to withdraw all U-boats from the Norwegian theatre and order an enquiry. Much of the blame came to rest upon the weapon testing department.

The traditional torpedo used on both sides had a simple percussion firing mechanism which exploded on impact. The trouble was that unless it hit the target fair and square it might not explode. The British had brought the Mark 8 torpedo into service in 1928. It had a range of 6.5km, packed 364kg of high explosive and it worked, so the British stuck to what they could rely on. By temperament the Germans are always trying to improve, particularly where gadgets are concerned. They developed a magnetic pistol. This would enable a torpedo to run at a predetermined depth and explode upon entering an enemy ship's magnetic field directly under the keel with deadly effect. There were however technical problems although the Germans largely solved these later in the war. For example the nearer one gets to the North Pole the stronger the magnetic field becomes. Thus on the Norwegian coast the firing pistol had to be set at a much weaker level often resulting in the torpedo failing to explode at all.

The Germans were not the only ones to have a proactive submarine service commander. The Submarine Service had in Vice Admiral Max Horton, an intrepid submarine captain in the Great War, a tough, imaginative and competent commander. On April 4 the Admiralty had decided to concentrate submarines on the Scandinavian coast in anticipation of any German reaction to Operation Wilfred, the plan to lay mines in Northern Norwegian waters. Three submarines were sent to the Kattegat, the most hazardous area to patrol, between Denmark and Sweden. Three were sent to the Skagerrak between Denmark and Norway and three more to patrol off the western Danish coast.

These were the submarines which had witnessed the long procession northwards of merchant ships, many of them flying neutral flags. By 7 April Admiral Horton was convinced that the invasion of Norway was imminent. Unfortunately an adjustment of patrol positions to cover Heligoland Bight at the bottom of the Danish peninsular left Stavanger and Oslofjord unmarked just at the crucial time.

The British were still complying with the Geneva Convention drawn up between the wars prescribing that a submarine should surface, challenge civilian ships and give the crew time to take to the boats before sinking the vessel. This invariably gave the ship time to send out an SOS signal which of course would include a position expressed in latitude and longitude. The Polish submarine *Orzel* had complied with the convention on 8 April which gave time for the German troops in uniform to take to the boats. On the same day HM submarine *Trident* complied with the convention before sinking the *Poseidon* laden with 8,000 tons of fuel destined for U-boats at Stavanger.

The problem for the submarine was that a destroyer or other anti-submarine vessel, travelling at a speed of 25 knots could be on the spot within a quarter of an hour. This gave the submarine just about enough time to dive but once under the water the pursuing vessel would know that with a speed under water of six or so knots, the submarine could not be very far away. The submarine's only defence would then be to stop its engine which could be heard by a destroyer's hydrophones. All navies developed more sophisticated sonar detection equipment later in the war.

It was not until 13.30 on 9 April that the Admiralty sent a signal permitting British submarines to sink enemy vessels without warning while submerged, thus bringing British practice into line with that of the Germans. At the time Lieutenant Commander Slaughter in command of HM Submarine *Sunfish* was watching the steamer *Amasis* through his periscope. His torpedo tubes were primed, the bow caps open, so he gave the order to fire. By 14 April the *Sunfish* had sunk three more steamers.

Each attack swiftly brought anti-submarine vessels to the spot. As Captain Macintyre put it, 'Then only stillness and silence could save them from detection and crippling damage from depth charges. For hour after hour they had to lie quietly and endure, while the air got steadily fouler, bodies weaker and brains more torpid. Only with nightfall might there come an opportunity to float secretly and softly to the surface and suck in the clean air while they sneaked away in the darkness to recharge their exhausted storage batteries.'

On 9 April off Kristiansand, the most southerly port in Norway, Lieutenant Commander Hutchinson was patrolling in HM Submarine *Truant*. The sound of fast moving propellers in his hydrophone warned him that it would have been madness to surface. The German light cruiser *Karlsruhe* had not waited long at Kristiansand. Having disembarked troops she sailed for home on the same day. At 18.30 Hutchinson suddenly saw her coming his way on a zigzagging course escorted by three torpedo boats.

The procedure to be carried out involved feeding into a calculator the following variables: an estimate of the enemy vessel's speed, in this case about 20 knots; an estimate of the compass course that the enemy vessel appeared to be steering; the estimated range to the enemy vessel; the speed of the torpedo, about 35 knots would be known. The answer would give the angle of deflection, that is to say the distance in front of the bows of the enemy ship that it would be necessary to aim off.

Just as Hutchinson was about to give the order to fire, the *Karlsruhe* altered course. Nevertheless he shortly after fired a full salvo of four torpedoes as the cruiser drew away from him. The torpedoes were actually sighted by the *Karlsruhe* which swerved. Just one torpedo struck her near the stern not only wrecking her steering gear but also putting both main engines out of action. Her main pumps were out of action and she began to sink. It became obvious to the German captain that he could not save his ship. The crew were transferred to the torpedo boats and it was eventually decided to sink her with one of their own torpedoes.

Lieutenant Commander Hutchinson had not had time to reload so he decided to dive as deep as it would be safe to go i.e. before the pressure becomes so strong that the hull would start to cave in. It was just as well that he should be lying at a depth of about 320ft because an anti-submarine flotilla came hurrying to the spot. In the course of the next two hours The *Truant* was harried remorselessly. At about 22.00 there was a break, but as Hutchinson approached the surface the noise of compressed air expelling sea water from his ballast tanks was picked up on the enemy's hydrophones and the attacks by depth charges began again. At 23.25 the *Truant* had been submerged for nineteen hours and her batteries were almost exhausted. At last Hutchinson decided that it might be safe to rise to the surface. The enemy had departed and he was able to head for home.

The hottest posting on the Scandinavian coast was the almost landlocked area of the Kattegat. Through this all vessels from the Baltic must pass and it was here that two British submarines were waiting: the *Sunfish* and the *Triton*. The supply ships for the invasion force for Oslo were held up for a day until the city had been taken, but on 10 April fifteen supply vessels together with escorts were sighted at 16.30 by Lieutenant Commander Pizey commanding the *Triton*. He managed to penetrate the screen of escorts without being detected and fired six torpedoes. Two transports were sunk sending 900 troops and much equipment to the bottom. Another torpedo sank an escort vessel. Retribution was immediate. The *Triton* had to endure no less than seventy-eight depth charges, some of which exploded perilously close, before the attacks were called off and she was able to creep away

For some reason the patrol vessels attacking the *Triton* were diverted to another target HM submarine *Spearfish* commanded by Lieutenant Commander

Forbes. Between 17.30 and 18.40 the Germans dropped no less than 68 depth charges. By midnight the sound of the pursuing vessels had died away. The *Spearfish* had been submerged for almost twenty-four hours and her batteries were well-nigh exhausted before Forbes at last felt that it was safe to bring his vessel to the surface.

How the German pocket battleship *Lutzow* came to be in the same area unescorted some 10 miles north of the tip of Denmark is a good illustration of the way in which chance plays a part in the fortunes of war. She had been designed as a deep sea raider and had been pressed into service for the Oslo expedition by chance. After the sinking of the *Blucher* in Oslofjord the Germans wanted to limit her exposure. It will be recalled that she had sailed into Oslo harbour a day later than planned. Arriving at noon, she landed the troops that she was carrying and set sail for home at 14.40. As no fast escort vessels were available it was decided to rely on speed and darkness.

On account of the activities of the *Triton* and *Sunfish*, the *Lutzow* had made a wide sweep to the west. About 01.00 on 11 April Lieutenant Commander Forbes thought he saw the bow waves of a destroyer. The *Lutzow*, which was equipped with an early form of radar, had detected the *Triton* and borne away for several minutes. What Forbes saw was in fact her stern wash. Some minutes later the *Lutzow* resumed course and Forbes realized that his target would rapidly recede. He therefore fired six torpedoes one of which struck the pocket battleship near the stern. The propellers and rudder were wrecked and she started to take in more and more water. While the *Lutzow* lay helpless expecting more torpedoes, Forbes had not stayed to admire his handiwork. He was on the surface with no battery reserves which would have enabled him to dive. He had therefore immediately hurried away to the west. The *Lutzow* was not able to be taken in tow by tugs equipped with pumps able to save her until the next morning. She then had to spend the next twelve months *hors de combat* in a dry dock in Kiel.

In the middle of March German intercepts of British radio traffic suggested that there were no less than fourteen British submarines operating in the Skaggerak and Kattegat. Admiral Doenitz had therefore decided to send eight of the smaller type of U-boat to try to hunt them down. It had also been embarrassing for the Germans, to say the least when one of them had run aground on the Norwegian coast and the crew interned. On 9 April at first light, the *Thistle* had sighted U-4 on the surface some miles off the south western tip of Norway. Torpedoes were fired but they were spotted and U-4 had time to dive. Just before dawn on the following morning the tables were turned. U-4 sighted the *Thistle* on the surface and one torpedo sufficed to send her to the bottom.

On 10 April HM Submarine *Tarpon* fired torpedoes at the *Shurbeck* which turned out to be an armed merchantman. For four hours the *Shurbeck* and a minesweeper hunted the *Tarpon* with depth charges and the latter was never seen again.

HM Submarine *Seal* had completed her task of laying mines near Gothenburg, when she became entangled with the anchor line of a German mine which exploded. Although the *Seal* settled in the mud 200ft down she was only partially flooded. After nearly 24 hours submerged, with her crew and batteries exhausted, she was brought to the surface in the early hours of 5 May. When Lieutenant Commander Lonsdale saw that his disabled vessel was sinking he surrendered to a seaplane. The *Seal* had the dubious honour of being the only Royal Navy ship to surrender in the whole war. Lonsdale had nevertheless saved his crew and at a post-war court martial he was exonerated.

Other British submarines scored. On 11 April the *Sealion* sank a supply ship, the *August Leonhardt,* in the Kattegat. It is harder to hit a target with torpedoes than gunfire owing to the time that it takes for a torpedo to travel to the target. At a speed of about 35 knots it may take 3, 4, 5, or 6 minutes depending on the distance to be travelled. This gives the target vessel time to take avoiding action if she sights the torpedoes in time. On 12 April the *Snapper* missed the *Moonsund* with her torpedoes but was able to surface and sink her by gunfire. Blow her up would be a more accurate description, for she was carrying aviation spirit. On 14 April the *Sunfish* sent the transport *Florida* to the bottom. On the very same day the *Triad* sank the German transport *Iona* in the very mouth of Oslofjord.

While the Admiralty's signal, 'You are all doing magnificent work', was richly deserved it had not come without a price. If a submarine is sunk while it is submerged there are unlikely to be any survivors. On 15 April HM Submarine *Sterlet* sank the gunnery training ship *Brumme*. However such was the ferocity of the subsequent attack by the escorting vessels that the *Sterlet* herself was shortly blown to pieces. Thereafter Admiral Horton drew the conclusion that since the Kattegat had effectively become a German lake, constantly patrolled by aircraft, it would be best to withdraw all British submarines from the area. This gave German convoys to Oslo a more or less clear run.

Chapter 14

We are coming as quickly as possible and in great strength

The decisive strategic advantage enjoyed by the Germans was that they were working to a single plan for which they had many months in which to prepare. The Allies later demonstrated that they could do the same in the many months which they took to plan the landings in North Africa and in Sicily. You cannot simply cobble together an amphibious expedition in a few weeks and expect it to succeed. From the start the British were hamstrung by lack of information as to precisely what was happening in Norway. In mitigation it is worth quoting from a speech in the Commons by Churchill: 'It is not the slightest use blaming the Allies for not being able to give substantial help and protection to neutral countries if we are kept at arm's length until these neutrals are actually attacked.'

Once the initiative had been seized by the Germans, all the Allies could do was to react. British plans after 9 April kept being altered to meet the requirements of a changing situation. It is easy enough to lampoon the 'brass hats' especially with the benefit of hindsight. Nevertheless the number of code words engendered by the Norwegian campaign invites ridicule. It is difficult not to draw the conclusion that the principle upon which staff officers at the Admiralty and the War Office were operating was 'think up a code word and you have a plan'. We have already met the following:

WILFRED	Churchill's plan to mine the Leads.
CATHERINE	Churchill's crackpot scheme to send an armoured flotilla into the Baltic. Wiser counsels prevailed.
PLYMOUTH	A plan to send two divisions to Trondheim, should it be necessary to go to the aid of the Swedes.
AVONMOUTH	The initial plan to land two brigades at Narvik and occupy the ore fields.
STRATFORD	The plans to send five battalions to occupy Trondheim, Stavanger and Bergen, should the Germans land in southern Norway.

R4	The plan to land troops at Narvik, Trondheim and Bergen merely on evidence that the Germans intended to invade.

One vice, of which the planners cannot be accused, is indolence. Following 9 April, the planners' minds went into overdrive. In the next few weeks they came up with even more code words:

RUPERT	A reference to the dashing Royalist commander in the Civil War [emanating from Churchill].
HAMMER	A proposed direct attack on Trondheim from the sea.
HENRY	The landing of seamen and marines at Namsos north of Trondheim.
MAURICE	An operation against Trondheim via Namsos.
PRIMROSE	Landing marines and seamen at Aandalsnes south of Trondheim.
SICKLE	A flank operation against Trondheim from Aandalsnes.
SCISSORFORCE	A later project to send independent companies to cover the retreat up the road to the North.

The planners could but do what the policy makers told them and the Norwegian campaign provides a glaring example of trying to run a war by committee. To a considerable extent this was changed when Churchill came to power. In the month following 9 April, the ministerial committee on military co-ordination held twenty-three meetings and the Chiefs of Staff committee met forty-three times. As Churchill pointed out, the Chiefs of Staff themselves had to attend both meetings.

The shifts in policy in the next three weeks which emerge from the minefield of Cabinet and committee minutes may be briefly chronicled. In the early hours of 9 April, Major General Ismay, head of the Chiefs of Staff Secretariat and also secretary of the Military Co-ordinating Committee, was woken by an agitated and incomprehensible staff officer. Ismay ordered him to put in his dentures and ring him back. At 06.30 the Chiefs of Staff held their first meeting. At the morning Cabinet meeting Churchill, stimulated at the prospect of shot and shell, took the lead.

The policy that emerged was that the plan to seize Narvik should go ahead. At that point the Cabinet were not aware that the Germans were actually in Narvik. Indeed despite unconfirmed reports at midday, the Prime Minister could tell the House in the afternoon, 'It is very possible to believe that the Germans had landed at Larvik in Southern Norway and not Narvik'. It was considered most important that the Germans should be turned out of Bergen and Trondheim and the Chiefs of Staff were instructed to prepare expeditions. However it was resolved that there should be no movement until the naval situation was cleared up. In words that he was soon to regret Churchill said, 'Our hands were now free and we could apply our overwhelming sea power on the Norwegian coast. We could liquidate their landings in a week or two.'

In the late afternoon the French contingent arrived in London for a meeting of the Supreme War Council consisting of Paul Reynaud, the new Prime Minister, his predecessor and rival Edouard Daladier, now Minister of Defence and the French Service Chiefs. General Gamelin, Commander-in-Chief on the Western Front was only too happy to abide by the decision of 5 February that the planning, command and transportation in connection with operations in the north west should be left in the hands of the British. Admiral Darlan seems to have had more prescience as to German intentions. The French force of about 40,000 men which had been assembled for the Finnish expedition: *Le Corps Expeditionaire Français en Scandinavie* had never been disbanded and was more or less ready to sail.

At 21.30 that evening, after the first of many long days, the Military Co-ordinating Committee met again. It was now known that the Germans were in Narvik in some strength and both Churchill and General Ironside thought that Narvik would fully occupy our available resources. It was resolved therefore that Narvik should take priority but that the possibility of procuring a foothold at Namsos and Aandalsnes, north and south of Trondheim respectively, should be explored. The next morning this policy was endorsed by the War Cabinet.

The planning of Rupert, the quick dash for Narvik thus came to dominate thinking for the first few days. A new appointment to command all naval forces in Northern Norway was made. The Earl of Cork and Orrery, a fiery First World War commander and Admiral of the Fleet, was Churchill's choice. The latter had a penchant for appointing blood and guts members of his own class to high command. The Irish earl's energy was as legendary as his irascible temper. Rupert was essentially based on R4, the plan to send an infantry brigade to forestall the Germans at Narvik and five battalions for Trondheim and Bergen. At this point the units which had been ear-marked for R4 were disposed as follows:

• 24 Guards Brigade. This consisted of 1st battalion Scots Guards which was already embarked on the Clyde. It was the only unit with Alpine training having spent the winter of 1939 in Chamonix learning to fight on skis. The 1st battalion Irish Guards were shortly despatched to join them. Little thought was given to security. As they drove out of Chelsea barracks slogans referring to holidays in the midnight sun were daubed on the sides of their coaches. They were joined by 2nd battalion South Wales Borderers.

• 146 Infantry Brigade [territorial]. The Hallamshire battalion of the York and Lancaster Regiment was already embarked on the Clyde. With Finland in mind the colonel had the foresight to have given them some excellent training on the Yorkshire Moors. The brigade's other two battalions were not so fortunate. Having been carefully embarked on cruisers on the Firth of Forth, they had recently been somewhat precipitately dumped ashore, about which more later.

• 148 Infantry Brigade [territorial] had been destined for Stavanger but both battalions had been similarly dumped ashore without much ceremony.

• There was also a French contribution to the force destined for Narvik consisting of six battalions of Chasseurs Alpins.

It should be borne in mind that the French Army was much bigger than the British Army. In the event they offered two battalions of the legendary Foreign Legion trained to fight in the sand but not the snow. They also offered a brigade of Chasseurs Alpins but it seems that they were not all Alpine troops. Finally they offered four battalions of Poles. The latter were largely recruited from miners and other migrant workers, but they were commanded by first class professional officers who had escaped from Poland. Thus both men and officers were driven by a deep hatred of the Germans and a burning desire to see their country eventually liberated.

A further build up was envisaged to a French total of 40,000 with a British contribution of 14,000 men. The main contribution from the British was of course the Royal Navy. Bearing in mind that the Norwegians were in the field and that Norway if properly fought was supremely defensible the Allied numbers were not unreasonable when compared with 60,000 Germans. Nor was training or the lack of it so unequal. Only the Germans bound for Narvik had Alpine training. Two British brigades allocated to Central Norway were regulars; two were territorials who had had only seven months full-time training. Only a minority of German troops were regular, the majority were reservists with one year's training.

Where the German forces proved superior was in equipment. The German infantry had a higher proportion of automatic weapons. Each infantry company was armed with sixteen sub-machine guns and twelve light machine guns. The British had three Bren medium machine guns per platoon. Otherwise Tommy Atkins relied on the Short Lee Enfield 303 rifle, albeit the finest weapon in its day: 1914. Tanks were not a decisive factor in Norway, although German road columns were generally led by a couple of tanks. Transport was a different matter and vital where stores were concerned. Such transport as the British possessed, and they were to be greatly supplemented by Norwegian civilian vehicles, was extremely vulnerable to German air attack. In Central Norway, apart from a few bombing raids mounted from Britain or occasionally from aircraft carriers, the

British had no air cover at all. The Germans had the right proportion of artillery to infantry. Such few guns as the British were able to spare for Central Norway were often the first items of equipment to be abandoned in a retreat. Initially only one battery of 25-pdr field guns was allocated to Narvik.

An important factor in the first few days was the lack of intelligence available to the Allies. Despite the fact that the telephone system in Southern Norway quickly fell into the hands of the Germans, the lines to Sweden remained open. Thus the main source of information about what was actually going on came from American and other journalists in Stockholm. It also put the newspapers in a commanding position to review what the options open to the Allies were. This no doubt the Germans found interesting when they bought the morning editions of *The Times* and *The Daily Telegraph* on sale in Zurich.

It almost beggars belief that the British should have had no military attaché in Norway. Lieutenant Colonel Salter the military attaché in Finland was immediately drafted into the post and a better choice could not have been made. This vigorous and competent Rifle Brigade officer immediately commended himself to the Norwegians. Alas the rapidly changing situation on the Norwegian front north of Oslo was such that he did not locate the makeshift Norwegian headquarters until 14 April.

On 9 April Sir Cecil Dormer, the British Minister accredited to Norway, was the first official British representative able to locate the Norwegian government near the Swedish border. The telegram which he sent to the Foreign Office on 12 April via the British Legation in Stockholm had a profound effect on strategic thinking in London: 'King and government more determined than when I last saw them at Elverum [north of Oslo]... Government are anxious to establish themselves at Trondheim as soon as the Germans expelled from there...the Norwegian government definitely do not feel capable of coping with the situation if British support is confined to naval operations only...I venture to urge that military assistance at Trondheim is first necessity. Seizure of Narvik of little assistance to Norwegian government.'

A glance at the map of Norway demonstrates the importance of Trondheim. It is the third city in size after Bergen and Oslo and incidentally the ancient political capital. It lies about halfway from north to south of the country at the confluence of the only two routes from the south through the mountains of Central Norway and the land route to the north. As early as 9 April an expedition to Trondheim had had its supporters, notably Sir Cyril Newall, Chief of the Air Staff. At a meeting of the War Cabinet on the afternoon of 12 April, Lord Halifax influenced by the telegram received from Sir Cecil Dormer warmed to the idea of an expedition to Trondheim, but many of the older military men were hag-ridden by the memory of Gallipoli. Churchill, whose political career had been almost ruined by Gallipoli responded by saying 'an opposed landing at

Trondheim would be a very difficult operation and if mounted without proper preparation might only lead to a bloody repulse'.

At the War Cabinet meeting on 13 April Chamberlain, supporting Halifax, said that he was impressed with the urgency of obtaining a firm foothold at Trondheim particularly from the political point of view and by the end of the meeting the decision was taken. Churchill went along with the majority. The next day a message was sent to the Norwegians over Chamberlain's name: 'We are coming as soon as possible and in great strength'. The news on the evening of 13 April that Admiral Whitworth had destroyed all the remaining German naval units at Narvik finally clinched the matter and for several days thereafter it was assumed that Narvik would fall quite easily. That night Churchill demonstrated his amazing ability to work all hours albeit facilitated by a regular sleep in the afternoon and the intake of a liberal amount of alcohol throughout the evening. Hitherto the Chief of the Imperial General Staff, General Ironside – known as Tiny on account of his massive height – had supported Churchill in maintaining that Narvik should remain a first priority. At 02.00, if you please, Churchill accompanied by Admiral Tom Phillips, Deputy Chief of the Naval Staff called at the Chief of Staff's flat. Churchill's opening gambit was, 'Tiny we are going to the wrong place, we should be going to Trondheim.' No doubt the general's initial reaction was coloured by the interruption to his sleep, but he came round to the idea.

Meanwhile, before the news of Admiral Whitworth's victory had come in, Operation Rupert, the quick dash for Narvik had been put in hand. At Scapa Flow the troops, who had arrived in transport ships, had transferred to cruisers and were scheduled to sail on 12 April. Major General Mackesy, a Royal Engineer of methodical if perhaps rather cautious temperament, had been appointed to command land forces in Northern Norway. He had arrived at Scapa Flow on 11 April and his orders were quite clearly written down. He was to eject the Germans from Narvik, but first he was to establish a base at Harstad on the Lofoten Islands. There was a single-track road between the two towns, a distance of about fifty miles. He was to secure the co-operation of the Norwegians; he was not to bombard Narvik if it was likely to lead to civilian casualties and a note was added, 'It is not intended that you should land in the face of opposition.'

Admiral Lord Cork & Orrery was known in the service as Ginger Boyle for his ginger hair and fiery temperament. On appointment to command all naval forces in the north, his orders had been only verbal, but he understood that he was to eject the Germans from Narvik as soon as possible. As yet command was still divided; Mackesy was in command of all land forces, Cork was in command of all seaborne operations. The two men had never met until they reached Harstad, when the difference in their characters and their orders immediately became apparent.

Progress along the single-track roads covered with snow, in many places with a fjord on one side and a sheer cliff on the other, the approach to Narvik whether from north south or east was bound to be hazardous. Mackesy argued that an attack from open ships boats against entrenched machine guns might turn out to be as disastrous as it had been in Gallipoli. In this he was supported by the majority of his army subordinates and the difficulties encountered in the final successful assault on Narvik confirm that he was right. The main obstacle was the snow and little improvement was likely before the thaw expected in a couple of weeks' time. When he first arrived, Cork might have taken any risk but a brief foray through the snow, for he was a short man, convinced him of the virtual impossibility of making much progress through snow which was on average 4ft deep. In the end it was concluded that the best thing to do would be to wait for the thaw and build up resources in the meantime. On 20 April one ambiguity was resolved when Lord Cork was given overall command of both sea and land forces within 100 miles of Narvik.

As early as 10 April, the Chiefs of Staff had decided to try to gain a foothold at Namsos and Aandalsnes (north and south of Trondheim) should Operation Rupert not require the whole of the Allied forces available. When the news of the naval victory at Narvik came in, the Chiefs of Staff authorized the diversion of 146 Brigade (territorial) from Narvik to Namsos. They also ordered a demi-brigade (three battalions) of Chasseurs Alpins bound for Narvik to divert to Namsos. The Military Co-ordinating Committee first considered Operation Hammer' a direct attack on Trondheim from the sea on 13 April. The initial reaction of Sir Charles Forbes, then off the Lofotens, was that it was too hazardous but when pressed by Churchill he thought that it could be done if the troops were covered by warships. The Navy was confident that it could breach the forts at the entrance to Trondheimfjord which is several miles wide. However their enthusiasm was considerably moderated when the cruiser *Suffolk* returned from bombarding Stavanger aerodrome with her gunnels awash from bomb damage.

After much deliberation Operation Hammer was cancelled but the more prudent option, which developed into Operation Scissorforce, a pincer movement on Trondheim from north and south was misconceived from the start. Moving over the ground in Norway is nothing like moving across the Home Counties. Distances as the crow flies are multiplied many times by the twists and turns of the fjords. Except for trained troops on skis or snow shoes it is well-nigh impossible to stray from the single-track mountain roads. Moreover conditions in the thaw about to set in and last for a month, would be just as bad. Added to this the streams and rivers were about to become raging torrents. In these conditions the distances were daunting, Namsos is 125 miles by road to Trondheim and Aandalsnes is 190 miles distant.

The reality of war eventually impinges on the men on the ground. It is the ordinary soldiers and sailors who have to contend with the consequences of changes of plan and the orders and counter orders which ensue. Some examples of this are as follows. On 7 April, the 1st Scots Guards were embarked on a transport in the Clyde bound for Narvik. A battalion of the Hallamshires (146 Brigade) was embarked on a transport on the Clyde bound for Trondheim. A further two battalions were embarked on cruisers in Rosyth on the Firth of Forth bound for Bergen. Two battalions of 148 Infantry Brigade were embarked on cruisers on the Forth bound for Stavanger. In every case their kit and equipment had been meticulously stowed aboard by their respective quartermasters.

Naturally, once aboard, army units are in the hands of the Navy. Thus when the Home Fleet was ordered to sea on 7 April, the Admiralty considered it necessary to press into service every single cruiser that could be made available. The four battalions embarked on the Firth of Forth were unceremoniously dumped on the quayside at Rosyth together with about 90 tons of supplies. The infantry were marched off to some bleak barracks at Dunfermline and their respective quartermasters were left to sort out the muddle as best they could. The irony is that if the cruisers had proceeded as planned they might even have scotched the German landings at Stavanger and Bergen.

The initial landings went reasonably well. Naval personnel and marines were landed at Namsos north of Trondheim on 14 April. To the south seamen and marines landed without opposition at Aandalsnes at the mouth of the cavernous Romsdal leading into the interior and the main route through to Dombaas and eventually Oslo. When the expedition finally got under way further consequences of the changes in plan emerged. Thus while 24 Brigade was sailing to Narvik, largely equipped for a peaceful landing, part of its equipment had been loaded onto ships which were diverted to Namsos. The 146 Brigade which was equipped with maps of the Narvik area was diverted to Namsos with no local maps at all. Its own vehicles, together with its commanding officer, were in another ship still on the way to Narvik. Meanwhile 148 Brigade, originally bound for Namsos but now diverted to Aandalsness, was still equipped with maps of Namsos.

Some more personal extracts from Jo Kynoch's book, *Norway 1940* could have provided the script for a music hall were it not for the fact that men's lives were at stake. Corporal Thomas of C Company 1/5 Leicester's, kept a diary in which he records:

'April 7 arrived Rosyth by train and boarded the destroyer *Alfridi*, disembarked a few hours later and boarded the cruiser *Devonshire*. April 8, given one hour's notice to get off the *Devonshire*. Our equipment was slung ashore willy-nilly in nets and dropped on the quay.

Some of our supplies were left aboard including vital signalling equipment. We were then marched through Dunfermline and nine miles beyond to a camp under canvas.'

On 13 April two companies of Leicesters together with half a battalion of Sherwood Foresters boarded the former liner *Orion*. Early on 14 April, the *Orion* weighed anchor and sailed down the Forth. Then as if commanded by the famous Duke of York, she was back on the anchorage by evening. Early on 17 April, while it was still dark and in a swell, the Leicesters were transferred to cruisers. Equipment overlooked included brigade headquarters wireless equipment and most of the Foresters' mortar ammunition. At the last moment a battery of Bofors anti-aircraft guns were put on board but since they were without predictors, they were for practical purposes useless.

On 17 April, the Motor Transport platoon of the Leicesters had been given the heavy work of removing vehicles and equipment from the *Orion* onto lighters and taken across the Forth to Leith docks onto a steamer called the *Cedarbank*. On 19 April the work party entrained for Aberdeen where then they embarked on the *St Magnus*, a 200ft coaster. They shortly made rendezvous in the North Sea with another coaster, two destroyers and the *Cedarbank*, which was carrying the battalion's brand new lorries and Bren gun carriers (small open topped tracked vehicles for transporting the Bren light machine guns and ammunition boxes).

The next morning Jo Kynoch's account becomes more personal:

'I hung on to the deck rail, retched again and realized that I would have to get down to the heads...the sea was boiling like some monstrous cauldron and washing past me on the deck...no sooner had I put my foot on the first step downwards than an assortment of stenches...hit me in the face like a blast from an oven. A pathetic scene met me head on. The non-commissioned officers allocated these quarters [ordinary soldiers had to sleep on the floor] were hanging over the sides of their bunks, groaning pitifully and retching onto the floor every few minutes.'

At 05.00 the following morning, off Aalesund, the *Cedarbank* was torpedoed and sank within ten minutes.

Chapter 15

The Norwegians Fight

Operation Weserubung had not gone entirely to plan, particularly in the key Oslo area and this gave time for Norwegian resolution to harden. In the event, could the Norwegian people, the heirs to the Vikings, be expected to do anything other than fight? The town of Hamar on Lake Mjosa, 70 miles north of Oslo had been selected as the first stop for the government because it had a radio station. However news that a party of Germans was only 10 miles away caused the government and the members of the Storting to entrain once more bound for Elverum some miles further east.

It was to Elverum that Dr Brauer drove under diplomatic immunity, demanding a personal interview with King Haakon. This was granted but since Brauer only asked for stiffer terms, his suit was rejected. Thereupon Captain Spiller, the German air attaché, acting on his own initiative, set out for Elverum. He led in a legation car still bearing corps diplomatic number plates. His intention was to capture the king and he was followed by an ad hoc motorized column of about 100 men. However at a makeshift road block, organized by Colonel Ruge he was held up. After a sharp fight in which Spiller was mortally wounded, the Germans were repulsed.

Having been alerted, the king and his government moved on to Nybergsund almost on the Swedish border. Shortly afterwards the college building at Elverum in which they had so lately been debating was blown to pieces by the Luftwaffe. Nor was it long before the Germans got wind of where the government had gone. The king, crown prince, the government and members of the Storting had to take refuge in the snow covered pine woods while they watched German bombers obliterate the little wooden town. The Norwegian Parliament then decided to disperse but not before delegating the conduct of the war to the king and his cabinet.

A proclamation was issued over the signature of Prime Minister Nygaardsvold and endorsed by King Haakon.

'The German government has demanded that the King of Norway shall appoint a government which enjoys the confidence of Germany...The King has been unable to submit to this demand which would make Norway a dependency. No other government can have control here but that which has the confidence of the Norwegian people... This government offered to resign...but the Storting unanimously requested it to remain in office... It now turns to the whole Norwegian people and asks their assistance in upholding a rule of the country according to law, the Norwegian Constitution, Norwegian liberty and Norwegian independence.'

As early as February Hitler had decided on a military plan which would not rely on diplomatic activity. He had told Rosenberg not to involve Quisling. The latter's intervention on the radio on 9 April had therefore been largely on his own initiative. It had undoubtedly confused many Norwegians, but combined with the growing Norwegian resistance, the government's proclamation on 10 April completely undermined Quisling's position. On 13 April the king made an emotional broadcast on the radio from somewhere in Norway:

'In this time of trial, the most difficult in which my people and country have been involved for more than hundreds of years, I address an urgent request to all Norwegian women and men to do all that lies in the power of each individual to save for our dear Fatherland, its liberty and independence.... our country has been exposed to a lightning attack from a nation with which we have always maintained friendly relations. This powerful opponent has not shrunk from bomb attacks on the peaceful population in town and country. Women and children are being exposed to death and inhuman sufferings...I ask all to remember those who have given their lives for the sake of the Fatherland. God save Norway.'

The king's words were certainly not lost on the American people and had a subtle effect on the large Scandinavian population of Northern America. It should be borne in mind that the indiscriminate bombing of towns and cities and of women and children did not come to be regarded as a generally acceptable means of conducting war, despite the reservations of many individuals, until adopted by the British and Americans some eighteen months later.

In general the reaction of the Norwegian people to the king's speech was much the same as the response of the British people to Winston Churchill's appeal to 'fight on the beaches' a few months later. The more cynical response was 'fight yes, but what with?'. Pacifism and myopia had gone, if anything, deeper into the Norwegian psyche than it had into that of the British. Thus, the same Dr Koht who had so robustly rejected Ribbentrop's ultimatum delivered by Dr Brauer on 9 April had said back in 1936 'so far as I understand it, everybody is agreed that we cannot and will not have in this country any strong military organization. And if we cannot create a strong military organization to defend ourselves, neither can we go to war for other people.'

Organized labour in Norway had not forgotten that the army had been used against strikers in the Twenties and in 1931. The Labour government had nevertheless increased the defence budget in the late Thirties. Conscription was traditional in Norway and to this Socialist governments were not opposed. Broadly speaking, the cadre of regular officers was regarded as a body of reactionaries and the Labour government was seeking to replace the regular army with a defence guard. If the Norwegian army had been equipped and trained on anything like say the scale and to the standard of the Finnish or the Swedish army, it would not have been greatly inferior to the German invasion force. The Germans, needless to say, had in the previous few months made a fairly accurate intelligence appraisal of the Norwegian armed forces and their depots.

The Norwegian system was not a bad one. Under the policy of a neutrality guard only pursued in the 1914-1918 War, six well-found divisions should have been drawn from the six command districts into which the country was divided. After an initial rigorous training of between 40 to 80 days reservists would serve 24 to 30 days each year with their field units. A full brigade consisted of four infantry battalions with cavalry, artillery, engineers, support units and the necessary supply depots. Unfortunately economies in the depression years had left their mark. There were no tanks and worse still there were no anti-tank guns. There were no manoeuvres for reservists. The fact that there was no systematic winter training did not matter so much as most Norwegian boys could ski. Rifle clubs were popular and a useful number of Norwegian men were marksmen.

The six command districts in 1940 were made up as follows:

1st Division under General Erichson at Halden south east of Oslo.
2nd Division under General Hvinden Haug north west of Oslo, who was also responsible for Oslo.
3rd Division under General Liljedahl responsible for the south based on Kristiansand.
4th Division under General Steffens responsible for Bergen and the surrounding area.
5th Division commanded by Colonel Getz at Trondheim, but under a brigade in strength.
6th Division under General Fleischer based on Harstad in North Norway. It was so far away that it was often referred to as the forgotten army. In point of fact because of the perceived threat of Soviet expansionism it was the only division that was reasonably up to strength.

As with other European countries the system relied on mobilization. This should have been carried out in two stages. Partial mobilization meant that each of the six field brigades would have been immediately brought up to strength. But partial mobilization relied on reservists being called up by post. Despite the warnings coming in from 10.00 onwards on 8 April, particularly eye witness reports of the German armada steaming through the Danish islands, the government did nothing. The fact of the matter was that enough people in high places were fully aware of the menace but feared what the German Air Force might do to Oslo if they made the slightest move. It had been made clear, in a somewhat unsubtle manner, when Dr Brauer had shown a film of the destruction of Warsaw to an invited audience at the German Embassy some days previously.

Only when the enemy were within the gates was an attempt made to call a general mobilization. By then it was too late for within twelve hours the Germans were in control of the main radio stations and newspaper offices. If the Norwegian army had been fully mobilized before the German invasion it would have made an enormous difference although it might not have affected the eventual outcome. Many Norwegian lads flocked to the recruiting centres only to find them occupied by the Germans. Others, for lack of instructions from the government were sent home in tears. Worse still, within 24 hours the Germans had captured the military depots in the towns and cities which they had been able to occupy, complete with arms, ammunition and stores of all descriptions.

While the army was in a parlous state, the air force was almost non-existent. In 1940, the Norwegian air arm consisted of about 100 planes. Thirty-two were serving with the navy as scout planes trying to enforce neutrality in Norwegian waters. Eighty-three were serving with the army, most were scout planes, nearly all were biplanes and there were a few bombers purchased from the Germans. Contracts had been placed abroad, but only nineteen American Curtis fighters had so far been delivered. These were captured at Oslo on the first day still in their packing cases. The seven operational Gladiators supplied by Britain performed admirably.

Once resistance began to materialize, scout planes did play their part in reconnaissance missions and conveying officers to different destinations. There were a few stirring incidents such as the scout aircraft that brought down a bomber over Horton near Oslo. Suicide gestures were made when scout aircraft tried to disrupt German transport formations. Feats of improvisation were performed using ordinary petrol when the high octane fuel ran out and landing on frozen lakes or other makeshift landing grounds where necessary. Generally speaking, the Germans had not provided much in the way of fighter escorts for their bombers as they did not expect much opposition in the air.

The key to the occupation of Norway was Oslo. Economically the largest of

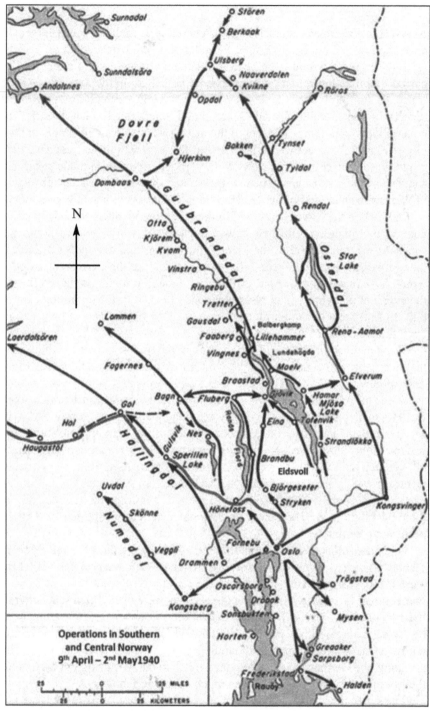

Fig. 7. German advance from Oslo

the industrial regions, routes led north and west to all the main provincial centres. Moreover the port was nearest to Germany and relatively safe from the Royal Navy. But things had not gone entirely to plan and by the evening of 9 April there were only seven companies of German infantry and two parachute companies in the city.

The first moves made by General Falkenhorst, commanding XXI Corps was to cover his flanks on the south-east of Oslofjord and south-west to Kristiansand. His main strategy thereafter would be to move west towards Bergen and then north towards the two central valleys of the Gudbrandsdal and the Osterdal (literally eastern dale). Both linked Oslo with Trondheim and the north.

Major General Pellengahr, commanding 196th Division detailed an infantry regiment, supported by artillery to advance down the eastern side of Oslofjord. Within days it had occupied the ancient fortress of Fredrickstad at the mouth of the river Glomma, the main river flowing down the Osterdal. Another regiment was sent east and soon occupied Kongsvinger higher up the river Glomma, the main railway junction for Sweden, Major General Erichson, commanding the Norwegian 1st Division in the south-east had decided to make his stand along the line of old forts built in the days when Sweden had been the main menace some 45 miles from Oslo. He was able to mobilize quickly and no arsenals or magazines fell into enemy hands. But as a result of the German capture of the Kongsvinger junction, he was effectively cut off from the rest of Norway and had difficulty in communicating with headquarters.

General Erichson and his men fought the Germans for a week during which their positions and supply lines were constantly bombed during the hours of daylight. It was not long before the Germans captured the main base at Halden and Erichson was forced to the conclusion that he had three options: firstly to fight on and be annihilated, secondly to surrender. By 15 April he decided on the third option. Thinking that Sweden might soon be drawn into the war, he crossed the Swedish border with his remaining 3,000 men.

By 12 April in the south-west, Major General Engelbrecht's 163rd Division had occupied Kongsberg, the junction for the roads to Kristiansand and Stavanger. The greater prize at Honefoss the road and rail junction for Bergen was taken on 14 April but it did not come without a price. There had been some loss of transport at sea but in any case the Germans made use of commandeered lorries and coaches. Norwegian roads, even in the foothills north of Oslo, twist and turn and hairpin bends are commonplace. A moment's inattention can result in a vehicle plunging a hundred feet or so into a ravine. Near Honefoss three coach drivers, each driving a coach carrying sixty German soldiers, by prior agreement and with almost unbelievable bravery, elected to do just that. In a fourth coach, the Germans only just managed to prevent the driver from following his comrades' heroic example.

One regiment from 163rd Division had been part of the seaborne force which occupied Kristiansand. The Norwegian commander of 3rd Division, Major General Liljedal, was presented with an ultimatum by the Germans, 'Abandon Kristiansand or the city and several neighbouring towns will be bombed out of existence'. He therefore withdrew the garrison some miles up the Setesdahl valley. This left the port open for the Germans to bring in reinforcements as and when they pleased. What should have been a fighting withdrawal in the south deteriorated into a dismal retreat. A tactic adopted by the Germans was to approach a road block and ask for a parley. Once the troops started to fraternize, and as often as not there would be groups of refugees milling about, both sides became reluctant to start shooting. On 14 April General Liljedal telephoned the Norwegian HQ, and it has been suggested that he exaggerated the strength of the Germans. Although urged not to give in, it was too late because the truce had become a capitulation.

Not all troops of the 3rd Division threw in the towel quite so easily, Lieutenant Hannevig refused to surrender and with two other officers and four men headed north in some trucks with some equipment and ammunition. Six days later he had 200 men and had set up road blocks and was sending out patrols. This was the nucleus of the force which from the remnants of the 3rd Division grew to 700 men. They fought on at Vinjesvingen in Telemark for several months until they ran out of ammunition.

On the Bergen front it was fortunate that the mobilization centre for the 4th Division was situated some 100 miles inland by road at Voss. Major General Steffens received orders to mobilize at 04.35 on 9 April. He therefore ordered Colonel Ostbye to attempt to hold part of the town with one regiment while he withdrew to Voss. Here in the next few days he was able to mobilize a complete field brigade. Bergen is built on a peninsula bordered on the south by Hardangerfjord which runs south-east almost as far as Voss. It will be recalled that as soon as the landing at Bergen had been accomplished, the German commander had decided to withdraw the cruiser *Koln* into Hardangerfjord for greater safety pending a quick dash back to a German port. Reports of the cruiser and two torpedo boats sailing into Hardangerfjord led Colonel Ostbye to fear a landing in his rear. Accordingly he withdrew his troops and marched east to Voss.

Eventually it was decided to concentrate Norwegian forces as far as possible in the central region north of Oslo. It was also decided that it was more important to stop the Germans advancing west from Oslo to Bergen than to hold up the enemy forces coming from Bergen. Voss was therefore abandoned to the Germans on 26 April and Steffens concentrated the 4th Division at Dokka at the northern end of Randsfjord. The smaller body of Norwegian troops at Stavanger was similarly withdrawn 25 miles into the hinterland to facilitate mobilization.

Chapter 16

General Ruge Takes Over

Spontaneously as it were, Norwegian resistance to the invader began to coalesce round Major General Hvinden Haug and the 2nd Division north of Oslo. This coincided with a change in Commander-in-Chief [C-in-C]. On 10 April the Norwegian government had, for once, acted decisively. They called on the 65-year-old Major General Laake, the C-in-C to give up his command and appointed Major General Otto Ruge in his place. This universally popular officer had until recently only held the rank of colonel, but he had made a name for himself as an extremely able and energetic inspector general of infantry. Anybody who ever met him was lavish in their praise of his qualities which included vigour, thoughtfulness, humanity and imagination. It was later said that perhaps he was not ruthless enough. In view of the more or less hopeless hand with which he had been dealt, in the event he did as well as could be expected. When Ruge finally reached the general headquarters [GHQ] at Rena in the Osterdal he immediately decided to concentrate Norwegian forces in the central region of the fjords north of Oslo. The Norwegian line thus stretched from the Bergen Road across Randsfjord and Lake Mjosa to the Glomma valley in the east. The same day he transferred his GHQ to Lillehammer at the northern end of Lake Mjosa.

On 12 April General Ruge issued instructions to his commanders. They were to delay the German advance as far as possible. It was hoped that this would give the Allies time to arrive in force. At the same time they were not to become heavily engaged, nor should they allow themselves to be cut off. General Ruge was under no illusions as to the nature of the units under his command as the following often quoted passage from his field diary makes clear:

'Remember what kind of army this was. From Oslo came hundreds of men who could not mobilize because the Germans held Oslo. They gathered round some leader and became a company, they met other groups of the same kind and became battalions under the command of some officer. Casually assembled infantrymen, artillerymen, sailors and aviators with cars and chauffeurs collected from God knows where, they became fighting units. A commissary department was improvised, the women on the farms doing the cooking and looking after things. Sanitary services, we had none, but they seemed to spring up out of the ground under the energetic and resourceful hands of physicians. I visited one hospital in the Gudbrandsdal which was full of wounded and fairly well equipped. The doctor in charge was a civilian who said that he had started at a crossroads near Eidsvold with one box of aspirins in his pocket.'

In a later passage General Ruge wrote:

'The railway station at Dombaas was bombed every day, burned and laid waste, the railway and telegraph connections broken, but every night it was repaired sufficiently to use. The unknown men who in great danger to their lives did this work night after night seeming never to sleep will not be forgotten...I remember the military labourers who were given guns at Midtskogen. Some of them had never held a gun in their hands before and were rather surprised to find themselves soldiers, but they stopped the Germans. The tough Opland squadron covered the retreat of the British until they themselves were surrounded by the Germans.'

In another passage he recorded:

'The so called Sorkedal Ski Company consisted of men who had escaped from Oslo and met in the hills of Nordmark...they turned up as a fighting unit thoroughly welded together... I remember the students of the Technical Institute in Trondheim who worked as volunteers...I remember the old taxi driver who by chance had given me a lift the first day and who stayed permanently. He was on the road day and night, bombed and machine gunned but always smiling and with a firm grip on the wheel. I remember the escaped college boys who served with the ordnance and all the courageous women who helped us, the nurses, telephone operators and Lottas [Women's Auxiliary Army].'

When Colonel King Salter, the British military attaché finally reached General Ruge's headquarters at Oyer in the Gudbrandsdal he found internal security checks in operation, roadblocks manned and all the paraphernalia of a GHQ. Moreover Ruge had got up from his bed at 01.30 to greet him at the station. The main forces at Ruge's disposal were those which composed the 2nd Division which became divided into four groups named after their commanders:

Group Hiorth, operating in the Osterdal.

Group Hvinden Haug, the Hedemark group operating north of Oslo and east of Lake Mjosa.

Group Dahl, the Toten Group operating north of Oslo and west of Lake Mjosa.

Group Mork, the Honefoss-Hadeland group north west of Oslo.

It is perhaps easiest to follow the confused fighting in the area of the lakes from the German viewpoint. The fact that most actions were on a small scale did not detract from their ferocity. Generally a German column would advance up a road no more than a battalion in strength. At the head of the column there were frequently a couple of tanks but owing to the rocky nature of the terrain they could rarely operate off the roads. Where the Norwegians decided to defend a village, the small log cabin homesteads would soon attract the attention of German aircraft which would bomb or machine gun the cottages. A road block frequently held up the tanks, but the Norwegians did not have anti-tank guns. The German infantry would then try to develop a flank movement through the woods although the snow might be knee deep. If the opposition were serious the Germans would bring up a battery of artillery to which the Norwegians did not have an answer. From time to time the Germans overreached themselves. Reports that the British were on the way at the port of Aandalsnes stimulated the Germans into dropping a company of parachute troops near Dombaas, the rail junction for Trondheim halfway up the Gudbrandsdal. This was 220 miles from Oslo and after moving around on the freezing cold plateau for some days they were entrapped and surrendered to Norwegian ski troops.

As early as 13 April two German battle groups had started to move north. Group Laendle had already reached Eidsvold by 11 April but then encountered strong Norwegian resistance at Minnesund on the southern tip of Lake Mjosa. The Norwegians then fell back to an even stronger position at Strandlykka where they managed to bring Group Laendle to a halt. Meanwhile in the Osterdahl, Group Fisher was advancing up the Glomma river, until it came up against the Norwegian Group Hiorth holding an entrenched position at Rena.

The German 163rd Division was likewise divided into battle groups. One advanced up the western side of Lake Mjosa and was able to cross the frozen lake where the bridge had been blown. Thus they were able to outflank the Norwegian force holding up Group Laendle at Strandlykka. The Norwegians then withdrew to the next strongpoint at Tangen.

Two German groups advancing north between Randsfjord and Lake Mjosa converged on a Norwegian strongpoint at Roa. To the west of Randsfjord a German group fought its way up the road that leads from Honefoss via Bagn into the central mountainous region. The reality of hand to hand fighting in the defence of Tonsaasen has been immortalized in the illustrations of the work by Major Andreas Hauge. As Ruge noted, 'The 4th division fought a suicidal battle at Tonsaasen for four days holding back a large German force and thereby easing the situation in the Gudbrandsdal at the point when British troops were landing.'

The German advance west of Lake Mjosa was halted at Toten, the last Norwegian strongpoint before the important rail junction at Gjovik. By 20 April three groups were converging on Gjovik. Here the Germans demonstrated their ability to switch units from one division to another by drawing on one unit from 196th Division and two from 163rd Division.

With the fall of Gjovik, General Hvinden Haug withdrew to a defensive position halfway between Hamar and Lillehammer. Hvinden Haug told Ruge that he thought that he could hold this position for several days but if forced to withdraw, he would cover the entrance to the Gudbrandsdal with two of his four groups. A third group 'Dahl' would withdraw into the Gausdal which runs parallel to the west. The line south of Lillehammer was the furthest point reached by two companies of the Royal Leicestershire Regiment and two companies of Sherwood Foresters on Sunday 21 April. At the same time a further company of Sherwood Foresters reached a position on the western side of Lake Mjosa.

Chapter 17

The Ill-fated 148 Brigade

Nothing that follows should cast a reflection on the small band of regular officers and non-commissioned officers or indeed their enthusiastic comrades of all ranks who found themselves in a well-nigh impossible situation. From the moment that 148 Brigade landed at Aandalsnes and Molde they did not stand a chance. Normally a brigade consists of three battalions of infantry together with supporting arms such as anti-tank guns but 148 Brigade was one battalion short and had no supporting arms. The brigade consisted of two territorial battalions, the 1st/8th Sherwood Foresters commanded by Lieutenant Colonel Ford and the 1st/5th Royal Leicestershire Regiment commanded by Lieutenant Colonel German.

We have already dwelt on the muddle and lack of inter-service planning that had attended embarkation. On 7 April, 148 Brigade had been ready to proceed to Stavanger. It then disembarked and had been selected to land at Namsos north of Trondheim. It then re-embarked but after two days was transhipped to the anti-aircraft cruisers *Carlisle* and *Curacao* which proceeded to Aandalsnes [pronounced Orndalsnes]. Much essential equipment like wireless equipment was mislaid. A and D Companies of the Royal Leicesters had sailed with the main body, but B & C Companies had followed on two days later. It was the latter who had witnessed the torpedoing of HMS *Cedarbank*, the only serious loss inflicted by the Germans on the invasion fleet. Nevertheless much of the Leicesters' equipment and stores, together with the whole of the battalion transport, had been lost.

Aandalsnes was a tiny port with only one concrete jetty 150ft long and had only one travelling crane. It is not much bigger today. The larger port of Molde is on the other side of the fjord some miles to seaward. Some troops were disembarked there then had to be ferried to Aandalsnes by local ferry. Aandalsnes lies at the top of a fjord where a dark gorge leads into the interior. It had increased in importance in the Thirties with the completion of a rail spur running down to the sea from the junction at Dombaas (pronounced Dombaws) on the main line through the Gudbrandsdal from Oslo to Trondheim.

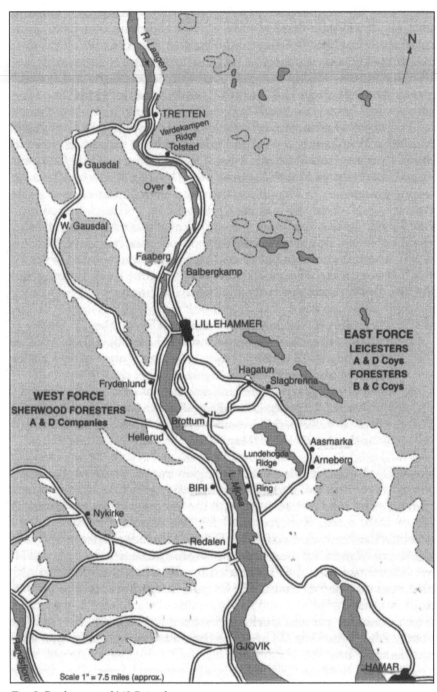

Fig. 8. Deployment of 148 Brigade

Several days before the arrival of 148 Brigade, the Navy had landed a party of Royal Marines at Aandalsnes under the command of Lieutenant Colonel Simpson. Supported by a battery of eight naval 2-pdr light anti-aircraft guns, Simpson had organized the defence of the port and it was he who met Brigadier Morgan, commanding 148 Brigade when he landed. By the time that Brigadier Morgan set foot on Norwegian soil he had received four sets of often conflicting orders. At the time of landing, the intention was a pincer movement on Trondheim. The orders stated: 'Your role to land Aandalsnes area secure Dombaas then operate northwards and take offensive action against Germans in Trondheim area.'

Dombaas situated near the top of the east/west watershed is the junction where the main line from Oslo leaves the Gudbrandsdal and turns north for Trondheim. Disembarkation of the brigade on the morning of 19 April had to be completed before it got light. The Norwegians had every incentive to lay on troop trains and D and A Companies of the Foresters were shortly moved up to Dombaas by rail. The brigadier was put in touch with Colonel King Salter at the Norwegian headquarters and both officers arranged to meet at Dombaas as soon as possible.

When they met that evening King Salter explained that unless 148 Brigade was diverted to the southern end of the Gudbrandsdal immediately, Norwegian resistance would in all probability collapse. Perhaps the Norwegians had been given to expect too much from the British for Colonel King Salter informed Morgan that General Ruge had received a telegram from the War Office informing him that he could call on 148 Brigade. Naturally Morgan was taken aback and felt that he should refer to the War Office. He ordered the rest of the brigade to come up to Dombaas while he and King Salter set off down the Gudbrandsdal valley to the Norwegian headquarters at Oyer, 12 miles north of Lillehammer.

The initial meeting with General Ruge was not entirely cordial. Morgan began by outlining the British plan for the recapture of Trondheim. Ruge for his part expressed some annoyance that the British had not kept him fully informed. He was even more upset when he heard that the British planned to blow up the bridges in the Gudbrandsdal which would have cut off the Norwegian forces' line of retreat. General Ruge was plainly disappointed at the size and the composition of 148 Brigade. He had requested three infantry battalions as well as field artillery and tanks. On the main point that he was in charge of operations in Central Norway, he was adamant. Part of the problem was solved by a War Office telegram received by Morgan on 20 April whereby General Ironside countermanded the order to move north from Dombaas towards Trondheim as operation Hammer had been cancelled.

On the question of command the telegram was more obscure: 'You should, if you can spare the troops co-operate with the Norwegian C-in-C,' but it emphasized, 'you remain under independent command of the War Office'. The telegram added, 'Now probable that you will be reinforced by another brigade - tell Norwegians'. Morgan and King Salter told the Norwegians about reinforcements but judiciously did not tell them about remaining under War Office control. For practical purposes Morgan had little option but to place his brigade under Norwegian command. He realized that he was largely reliant on the Norwegians for rations, artillery, maps and transport. When the Foresters arrived at Lillehammer Station at 02.50 on 20 April such were Norwegian expectations and typical of the Norwegian C-in-C that General Ruge, immaculately dressed albeit red-eyed from lack of sleep, was on the platform to greet them, along with Brigadier Morgan and a staff officer, Colonel Dudley Clarke. Brigade headquarters was set up at Lillehammer but there was to be little operational control and the tiny British force was shortly divided into three.

The troops allocated to support Dahl Group were known as West Force. Most of them had travelled down from Dombaas in open freight wagons for which they had been issued with blankets and tins of bully beef. On the way they had been bombed and machine-gunned lightly by a few aircraft but they reached Lillehammer unscathed. At 19.00 just as the light was fading, A and D Companies of the Foresters plus half HQ Company were loaded onto lorries and sent down the west bank of Lake Mjosa to Biri. By the time they arrived it was freezing hard. The British officer in command Major Roberts was told by Colonel Dahl commanding Dahl Group that the enemy was being held south of Gjovik. Dahl Group consisted of three battalions of infantry, one battalion of field artillery together with engineers and a supply column. What Colonel Dahl needed were troops to cover his western flank.

Roberts and his men were thereupon sent about 15 miles up a side road to a little village called Nykirke. They arrived tired and half frozen at 02.00 on Saturday morning where they sought shelter in the parish church which fortunately was heated. At dawn they deployed to positions round the village, but there was no sign of the enemy and at 11.00 a Norwegian officer arrived to tell them that Gjovik had fallen and they were to be withdrawn to Biri. Later they heard a massive explosion as the bridge at Lillehammer was blown up by Norwegian engineers. They knew what that meant; they were cut off from the main body of British troops on the eastern side of the lake. When finally withdrawn in Norwegian trucks on the night of 22/23 April they had to be driven miles round a parallel valley, the Gausdal, to the bridge at Tretten in the Gudbrandsdal.

Colonel Ford and the main body of the Foresters were allocated to General Hvinden Haug's 2nd Norwegian Division on the east bank of Lake Mjosa. The Norwegians were holding the Germans on the Lundehogda Ridge with 500 infantry, one battalion of ski troops and one battery of artillery. Some miles further to the east just south of the lake, at Aasmarka, Colonel Jensen was in position with 1,000 Dragoons. By 10.00 Ford reported to General Hvinden Haug at his HQ at Ring with B and C Companies of the Foresters. They were then deployed to provide a reserve for the Norwegians on the Lundehogda ridge. Lieutenant Dolphin and the 3-inch mortar section were moved forward to an isolated spur between the Lundehogda Ridge and Lake Mjosa, but German artillery fire was soon brought to bear on them and they ceased firing. The rest of the Foresters saw no action and were moved across to the rear of the Aasmarka position.

The third British force was composed of a body of Leicesters which was sent to support the Norwegian Dragoons south of Aasmarka. In the meanwhile the other half of the Leicesters, under their commanding officer Colonel German, had caught up and were brought forward by lorry. While in transit the Leicesters had their first taste of being strafed from the air. The effect on raw troops of the terrifying explosions and machine gun fire was bound to be considerable. Nevertheless they came through unscathed. As was proved time and time again in the early part of the war, the strafing of foot soldiers from the air was relatively harmless when compared to sustained and accurate fire from field artillery.

On the morning of 21 April, the German commander, aware that British units had arrived, launched a more determined offensive. He had at his disposal about 4,000 men made up of two infantry battalions, a motorized machine gun battalion and a battery of artillery. It was not the weight of numbers which made the difference, although the Germans comfortably outnumbered the British and the Norwegians combined, it was the integrated balance of supporting arms and total command of the skies which counted.

The Norwegian positions at Aasmarka were on a freezing hillside about 1,200ft above sea level. There were several farmsteads spreading into the woods on either side. The ground was covered by about 3ft of snow, making movement off the roads and tracks well-nigh impossible for British troops. The Germans had moved up their field artillery which was brought into action at about 3,000 yards, comfortably out of range of small arms fire. The Dragoons continued to hold the enemy at bay but gradually superior fire began to tell and the Norwegian positions were driven in from both flanks. The Norwegian commander concluded that his position must be abandoned and this opened the lakeside road to further German advance.

It came as a shock to the British when General Hvinden Haug requested that the flimsy British units should hold the line temporarily while the Norwegians withdrew through their positions. The Norwegians had every justification for making this request because although not necessarily heavily engaged, they had been in action continuously for the past ten days almost without respite. It was on the Aasmarka ridge that Sergeant Rowlinson, commanding a platoon of about thirty men held out until overrun by the enemy. Despite being severely wounded, he undoubtedly held up the German advance and was later awarded the Norwegian Military Cross. He would not have been awarded a British Military Cross which was reserved for officers. One is entitled to ask however, why was he not awarded the British Military Medal which was the equivalent awarded to other ranks?

By about 20.00 on Sunday 21 April, the Norwegians had completed their withdrawal to a line above Lillehammer. The Norwegian transport evacuated the Norwegians, but the civilian drivers were not told to return for the British. By midnight no transport had materialized so Colonel German and the main body of the Leicesters set out on a 14-mile tramp over the snowbound roads to Lillehammer. It was their second night out in the open although they had the modest consolation of a hot meal on arrival in Lillehammer. Transport then took them up the valley to new positions.

At this early stage of the campaign, the Germans had the good sense to appreciate that trying to fight at night in those semi-Arctic conditions was a near impossibility. This enabled the British to seek what shelter they could during the hours of darkness and when necessary to make their escape. Unhappily a large party of Leicesters and six officers did not make it to Lillehammer and were later captured. Captain Cripps of the Leicesters recounted how a platoon from D Company was left as a rearguard. After dark, finding that they had been left behind, they set out to march to Lillehammer. By mistake they took a left fork which took them via a longer route. Arriving at Lillehammer at dawn he enquired at the main hotel whether he and his weary men could have a wash and a meal only to be informed by the manager that the hotel had already been booked over the telephone by the Germans as their intended headquarters and that the new guests were expected shortly.

The British contingent didn't waste much time before heading for the mountains and what subsequently happened no doubt fuelled stories of British troops looting. For ten days the party tried to outflank the enemy's relentless progress up the Gudbrandsdal. The only way that they could survive was to seek food and shelter at night by breaking into empty ski chalets or farmhouses or by imposing themselves upon the kind hearted crofters. After ten days the party gave up the idea of reaching the coast and doubled back towards the Swedish border. This they eventually reached and were interned by the Swedes. The latter, while desperate not to upset the Germans, were fairly liberal in allowing repatriation of British troops through Finland which was still a neutral country.

At this stage of the campaign German broadcasts made it clear that civilians aiding the British ran the risk of being shot. As early as 14 April the C-in-C

General von Falkenhorst had issued the following chilling proclamation:

'The Norwegian government has declined several offers of co-operation. The Norwegian people must now themselves determine the fate of their Fatherland...if opposition is offered and the hand of friendship is rejected I shall be forced to employ the severest and most relentless means to crush such opposition. Anyone who assists the mobilization ordered by the former government, now evacuated or anyone who spreads false rumours will be court-martialled. Any civilian who is found carrying arms will be shot. Anyone found guilty of the sabotage of the means of transport or communications or of public undertakings will be shot.'

The new position taken up by the Allies was at Faaberg north of Lillehammer. Just below the bridge the valley narrows. The Allied position had the River Laagen which flows south-east on the right facing downstream and the high ground rising 2,000ft up to the Balbergkamp ridge on the left. Despite Brigadier

Fig. 9. Action at Balbergkamp

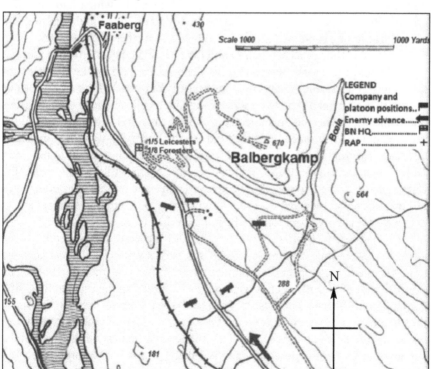

107

Morgan's protest, the Norwegian command asked that the British should hold this position while the Norwegians regrouped further up the valley. Brigadier Morgan, now in operational command of all British troops, had to make do as best he could with troops which had only reached the position piecemeal, ill-fed and tired and who had been forced to abandon essential items such as signals equipment in the course of their retreat. Morgan disposed of his mixed force of Leicesters and Foresters, about 650 men, as follows: two companies were placed forward astride the main road and two companies to the rear, while a further company covered his flank on the Balbergkamp side halfway up the hill.

The one thing for which Morgan could not provide would be a wide flank attack on his side of the river. The Germans did not in fact open their attack until noon when incendiary bombs were dropped from aircraft which set the woods alight. By 15.30 small numbers of Bavarian ski troops had reached points behind and above the British positions. A ski patrol armed with machine guns even made a surprise attack on brigade headquarters. There was only one thing to do and that was to pull back. A Norwegian commentator later described the loss of the Balbergkamp position as the first serious defeat of the war. Be that as it may, the blame can hardly be laid at Brigadier Morgan's door.

In the late afternoon a new position was taken up further along the valley with the support of two fresh companies of Leicesters which had only just arrived. But this position too came under heavy fire both from the ground and air and had to be abandoned after several hours. A further position 10 miles up the valley at Tolstadt was held until noon the following day. Two miles north of Oyer, Second Lieutenant Jessop and his platoon had held up the Germans for four hours at a roadblock. This had been hastily constructed out of tree trunks so that all the Germans had to do was to bring up a tank and nose the barricades out of the way. After being subjected to both heavy and short range machine gun fire, not to mention being outflanked, Jessop and most of his men managed to escape up the mountain side and to rejoin the battalion eight hours later. Jessop was duly awarded a Military Cross. After withdrawing from the Balbergkamp, some Foresters had been overtaken and captured. Two companies of Foresters never received the order to withdraw, although they did manage to get away. Inevitably more food and equipment had to be left behind.

This had been no blitzkrieg offensive and the Germans appeared to be advancing at an almost leisurely pace. Their tactics were predictable: advance until checked then regroup and attack from either one flank or both. The effectiveness of German tactics were put more luridly in the recollections of a corporal in the Sherwood Foresters: 'you can't see the Jerries for bleeding trees, then before you can even cock your rifle they are on top of you and they've all got automatic rifles that spray you with bullets'. Particularly effective was the support the Germans were able to give their troops with mortar fire. The

Chamberlain's War Cabinet 1939
Top: Lord Hankey, Hore-Belisha,
Winston Churchill, Kingsley Wood.
Seated: Admiral Chatfield, Samuel
Hoare, Neville Chamberlain, John
Simon, Lord Halifax. *Imperial War
Museum.*

First Cruiser Squadron off
Norwegian Coast.
HM Ships: *York; Sheffield;
Birmingham; Manchester.*
National Museum Royal Navy.

HM destroyer *Bedouin* in Narvik Fjord. *National Museum Royal Navy.*

HM destroyer *Eskimo* after bows blown off. *National Museum Royal Navy.*

General Ruge
appointed
Norwegian
commander.
Imperial War Museum.

Norwegian ski troops in action. *Imperial War Museum.*

German troops taking cover in Valdres uplands. *Imperial War Museum.*

The Gudbrandsdal at Kvam. More British troops lie buried in the churchyard at Kvam than anywhere else. *Epsom Print Centre.*

British troops search ruins of Namsos for survivors. *Imperial War Museum.*

View of burning ship through port hole. Namsos Fjord. *National Museum Royal Navy.*

Troops of 24th (Guards) Brigade land at Harstad. Lofoten Islands, 15th April 1940. *South Wales Borderers. Regt. Museum.*

British anti-aircraft battery at Harstad. Puffers in background. *Imperial War Museum.*

The French Foreign Legion at Bjerkvik with Hotchkiss tank. *Imperial War Museum.*

The final prize – Narvik (Luftwaffe photo). *Imperial War Museum.*

HMS *Glorious* in happier times. *National Museum Royal Navy.*

French and Polish troops on their way back to Britain. *National Museum Royal Navy.*

Germans were equipped with 100mm mortars, that is to say over 4-inch, whereas the heaviest British mortars were only 3-inch. Again an incident recounted by a Sherwood Forester brings out the reality of those early days: 'we had a couple of 3-inch mortars which we set up to fire at an enemy machine gun post which was pinning us down; but when we fired our first two bombs there was no explosion - oh no, just this bloody cloud of smoke' [they had been issued with smoke bombs instead of high explosive].

Having endured their baptism of fire in the course of these few days, the Foresters and Leicesters had to get used to too little sleep, intermittent meals often provided through the generosity of the villagers, short freezing nights and the slush of the April thaw by day. As a Norwegian colonel put it: 'a difficult job in a strange land in frost and snow with thick dark woods in all directions. It might be difficult for us - for them it was infinitely worse'. Bearing in mind the state that some British troops were in their performance can only be described as beyond reproach. Remember they were for the most part volunteer territorials who nine months earlier had been in civvy street. Consider what some of them had already been through. The two and a half companies of Sherwood Foresters isolated on the west bank of Lake Mjosa had commenced an eleven-hour journey in open trucks on secondary roads after nightfall when it was safe to move and in temperatures below freezing point. For some reason which remains unexplained, the men were without their greatcoats.

The Gudbrandsdal gorge proper begins some two miles short of Tretten at Vardekamp. A bridge over the river Laagen at Tretten links the Gausdal valley with the Gudbrandsdal. Steep sides to the main valley render the position much easier for a small force to defend. A ledge on the west bank carries the railway and a ledge on the east bank carries the main road. The mountain rises about 1,200ft and is traversed by a farm track. The biggest building in Tretten was a cheese factory and here several platoons spent the night. If the British helped themselves to the cheese throughout the night it was understandable. It wasn't missed because the following afternoon the cheese factory was blown to pieces.

The Norwegian command considered it vital that the position at Tretten should be held for twenty-four hours to enable Colonel Dahl's West Force to withdraw over the bridge. This unhappily was not to be and Dahl Force had to retreat higher up the Heidal valley. The Norwegians had placed the remnants of three squadrons of Dragoons with four medium machine guns and a mortar on the mountain saddle. The final position taken up by the remnants of 148 Brigade was as follows: two companies of Foresters were placed on the main road and the fresh company of Leicesters up on the saddle. One company of Foresters was placed astride the railway on the west side of the river on the outskirts of Tretten.

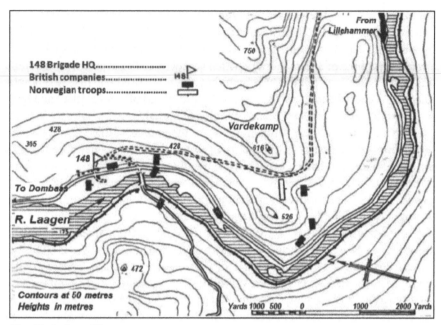

Fig. 10. Action at Tretten

Fighting began about 13.00. The opening paragraph of Jo Kynoch's account runs:

'Do you remember that St George's day? Do you remember Tretten Gorge? Do you remember the hellish din of warfare on that late sunny afternoon? The confusion, men shouting orders, wounded men screaming in pain, the horrendous shriek of the dive bombers and the explosion and dust of their bombs and the deadly sing of flying shrapnel.'

While enemy troops worked round the eastern flank, the weight of the attack came along the main road led by three or four tanks. Each British platoon had been issued with a Boys anti-tank gun which fired a half inch armour-piercing bullet. Unfortunately when fired at tanks the bullets simply bounced off the tank's armour. The general failure of the weapon was to cause particular bitterness in France a month later. By chance however, at one point in the fighting, Colonel German took an anti-tank rifle from one of his men and with a lucky shot broke one of the tank's tracks causing it to skid into the ditch.

Fighting continued until after 16.00 by which time the Foresters had suffered considerable casualties and a number of men had run out of ammunition. Steadily the forward troops were driven back. Any position retaken was soon lost again. Captain Ramsden, the C Company commander, led a charge in the old style at the point of the bayonet and silenced a machine gun, but he paid for it with his life. Despite the reserve company of Foresters being moved forward several tanks moved into the British positions. Fighting every inch of the way, the battalion was forced back to the bridge where a last stand was organized by the adjutant Captain Ford-Smith who was also killed.

The troops up on the farm track to the east held their positions but the German advance along the main road effectively cut off all troops on the Vardekamp ridge. Meanwhile the village of Tretten had come under heavy bombardment from German 5.9cm (2.5-inch) close support guns. To cover the inevitable withdrawal, a rearguard was set up in the late evening a mile north of Tretten. This enabled the remnants of 148 Brigade to be withdrawn by means of Norwegian buses under cover of darkness. The brigade, now down to nine officers, four Foresters and five Leicesters, was initially withdrawn to a position some 45 miles up the Gudbrandsdal.

This was not the end of the story. Small parties of men who had been cut off made their way back by mountain paths. The Leicesters up on the Vardekamp were not so lucky, their position was overrun and they were captured. One party led by Colonel German reached Ringebu. As they marched through the village in the fading light there seemed to be a number of troops about whom they took to be Norwegians. Suddenly someone said 'It's the Jerries'. On they marched but they were challenged at a roadblock and forced to surrender.

Earlier a company of Leicesters had been told to take up a position in an old barn. In the afternoon they saw a light tank closely followed by troops coming up the road. German troops habitually fight more closely with their tanks than do the British. Then they saw a 150mm field gun take up a position and start shelling the village of Tretten. Opening up with their Bren guns they were dismayed to discover that their magazines had been loaded with tracer bullets for firing at aircraft which exactly pin-pointed their own position. This soon attracted heavy fire; then three tanks appeared against which their anti-tank rifles were useless. One of the tanks even moved right up to the barn. By this time the hay in the loft was ablaze and the Germans simply waited for the British to come out with their hands up. Their first face-to-face contact with a German was when a Feldwebel (sergeant) said 'for you the war is over'. They were then put on a lorry and driven down to Oslo and later transhipped to a prison camp in Germany.

Treatment of British and Norwegian soldiers captured by the Germans was variable. For the most part the Germans in Norway played by the rule book. As a Polish officer who took part in the recapture of Narvik remarked ruefully to a

Norwegian: 'The Germans behaved like angels in your country'. It is difficult to make comparisons with the behaviour of Allied troops. In the first place an advancing army takes many more prisoners than an army in retreat. Secondly atrocities committed by British and later American troops in the Second World War do not, as yet, seem to have been adequately chronicled.

Colonel King Salter was among one group of stragglers who were surprised when they cautiously approached the main road. As the colonel tried to make good his escape he was wounded in the leg. The young Germans who shortly picked him up seemed genuinely concerned at the state of his shattered foot. After administering first aid, they made a makeshift stretcher with their rifles and a greatcoat and carried him down to a farmhouse and put him to bed in the farmer's bed. Not all stragglers from Tretten received such considerate treatment. A truck picked up some of the men in a mixed party of Foresters and Leicesters. An officer then told the rest that transport would come back for them. But it was a German tank which came up the road and the men hastily took cover in the trees. A voice shouted out 'come out Englishmen it is all right'. The first man to stand up was shot down, then the tank sprayed the trees with bullets and a number of men were killed.

Small parties of men continued to try and reach the coast, others made it to Sweden. Some even commandeered fishing vessels and sailed back to England. The Germans hunted these parties of fugitives relentlessly with spotter planes and ski troops and a considerable number were taken prisoner. One party thought that they were safe and were cooking a meal in a mountain chalet when a knock came at the door. Some Austrian ski troops had seen the smoke from the chimney.

Chapter 18

A Fighting Retreat Through the Gudbrandsdal

On 21 April the OKW, through a Hitler directive, decreed that the main strategy of XXI Group should be directed towards establishing the land link between Oslo and Trondheim. To this end 196 Division under General Lieutenant Richard Pellengahr had been reinforced. Colonel Herman Fischer's group was transferred to the direct command of 196 Division and was proceeding up the eastern valley, the Osterdal. Group Fischer had been assigned three infantry battalions, two artillery regiments, one engineer company and two motorized companies of the General Goring Regiment, one motorized machine gun company and two squadrons of tanks. Thus while Group Fischer was not much bigger than a British infantry brigade, it was the wealth of supporting arms which enabled it to drive the Norwegians relentlessly before it.

On 23 April forward units of Group Fischer reached Rena, but the main body was held up by demolished bridges and did not come up until the next day. Meanwhile Colonel Fischer formed his tank and motorized troops into a flying column and sent them off to Tynsett which they reached on 25 April. While the main body was pushing along the Trondheim road, a small reconnaissance party was sent east along the railway to Roros, the mining centre, where it encountered some Norwegian resistance.

By 27 April, the main part of Group Fischer had moved up to Tynsett and the next day a motorized unit reached Ulsberg and turned north towards Trondheim. By 30 April the motorized unit had made contact with troops of 181 Division advancing south from Trondheim. The significance of this was that the Germans had possession of a virtually undamaged railway line running south from Trondheim to Dombaas and were thus in a position to menace the British on their northern flank.

The Allied defeat at Tretten on 23 April had an important effect on German strategy. General Falkenhorst in overall command of XXI Group no longer considered that the drive to Trondheim was so urgent whereas retaining the initiative by harrying the British and Norwegians in the Gudbrandsdal was seen to be of cardinal importance. General Pellengahr commanding 196 Division had at his disposal seven infantry battalions, one motorized machine-gun battalion, two artillery regiments one company of engineers and a squadron of tanks.

On 21 April units from 163 Division were withdrawn from the northern advance and turned west towards Bergen and also Sognefjord. At Bagn they encountered stiff resistance and were repulsed by the Norwegian 4th Field Brigade under Colonel Gudbrand Ostbye. The Germans then sent reinforcements with strong dive bomber support and they broke through on 27 April. The 4th Brigade was then driven up into the mountains.

Several days after the action at Tretten a battalion from 163rd Division entered the Gausdal at Vignes. General Pellengahr diverted a detachment, including tanks and motorcycle troops, south-west from Tretten. The Norwegian troops in the Gausdal were thus trapped. If the British had been able to hold Kjorem in the main valley, the Norwegians would have had a chance to regain the Gudbrandsdal by making a long detour via the Heidal. In the event, Colonel Dahl together with 250 officers and 3,500 men were forced to surrender on 29 April.

15 Infantry Brigade
As Norwegian resistance in the central valley inexorably declined, the campaign largely devolved onto 15 Brigade. This was made up of three regular battalions: 1st Battalion King's Own Yorkshire Light Infantry (KOYLI); 1st Battalion York and Lancaster Regiment; 1st Battalion The Green Howards. The brigade landed on 22 April and the last ship of the final evacuation of the entire British force in Central Norway left Aandalsnes at 02.00 on 2nd May. The brigade was in Norway just twelve days!

The brigade had previously been stationed near Lille in Northern France when suddenly they were told to pack up their bags and prepare to move by train. All motor vehicles and drivers were to be left behind and within 36 hours the brigade found itself at Dunfermline. The original objective of Sickleforce had been the Trondheim area, but the Germans were by this time too strongly entrenched and the Navy did not like the idea of risking ships in the confined waters of Trondheimfjord. Plan Sickleforce had therefore been abandoned. The command structure of 15 Brigade was plagued with setbacks; the Brigadier had a stroke and was succeeded by Lieutenant Colonel Smyth, promoted to brigadier. With little time to prepare, Major General Bernard Paget, until recently the Commandant at Sandhurst was given overall command in Central Norway and arrived at Molde on 25th April and the Norwegian destroyer *Sleipner* transported him to Aandalsnes.

One of General Paget's first acts had been to study the reports from Brigadier Morgan and based on these he made strong representations to General Massy, the GOC Central Norway, still in England, about the lack of air cover. The demands on the Royal Air Force were based on the priority of the British Expeditionary Force in France and maintaining forty-five fighter squadrons in the UK, considered to be the minimum necessary for the protection of Britain. The Air Staff decided to send just one squadron of eighteen aircraft. This was hardly enough to maintain a constant patrol of six aircraft over the battle area and protect the railway line, not to mention the port of Aandalsnes. Moreover the aircraft were to be Gloster Gladiators, a robust little fighter but an out-of-date biplane and no match for any of the Messerschmidt aircraft.

The saga of Lake Lesjaskog was as short as it was predictable. The lake is about eight and a half miles long and half a mile wide. It was a good choice as a landing ground. It is almost at the top of the watershed between the Gudbrandsdal and the Romsdal and the ice was practically frozen solid. Both the road and the railway linking Aandalsnes and Dombaas ran alongside the lake. A runway about 800 x 75m had been swept by local labour and essential equipment and a servicing flight arrived on 23 April. By 17.00 on 24 April fuel and ammunition had been laid out along the runway. But there were only two refuelling troughs and the starter trolley was out of action. The batteries had no acid. For defence two Oerlikon anti-aircraft guns had been sent up from Aandalsnes.

Vice Admiral Wells commanding, the aircraft carriers *Ark Royal* and *Glorious* were recalled from the Mediterranean and left Scapa Flow on 23 April. The fighter aircraft could not possibly have flown the distance from Britain so the Gloster Gladiators of 263 Squadron had been brought over on the aircraft carrier *Glorious*. An experienced pilot, Squadron Leader J. Donaldson, took off from the *Glorious* and with only four maps between eighteen pilots it was a wonder that he brought all aircraft over the mountains, especially as at one point they had to fly through a snowstorm. The night was, as usual, bitterly cold. By daylight the controls and the carburettors were frozen stiff. With no starter trolley, to say that there were starter problems is an understatement. Nevertheless the first aircraft got off the ground two hours after first light and two aircraft were sent off to patrol the battle area at Kvam.

The Germans had a good look at what was happening and one Heinkel was shot down after dropping a few bombs. At 08.30, while the servicing party was struggling to get more engines started, the main attack started. Heinkel bombers approached in threes and then broke off to bomb and machine gun the lake. Five Gladiators were destroyed before they could take off. A number of ground staff were strangers to the unit and unfamiliar with the aircraft. Some took refuge in the trees. The marines and naval contingent stuck to their posts firing their two anti-aircraft guns furiously. They also had some Lewis heavy machine guns. The tragedy was that it was taking an hour to refuel a single Gladiator and some aircraft, while waiting on the ground to refuel, were set alight or damaged by bombs.

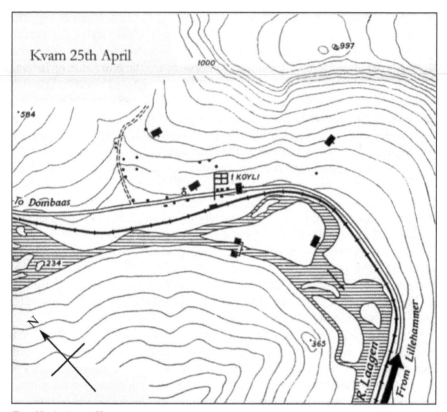

Fig. 11. Action at Kvam

In the late morning two sections of three aircraft got into the air and appeared over the battlefield at Kvam. This was greatly encouraging to the troops. In all forty sorties were flown and six enemy aircraft shot down. By the afternoon heavier bombers of the Junkers 88 variety were appearing and the lake was beginning to break up. After just one day in action, four surviving aircraft were flown to an emergency landing ground at Aandalsnes. All remaining damaged aircraft had to be destroyed and after dark the ground staff were evacuated.

The Kings Own Yorkshire Light Infantry at Kvam 25/26 April
Brigadier Morgan commanding 149 Brigade had established his latest HQ 45 miles north of Tretten and although stragglers kept on coming in, he was down to about 450 men and had no officers of company commander rank. It was therefore agreed that Morgan's men should be placed in reserve to Smyth's 15 Brigade which took up a position at Kvam. On Smyth's promotion to brigadier, Major Cass, holder of the Distinguished Service Order and Military Cross from

116

the First World War, took command of 1st KOYLI. To mention that he had at one time played rugby for the Army team is by no means irrelevant, for the qualities that a man displays on the sports field often give a good indication as to how he is likely to conduct himself on the battlefield.

By the time that the battalion landed at Aandalsnes on the night of 23/24 April, the campaign was as good as lost. Two companies, C and D had been landed at Molde, further down the fjord. By 02.00 the main body of the battalion steamed out of Aandalsnes bound for Dombaas and beyond. At each station Smyth telephoned to find out if the next station was clear. The battalion then detrained and took cover in the trees. For most of the day they had to watch the village being set alight by intermittent bomb attacks. In the evening they were moved a further 20 miles down the line to Kvam. That night C and D Companies rejoined the battalion. They had only succeeded in doing so by boarding a trawler at Molde and forcing the captain at the point of the bayonet to ferry them across the fjord to Aandalsnes.

From the direction of Oslo, the road and railway run up the east bank of the river Laagen which takes a right-angle turn to the left about a mile below the village of Kvam. As the river turns west it flows past a large pear-shaped island covered with bushes and small trees and this is where Brigadier Smyth posted A Company. He then posted B Company halfway up the slope on the northern side and put his own headquarters in front of the parish church. The ground slopes gently on the northern side of the river but much more steeply on the southern side. Two companies were posted in the village and C Company, York and Lancaster up a small road leading out of the village to the north. The snow had receded from the centre of the fields, but a few hundred feet up it was near impassable except for ski troops. It was a glorious spring morning. 'Just the day for a battle', the CO remarked. Fairly early on in the battle Brigadier Smyth was wounded and command of the brigade passed to Lieutenant Colonel A. Kent-Lemon of the York and Lancasters.

At 07.30 a Norwegian battalion started to withdraw through the position as prearranged. As soon as the sun was up the temperature started to rise and the men were digging in their shirt sleeves, when at 11.30 the Germans appeared. In the lead were a medium tank, followed by a light tank and an armoured car, followed by fifty infantry. Then came motorcycles with side-cars mounted with machine guns. There were towed guns and lorries full of infantry stretching down the road for five miles - an artillery man's dream. Unfortunately the British had no artillery except for six 25mm Hotchkiss anti-tank guns.

The KOYLI fire discipline was excellent and both A and B Companies held their fire until the enemy were about 150 yards distant. The Germans immediately went to ground leaving a number of bodies by the roadside. The Germans then brought up their 5.9cm close support artillery to a point some

2,000 yards down the road just out of range of small arms fire. They were thus able to bring an accurate fire to bear on the positions on the island and on the village, each house receiving a couple of well placed rounds of shell fire.

The Germans launched their first infantry assault on B Company up in the woods on the British left, but the Yorkshiremen were well dug in and the Germans were easily repulsed. They then launched their main attack on A Company on the island. Unfortunately the island was lower than the land on the road side of the river and the enemy were able to pour down machine gun and mortar fire onto the British positions. Many men of A Company were killed and even more wounded. Shortly after 14.00 the adjutant found that some of A Company had been pushed back to the village end of the island thus leaving the flank of B Company on the hill dangerously exposed.

Captain Fox commanding C Company, KOYLI was summoned forward but soon every German gun was brought to bear on the advancing troops. Through the exploding shells the gallant captain was to be seen urging his men on. The KOYLI line was restored just in front of the railway station. During the afternoon the Germans made a determined effort to outflank C Company along the river but Captain Fox, armed with a Bren gun, put a stop to that. Later in the day Captain Fox was killed by a mortar bomb.

The Germans then turned their attention to B Company, but they were so well dug in that the casualties were remarkably light. Not so the Germans; no less than fifty bodies were counted in front of the B Company position. It might have been otherwise if Corporal Binns had not spotted a German machine-gun crew setting up their guns behind a large rock on the flank. Leaving his position he crawled through the trees with his Bren gun and wiped out the entire crew. Corporal Binns, who was awarded the Military Medal, was killed in Italy in 1944.

The position in the evening was that A Company with four officers and eighty-five men having either been killed, captured or wounded, had ceased to exist. Major Cass, the commanding officer, therefore decided to move C Company, York and Lancaster, previously in reserve, up the hillside behind B Company which he had ordered back to a position nearer the village. The short night was bitterly cold; it was the men's third night without sleep. By 02.30 it was getting light, but the hours of darkness had not been wasted. Those in the open dug furiously and others put the houses and sheds into a state of defence, despite a Tommy's aversion to smashing up people's homes.

At 05.30 the German bombardment started and it became clear that the artillery had received reinforcements during the night. When the German machine guns opened up they were firing whole belts of ammunition at a time. At 06.30 the Germans attacked C Company, York and Lancaster which was among the trees on the hillside. Nevertheless, with their Bren guns carefully concealed among the trees, the York and Lancasters held their ground. A second attack at 09.00 was held, but a third attack on B and D Company on the flatter ground led to some heavy fighting and casualties began to mount.

There were some notable examples of individual courage. Two Yorkshiremen remained behind a low wall working their machine gun, cracking jokes all the while as the houses round them were blown to pieces. In the early afternoon a shell landed on top of them. At 13.00 a light tank appeared along the road. Corporal Stokes was manning an anti-tank gun sighting down the road through the village. To his chagrin, his field of fire was obscured by some tree trunks which had been put up as a roadblock. Captain MacRiggs crawled along the road under fire and started to dismantle the roadblock. When the job was nearly finished a bullet hit him in the shoulder and he was knocked into the ditch. Corporal Stokes was then in a position to take a sight and his first shot stopped the tank. A second set it on fire. A further tank appeared and Stokes waited until it was level with the first tank before finishing it off with a couple of shots. Unbelievably an armoured car appeared round the corner and Stokes waited for it to draw level before knocking it out with a single shot. The road was then completely blocked and Stokes and his crew prudently withdrew before a German shell knocked out their anti-tank gun.

By early afternoon the Germans had made little progress. They moved into a sawmill on the outskirts of the village but were driven out by two sections of C Company led by Lieutenant French who was wounded. The Germans did succeed in placing heavy machine guns in the woods on the flanks of the battalion and were pouring fire down into the village. Casualties began to mount. By 17.00 news came in that the York and Lancasters had taken up a position several miles up the valley. A rearguard was set up under Sergeant Rowan with three Bren guns and an anti-tank gun and at 23.00 the battalion was ordered back to Dombaas. B, C, and E Companies together with HQ Company were successfully withdrawn but D Company did not receive the order. Captain Vickers organized his company into three fighting patrols, and they set off over the hills. In general the Germans did not pursue them although they had several skirmishes in the woods. After regaining the woods higher up and a 12-mile march, they arrived at brigade headquarters. So ended the battle and today there are more British graves in the little churchyard at Kvam than anywhere else in Norway.

The York and Lancasters at Kjorem

While the battle was raging at Kvam, General Paget met General Ruge at Norwegian headquarters. The latter, facing up to the reality of the situation, handed over command in the Gudbrandsdal to Paget from Dombaas southward. This meant that Paget could call on General Hvinden Haug's supply and transport. General Ruge's last message to London had been that his men were exhausted and that unless immediate help were forthcoming a debacle would

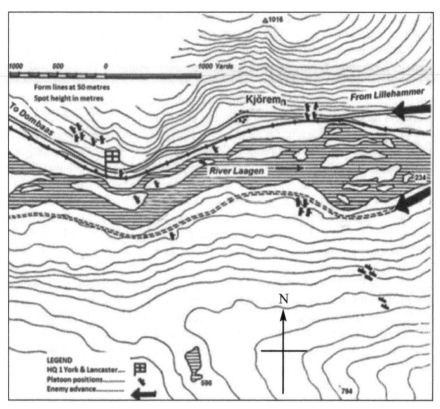

Fig. 12. Action at Kjorem

occur. General Paget had decided to make his next stand at Otta pending the arrival of a regiment of artillery and a further infantry brigade for which he had asked. His most immediate concern however was to fight a rearguard at Kjorem about five miles north of Kvam which was about the last point at which Colonel Dahl could get his troops back into the main Gudbrandsdal valley from the Gausdal. The 1st Battalion York and Lancaster were allotted this task, the plan being that the KOYLI would withdraw through their position.

Although General Paget was primarily concerned with holding the Germans in the Gudbrandsdal. He could not overlook the fact that the Germans advancing up the Osterdahl would shortly link up with the force at Trondheim. On 27 April Paget received news that the Germans had sent a force up a side valley which would lead them to cutting the Dombaas/Opdal route only 20 miles to the north of Dombaas at Hjerkinn.

The approach of the York and Lancasters to the fighting zone had been similar to that of the KOYLI. Thirty-one officers and 690 men had embarked on 29 April under the command of Lieutenant Colonel Kent-Lemon. B and D Companies were landed from destroyers at Aandalsnes and had been sent up to Dombaas to support the KOYLI. The cruiser *Sheffield* had been too large to proceed up the fjord so had landed the rest of the battalion at Molde. Here they were transferred to trawlers and ferried to Aandalsnes. The port was continuously bombed so the troops took cover in the woods up river and they did not catch up with the rest of the battalion until Dombaas. While there the little railway junction was continuously bombed and the battalion to its credit brought down three enemy aircraft with their Bren guns. They were then put on the train for Otta. No sooner had they arrived and detrained and got their equipment under cover than they got the sort of order which makes men doubt the infallibility of their officers, 'Get back on the train'. Their final destination was Sjoa a few miles above Kvam.

Major Jordan was sent on to Kvam with C Company where he arrived in time to take part on the second day of the battle, while lorries took the rest of the battalion to Kjorem, a mere hamlet on the north side of the river. The lie of the land at Kjorem is a bit different to that at Kvam. The valley rises steeply on the northern bank. Road and rail continue to run along the northern side of the river but on the south side there is a farm track parallel to the river and the valley sides rise more gently. The York and Lancaters dug in as best they could astride the road with standing patrols at a considerable height among the woods and the broken ground with occasional farmhouses on the hillside. Nevertheless numerous woods restricted the field of fire. A & B Companies occupied a position on the right with D Company on the left. The gap through which the river flowed was covered by the dismounted Bren guns of the Carrier platoon, with the Pioneer platoon in support. There was further a company of Green Howards to the rear.

At midnight the KOYLI began to pass through the position and C Company, which had fought so courageously at Kvam, rejoined the battalion and was placed in reserve. Promptly at 08.00 the enemy, covered by artillery, advanced on the battalion position. As the morning wore on the strength of enemy infantry attacks increased with tanks and mortar fire in support. Not only did the enemy bring up this support along the road but also along the farm track. At noon tanks and mortars were brought into action and the trees in front of D Company were set alight by mortar bombs. This forced D Company to withdraw which exposed A and B Companies to enfilade fire from across the river. Finally it was decided to withdraw A and B Companies several miles up the road to a position in front of Sjoa which could then cover the battalion's withdrawal after nightfall.

Meanwhile B Company of the Green Howards was deployed on the south side of the river and spent the night of 26 April digging in approximately level with the York and Lancaster HQ on the northern bank. The next morning they could see pressure mounting against the York and Lancasters on the north bank and British prisoners being marched back. There were KOYLI platoons in front of the Green Howards and they began drawing back through the Green Howard position in the afternoon. That night B Company started stumbling in file through the woods and along the river back to the bridge at Sjoa. They were then required to leap frog by platoon back along the road on the north bank to Otta. The Carrier platoon (without carriers) suffered heavily when several German armoured cars surprised them. Captain Lidwill was killed and armoured cars moved up and down the road machine gunning the men who had taken refuge in the trees.

Throughout the day, the number of casualties had mounted and the evacuation of the wounded, which included Regimental Sergeant Major Haggerty, became increasingly difficult. Strong parties of the enemy kept trying to work round the flanks of the battalion. Finally orders were received to move back to Otta where the main body of Green Howards had taken up a position. This time the Germans were determined not to let the British get away quite so easily. They had succeeded in getting round to the rear of the forward companies thus cutting them off from the two companies at Sjoa.

Lieutenant Willis was sent out with a fighting patrol which found the roadblock strongly held and covered by machine guns on either flank. Sergeant Cully was later awarded the Distinguished Conduct Medal and Private Ryan, the Military Medal, for their part in silencing the machine guns. This enabled the civilian transport with battalion stores to get through, but when C and D Companies moved down the road, machine gun fire from the flanks forced them off the road. For several hours during the night, platoons and sometimes individual sections were forced to fight independent actions in the woods. Those who reached Sjoa were then moved back to Otta. Some groups of men lost their way and arrived later. Others were captured. One party with Lieutenant Colonel Tennent walked for a hundred miles over mountain tracks to the Swedish border and was eventually repatriated. Captain Wilson took an even more tortuous path over the mountains to the coast. Here he and his men both bribed and cajoled a Norwegian fishing vessel to take them over the North Sea to England.

The Green Howards at Otta 28 April

Otta is a small market town situated about ten miles north of Kjorem where the River Otta flowing from the west joins the River Laagen. The main road follows the east bank and the railway the west bank. The valley floor on the west bank on which the little town is situated is fairly flat. On the east bank a steep spur just below the town practically comes down to the river. This is the historic spot where in 1612 the local peasantry massacred a party of Scottish mercenary

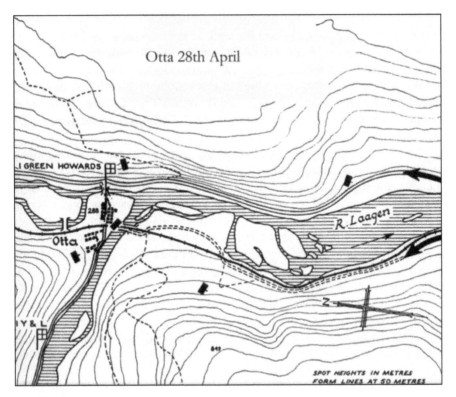

Fig. 13. Action at Otta

soldiers by rolling boulders down on top of them. The 1st Battalion, Green Howards was short of A Company which had been detached to defend Dombaas from the incipient threat of German forces coming down the railway line from Trondheim. It was also short of B Company which had been in action at Kjorem and did not limp into Otta until 07.00 on 28 April.

The Otta position, the last place where a stand could be made before Dombaas, really required two battalions to hold it. In the event, the KOYLI had been evacuated bloodied but unbowed to Dombaas and the York and Lancasters had suffered similarly while extricating itself from Sjoa. So it was down to the Green Howards. Lieutenant Colonel Robinson placed C Company just in front of the spur on the east bank and D Company on the west bank in front of the little town. B Company and Brigade HQ occupied the town behind the River Otta. Y Company made up of transport drivers and despatch riders, for there was no transport, was placed on the east bank together with the battalion anti-tank platoon.

About 10.30 some 150 enemy infantry, advancing behind several tanks and armoured cars, approached along the track on the west bank. D Company held its fire until the enemy were about 400 yards distant. The ensuing fusillade was deadly and the enemy retired leaving a number of dead and wounded on the track. No. 16 platoon higher up the hill was heavily bombarded while No. 17 platoon held its fire until the enemy were down to 150 yards before opening up. At 18.00 the enemy made their final assault and all troops were ordered to retire across the Otta Bridge.

On the east bank of the river several light tanks were seen advancing along Y Company's front at lunchtime. Lieutenant Harrison succeeded in knocking out one tank with an anti-tank rifle one of the rare occasions on which the Boys anti-tank rifle was effective. Later the enemy tried to cross the river in collapsible boats but were stopped by fire from Y Company. A party of Germans were observed trying to filter through the woods above C Company's left flank. Captain Armitage sent No. 15 platoon up the hill to stop them. By 17.00 in the evening there were no less than four groups of enemy troops in front of Armitage's position. Lance Corporal Headley seized a Bren gun and ran 20 yards to the flank and brought a deadly fire to bear on the attackers. On another occasion Sergeant Roche left his cover and drove the enemy back with hand grenades. Eventually C Company was down to twenty-three men of all ranks with a second lieutenant in charge. Nevertheless they held a party of fifty Germans at bay.

Earlier in the day Lieutenant Rawson had observed a party of about thirty German officers in conference. With a small party he left the relative safety of the British positions and crept forward. Surprise was complete and he caused heavy casualties with his Bren gun. Unfortunately the gallant lieutenant went missing later in the day. At 22.00 the road and rail bridge were blown up and D Company was forced to ford the river about half a mile north of the bridge. As soon as they had vacated the spur, the battalion mortars laid down a barrage of fire and smoke. B and Y Companies opened rapid fire which enabled the battalion to get clean away. C Company were lucky enough to get back to the railway line and effect a rendezvous with the Norwegians who had laid on a train to take the Yorkshire men back to Dombaas.

Captain Armitage's C Company finally beat off an attack by a force twice their number. He then divided his company into four groups and set out for Otta. The path he took was some hundred yards below the crest of the mountains. Progress through the thick snow was slow and it took seven hours, part of which the men had to crawl on their hands and knees. By the time that they reached Otta it was in enemy hands, so dividing his men into even smaller groups, the company made its way back to Dombaas. Armitage's courage and resourcefulness earned him a Military Cross.

Chapter 19

Trondheim

Trondheim, the ancient capital of the kingdom, is the third largest city in Norway. It is situated at the head of Trondheimfjord and has a broad and safe anchorage. It lies at the confluence of the main road and rail routes from Oslo via Dombaas through the Gudbrandsdal and from Oslo via the Osterdal Eastern valley. It is a starting point for a road and rail route due east to Central Sweden. The main road to the north starts at Trondheim as does the railway, although in 1940, the railroad only ran for a couple of hundred miles.

The original intention of the British Service Chiefs had been to occupy Bergen, Stavanger, Trondheim and Narvik. The first two were crossed off the list when the Navy concluded that operating in narrow fjords several hours steaming from the open sea was too hazardous without adequate air cover. At sea ships could keep up a reasonable speed making them far less vulnerable to high-level bombers. In the fjords they had to greatly reduce speed. This was the main reason why Operation Maurice, the plan to land troops in Trondheimfjord itself was abandoned. In the end the plan code named Scissorforce was adopted which envisaged landings to the south at Aandalsnes and Namsos which lies about 100 miles to the north of Trondheim.

Vice Admiral Edward Collins commanding the Second Cruiser Squadron was diverted with 148 Brigade to Aandalsnes, while Vice Admiral Layton's Eighteenth Cruiser Squadron was escorting convoy NP1 bound for Narvik. When news of Admiral Whitworth's victory at Narvik came in, the Chiefs of Staff decided that one of the two brigades destined for Narvik, should be diverted to Namsos. Thus it was that on 14 April, Layton's squadron, consisting of the cruisers *Manchester* (his flagship), *Birmingham* and the anti-aircraft cruiser *Cairo*, together with three destroyers altered course south. They were escorting the troop ship *Chobry* and the rather grander *Empress of Australia* bearing 146 Infantry Brigade.

For the past couple of days, Captain Pegram with two cruisers, the *Glasgow* and the *Sheffield* plus six destroyers had been patrolling the Leads south of Trondheim, searching for enemy shipping. Pegram was ordered to land a force of sailors and marines at Namsos and also the smaller harbour of Bagsund next door. The anchorage was good but the fjord leading in from the sea was tortuous and narrow. Namsos only possessed one stone quay for ocean-going ships and a smaller wooden quay.

Captain Pegram's landing had been successfully accomplished at night by the destroyers which returned seawards in order to escort Layton's ships coming south leaving only Captain Nicholson's *Somali* in the fjord. Two staff officers had already signalled home a gloomy report about lack of air cover and the next day the *Somali* was heavily attacked. By the evening most of the *Somali*'s anti-aircraft ammunition had been used up. Nicholson then cabled the Admiralty that to bring troopships into Namsos would be extremely hazardous and acting upon this information the Admiralty ordered Layton to take his ships into the anchorage at Lillesjona just north of Ranafjord some hundred miles from Namsos. This provided the troops with their first view of the land of the midnight sun. As one eyewitness recorded, 'Snow lay thick on the hills, ice flows dotted the sea and bitter winds laden with snow swept the fjord'.

One of the larger than life characters thrown up by the First World War had been Lieutenant General Sir Adrian Carton de Wiart. Having lost both an eye and an arm and also winning the Victoria Cross in that conflict, he was beloved by the military establishment and by Winston Churchill in particular. In his memoirs Carton de Wiart recounts how in the middle of the night he received a telephone call summoning him to the War Office. 'It dawned upon me that the reason might well be Norway especially as I had never been there and knew nothing about it.' He had guessed correctly and was duly appointed general officer in command of Central Norway and flown out to Namsos in a flying boat. As the flying boat landed on the fjord a German fighter swooped down and strafed the flying boat with machine gun fire. The general survived unscathed but his only staff officer was wounded. A tender transferred the general to the *Somali* which that night took him up to Lillesjona to confer with Admiral Layton and Brigadier C. Phillips commanding 146 Infantry Brigade.

Even at Lillesjona, Heinkel bombers sought them out although the raids were light and intermittent. Nevertheless it was enough to convince the admiral that he should not risk the *Empress of Australia*. When his five destroyers had completed refuelling they ran alongside the liner and took aboard the Lincolns and the York and Lancasters. That night they steamed back down the coast to Namsos. The next body of troops to be landed were the rest of 146 Territorial Infantry Brigade, the Kings Own Yorkshire Light Infantry. They were transferred to the *Chobry* which was carrying most of the stores. The convoy put into Namsosfjord at sunset. The *Chobry* had to remain at anchor and four destroyers worked throughout the night ferrying troops and stores to the quayside.

The way in which the equipment was discharged is interesting. Chutes were lowered onto the decks of each destroyer and down them hurtled kitbags, ammunition boxes, cartons of food and so on. Some of the items fell into the sea, others were left aboard. Each man was supposed to be able to handle three kitbags which contained the regulation kit drawn up by the War Office for the last expedition to an Arctic region. This happened to be for garrison duties during the Boxer Rebellion in China at the end of the nineteenth century. Each man had been issued with: one pair Arctic boots, one pair rubber boots, eight pairs of socks, three pairs of gloves, two sweaters, two leather jerkins, one double Kapock sleeping bag and one Arctic coat lined with lambswool weighing 15lbs. When it came down to it, all the men really needed to carry was a thick greatcoat and enough ammunition.

On the morning of 20 April enemy bombers undertook the destruction of Namsos. Attacks started at 10.00 and carried on until 16.00. In all about sixty aircraft took part. In the late afternoon Commander Ravenhill commanding the destroyer *Nubian* described the effect of incendiary bombs on a little town largely constructed of wooden buildings: 'The whole place was a mass of flames from end to end and the glare on the snows of the surrounding mountains produced an unfortunate spectacle.' Unfortunate indeed for the civilians who returned to what had been their homes and livelihoods. As in other Norwegian towns the local authorities had learned to evacuate civilians as soon as Allied troops appeared but still twenty-two civilians lost their lives.

The next troops to arrive were the French. General Audet with his full staff had sailed from the Clyde in four troopships escorted by Admiral Derrien in the cruiser *Emile Bertin* together with four destroyers. The French force included the 5th Demi Brigade of Chasseurs Alpins composed of the 13th, 53rd, and 67th battalions under Brigadier Bethouart. The Chasseurs Alpins were brought in on the night of 19/20 April and deployed among the woods round the town as soon as it got light. This was lucky because that very morning the Germans undertook the destruction of the town. It has to be admitted that the French were rather better organized than the British because the force assembled for the Finnish expedition had not been disbanded. It was also a huge advantage that General Carton de Wiart spoke fluent French.

The last troops to arrive on 21 April were aboard the liner *Ville d'Anger* which had to remain offshore. Smaller vessels brought the troops ashore but not the heavy stores such as an anti-aircraft battery, and some anti-tank guns. Raids by the Luftwaffe were mounted with increasing ferocity. Throughout the hours of daylight, warships were selected as targets and the French cruiser *Emile Bertin* was hit and had to be withdrawn. None of the troopships was hit but the near misses were terrifying for those below decks. Those on the decks amused themselves by taking bets on whether the next stick of bombs would straddle the ship.

The Germans had been about a week ahead of the Allies. The German bridgehead at Trondheim was initially vulnerable, but by 11 April the airfield at Vaernes just east of the city could accommodate transports and bombers including seven dive bombers. On 13 April a battalion of infantry was brought in by air. The steamer *Levanter* had managed to slip through the Leads bringing in 100mm field guns plus ammunition and the all-important aviation fuel. A mistaken report that the British had landed at Aandalsnes on 14 April attracted one of the Führer's 'with greatest emphasis' missives. Hitler ordered that Trondheim should be reinforced by air. Group XXI accordingly shifted its attention north. The upshot was that General von Falkenhorst decided that the priority should be an advance on Steinkjer, which lay halfway between Trondheim and Namsos.

The enemy's secondary objective was to secure the railroad running to the Swedish border, which proved easy enough to achieve. The Germans believed that they would be able to get the Swedish government to agree to bringing supplies to Norway through Sweden. It is worth remarking that for the rest of the war the Swedes tried to keep in with all parties. They helped Norwegian and Allied soldiers to escape the occupying forces but at the same time they humoured the Germans by allowing war materials to pass over Swedish railroads. There does not seem to be any documentary evidence to corroborate the latter contention.

The advance along the railroad to the Swedish border began on 15 April with an improvised armoured train. By nightfall the line was in German hands despite shelling at a distance from the fort at Hegra. The defence of Hegra, an old fort designed, as were most Norwegian strongpoints, to guard a main road from Sweden their hereditary enemy, was heroic but nevertheless irrelevant to the outcome of the campaign. Major Holterman with a garrison of 300 men and one nurse, held out against German attacks for a month. The fort was equipped with four vintage 10.5cm guns, undoubtedly manufactured by Krupp, and two 75mm field guns. With these he was even able to shell Vaernes airport.

Mobilization of the Norwegian 5th Division had been frustrated by the sudden descent of the Germans on the main supply depot at Trondheim. The Germans had also captured most of the divisional artillery. The worst aspect was that young reservists had nowhere to report to. It occasionally happens that the shock of command on active service finishes off a commander. This happened to the elderly General Laurentzen commanding the Trondheim area who fell ill on 15 April, but not before meeting a British staff officer to arrange Norwegian transport to be placed at the disposal of the British. Fortunately command had devolved onto the altogether more energetic and younger Colonel Getz. The only troops at Colonel Getz's disposal were two battalions of reservists and a machine-gun squadron of dismounted dragoons. Moreover each

128

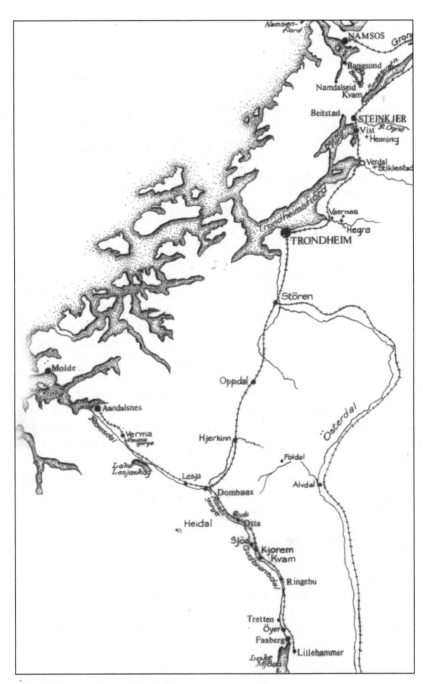

Fig. 14. Approaches to Trondheim

Norwegian infantryman had only 100 rounds of ammunition and each machine gun had only been allotted 2,500 rounds.

A glance at the map will show the line of advance of the Germans and the features that they would encounter. Leaving Trondheim and moving east along the shore of Trondheimfjord, one reaches Stjordal and the airport at Vaernes. The main road to Sweden branches off and runs due east past Hegra. The main road to the north continues north-east along the fjordside to Levanger. A few kilometres on, a minor road runs due east to Stiklestad, about the most famous place in Norwegian history. As every Norwegian child learns it was here that King Olav-Haraldsson was killed in battle fighting the pagan king, overlord of England, Denmark and Norway, none other than the illustrious King Canute who had been wise enough not to have attempted to stem the tide. The battle came to symbolize the conversion of Norway to Christianity with Olaf becoming the patron saint and the foundation of a united kingdom of Norway.

Continuing north from Levanger the main road leads to Steinkjer past a small lake to the left. A minor road passes south of the lake due west along Trondheimfjord to the narrows of Skansund giving access to Beitstadfjord on which Steinkjer is situated. A major road then runs north from Steinkjer to Namsos, then turns east and rejoins the main highway just above Grong.

The situation facing Carton de Wiart was not dissimilar to that in the Gudbrandsdal. While the Germans had nearly ten days in which to plan their advance, the Allies had only two. The French divisional commander, General Audet would not be ready to move for a couple of days so the French were allotted the left flank in support of the Norwegians. The main body of Norwegians was posted to guard the isthmus north of Steinkjer and the road to the north at Grong, the dismounted Norwegian Dragoons with their machine guns were posted to Stiklestadt.

Brigadier C.G. Phillips commanding 146 Brigade made his dispositions as follows: the KOYLI were sent south on the main Steinkjer-Trondheim road. The Lincolns were posted in the rear of the KOYLI holding the road and the railway south of Steinkjer as far as the crossroads at Vist where the coast road branches off. The Hallamshires, the territorial battalion of the York and Lancasters, were posted north of Steinkjer. This was for two reasons: first they constituted a reserve and secondly they were to guard the flank in case the Germans attacked along the north bank of the Beitstadfjord from the west.

In the KOYLI Regimental History Colonel Hibbert records that he protested strongly to brigade headquarters. There were 55 miles between forward and rear troops. The only transport consisted of thirty Norwegian trucks, communications were unreliable, often consisting of a man on a motorbike or a runner. Hibbert records 'such dispositions might be thought odd in any circumstances, but under conditions such as they were, they were frankly astonishing'. He pointed out at

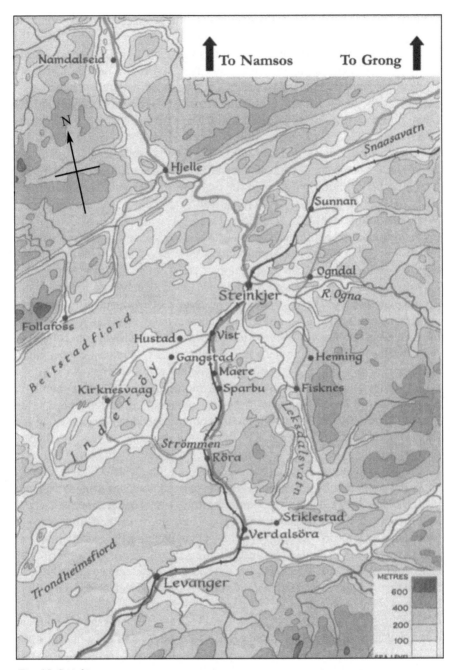

To Namsos   To Grong

Fig. 15. Steinkjer

131

the time that if the bridge over the river at Steinkjer were destroyed by bombing or the Lincolns were to lose control of the Vist isthmus, the whole KOYLI battalion would be trapped. In the event this was more or less what happened.

On 20 April, Generalmajor Kurt Woytash commanding the German 181st Division had taken command of group Trondheim and ordered an advance on Steinkjer to begin the next morning. The Germans were aware that they did not outnumber the Allies by any great margin. The plan was that the advance was to halt at Steinkjer and await reinforcements. Initially Woytash had at his disposal five and a half battalions of infantry, part of two batteries of mountain artillery and a company of engineers. Invaluable were some Austrian ski troops.

The actual fighting only lasted for two days, but for the last four days a Henschel spotter plane had been cruising at leisure around the Steinkjer area. While the troops on the ground almost developed an affection for 'George' and his clockwork appearance each morning, the significance was more sinister. It meant that the Germans had a pretty accurate idea of the Allied dispositions whereas we had but the sketchiest notion of theirs.

At this point the Germans played their master card - naval domination within Trondheimfjord. As early as 10 April a couple of German destroyers had penetrated the Beitstadfjord through the narrows, but the ice had been too thick to reach Steinkjer. A week later the ice was breaking up fast and the colonel of the Lincolns reported that a number of small vessels were in the inner fjord. Early on the morning of 21 April a small tanker and a German warship had sailed through the narrows. Later in the morning elements of a mountain battalion landed from a destroyer at the jetty of an old sawmill just beyond the narrows. These troops, about 400 in number, proceeded to advance along the shore of the Beitstadfjord towards Steinkjer. Another small group advanced in the opposite direction south-west aiming to cut the road south of Vist.

The Norwegians were already engaged at Verdalsora with a German infantry company supported by a mountain battery that had come up from Trondheim by rail. The Norwegians were supported by a small detachment of Royal Engineers (useful for blowing up bridges). A further German infantry company was landed by torpedo boat north of Verdalsora thus cutting the road to Steinkjer. After three hours of house to house fighting in a blinding snow storm, the Germans took the town. The engineers did succeed in blowing up the rail bridge but the road bridge remained intact. Fortunately the Norwegians and the British engineers were able to get away to the east to Stiklestadt.

The brunt of the fighting fell upon the Royal Lincolnshire Regiment commanded by Lieutenant Colonel R.W. Newton. It was not unusual for a territorial battalion to be commanded by territorial colonels, men who, as in this case, had won a Military Cross in the First World War knew all about fighting. On 19 April, the battalion had been brought down to Steinkjer from Namsos on lorries in the early hours of a bitterly cold morning. Both B and C Companies together with HQ Company remained in Steinkjer while D Company was sent on to Vist, several miles further south. Here the road forks down the side of the lake. A Company was held in reserve north of Steinkjer.

When news came in that the Germans had landed inside the Beitstadfjord, B Company was sent down to Vist and then along the shore of the fjord. Within two miles the troops came under fire. Although movement off the road was difficult, B Company was able to occupy a farmhouse and several other buildings on either side of the road. Enemy small-arms fire and bombardment by mortars became increasingly intense. By 18.00 the hayloft of the farm had been set on fire by incendiary bullets and it was not long before the whole range of the buildings was ablaze.

The commander of B Company was forced to order a withdrawal to the woods in the rear and, providing their own covering fire, withdrew to Vist. Unfortunately the order to withdraw did not reach two sections. They fought until their ammunition ran out when they were forced to surrender. Three men tending the wounded were also captured by Austrian mountain troops equipped with skis or snowshoes. Whatever the reputation of the Austrians in some other theatres like the Balkans, they treated their prisoners well. In the evening they buried Private Roe, who had died of his wounds, by the side of their own dead and fired three volleys over the graves.

Up until midday on 21 April Steinkjer was a pleasing town built almost entirely out of wood. As was becoming the usual procedure most of the town's 4,000 inhabitants had been evacuated before the air raids started. By the late afternoon nearly every building was ablaze. The Lincolns had to move their HQ several times and during the afternoon most of their stores were lost. Meanwhile Colonel Newton sent part of HQ Company forward to Vist and ordered C Company forward to fill the gap between B Company and HQ Company. However they never reached their objective as they had to keep jumping out of the lorries and take cover while German aircraft strafed them. By 21.00 they were in contact with HQ Company but by the next day the enemy were in the woods opposite them.

On the afternoon of 22 April D and B Company were subjected to heavy machine gun, mortar and light artillery fire. It was decided therefore to order a general withdrawal. B and D Company disengaged successfully from Vist and withdrew to Steinkjer but it was not easy. The troops kept having to scatter and lie in the deep snow on either side of the road as enemy aircraft bombed and machine gunned them. Incidentally no one was killed by attack from the air. At Steinkjer the road bridge over the River Ogna had been destroyed but the damaged rail bridge served as a footbridge. A, B, and D Companies got clean away and after marching some miles north were picked up by Norwegian lorries and transported back by stages to Namsos. It should be emphasised that the Allies benefited by German caution, as at Dunkirk, for the Germans decided to call a temporary halt at Steinkjer.

The going for HQ and C Companies of the Lincolns, was much rougher. Part of the way, the runner with the order to withdraw had to crawl through deep snow. HQ Company had been under heavy machine gun fire for several hours. By 17.00 C Company was able to withdraw from its position under fire and joined up with HQ Company. The Germans assumed that all British troops were heading north to Steinkjer, whereas in fact the only hope for HQ and C Companies was to make their way east to Henning and bypass Steinkjer on a side road.

With all essential equipment jettisoned, a column of about 200 men got on the move marching in file with linked hands. A Norwegian had told them that both Vist and Steinkjer were in German hands. By 21.30 they had reached the woods on the far side of the open valley without detection. With the aid of a compass and a local map, the troops stumbled up the mountain side for four and a half hours with the flames of Steinkjer as a reference point. At 03.00, having covered one and a half miles, exhausted by crawling over the frozen snow, they reached a barn and were able to have a short sleep. By next morning they were on the move by 07.00 and at midday reached another barn, the very same that had been occupied by the KOYLI the night before. Luckily the KOYLI had abandoned some provisions. After a rest and a meal they were again on the move.

Major Stokes, ably supported by Captain Craggs of C Company, decided to march up the northern shore of Lake Snaasa to Grong where there was direct access to Namsos. There were some anxious moments. At one point they were challenged by Norwegian sentries who took some convincing that they were not Germans. Eventually the Norwegians confirmed that other British units had gone up the main road direct from Steinkjer to Namsos. The night was again spent in barns and the quartermaster was able to produce a hot meal. Their luck then really looked up when one of the Norwegians they met turned out to have been a missionary and spoke excellent English. He confirmed that the main road from Steinkjer was reasonably clear and offered to guide them by side roads to it. This meant doubling back to the main road and eventually a telephone was located and lorries came to pick them up. They had marched 45 miles in 49 hours and all ranks still bore their arms and ammunition.

The experience of the 1/4th KOYLI was more a record of endurance than of actual fighting and in this they were singularly fortunate in having had Lieutenant Colonel H. Hibbert as their commanding officer. As late as January 1940 the battalion had been without a commanding officer for several months and morale was low. On Hibbert's appointment they were told to be ready for active service within eight weeks. The colonel immediately imposed a regime of tough physical training and discipline. No less than 30 per cent of the men were physically downgraded and replacements found. The battalion had disembarked at Namsos at 03.00 on 18 April and got on a train for Steinkjer. Once they had detrained and dispersed 'passive air defence' was the order of the day. Concealed, where possible in the farms and villages, the men were ordered not to fire at enemy aircraft in order to prevent giving their presence away.

Largely at Brigadier Phillips's insistence, Hibbert had ordered C Company to Sparbu where the battalion headquarters would be situated. A Company was sent south to man the Trondheim fjordside at the village of Strommen with a watching patrol on the Narrows at Skaansund. D Company was astride the road at Rora and B Company was posted to Stiklestad to link up with the Norwegians. Once the German landings inside the Beitstadfjord were known, Hibbert ordered C Company to leave Sparbu and move forward to support A Company. They set off in two old buses but one platoon had to march. There was not therefore much capability for carrying reserves of ammunition. They were not able to move much off the roads whereas the Germans were partly equipped with skis and snowshoes and the Germans were more resourceful in commandeering the light sledges to be found on most Norwegian farms.

Further south the Norwegians had destroyed the railway bridge at Verdalsora, but the road bridge was still intact. The Norwegians were holding the road bridge with six machine guns, but just as the party of Royal Engineers went forward to deal with the road bridge, the Norwegians were forced to give it up. Both the Norwegians and the British then fell back on Stiklestad. Having anticipated that the Lincolns would lose the fjordside, Colonel Hibbert ordered A Company to move at dusk to Maere. He also ordered D Company to pull back from Rora to Sparbu. He then sent word to B and C Companies to withdraw to the east side of the small lake to the village of Fisknes. He would then have the whole battalion in hand over a much smaller area. However, such are the vicissitudes of war that on the morning of 22 April he received orders that the whole brigade was to pull back 50 miles to Nandalseid well to the north of Steinkjer.

Colonel Hibbert's fears were duly confirmed when a message was received that under a barrage from German destroyers the Lincolns had been forced to retreat. The KOYLI were thus well and truly cut off from the north. Hibbert's options were threefold: to stand and fight until killed or captured, to make for the Swedish border or to try and march across country and round the top of Lake Snaasvatn. After conferring with his officers it was decided to opt for the latter course.

At Stiklestad B Company was able to disengage from the enemy quite easily on 21 April and set off up the east side of Leksdal lake. The next day it was able to rejoin the rest of the battalion at Fiskness. Major Dugmore's C Company were in a much more difficult position. They had already marched across the enemy's front and were clearly observed from a hill at the crossroads. In order to slip away therefore, they had to wait until dark. Already tired, nevertheless as soon as it got dark the men set off. Snow was falling and temperatures fell below freezing. By 04.00 the following morning they had reached a large farm and it was decided to halt. Several men had already collapsed and had to be carried into the barn. The men climbed into a hayloft and almost immediately fell asleep in the hay. The company did not take the road again until 10.00 and, footsore but relieved, they were able to join up with 'B' Company at Fiskness in the early afternoon.

The position of the rest of the battalion was dire. A Company was being attacked from the north at Maere and D Company was being attacked from the south of Sparbu. Hibbert had already moved HQ Company into the woods east of the village. At 10.00 he ordered D Company to pull back to Sparbu and get away to the east. They had already ambushed a German cycle patrol armed with Tommy guns and six men had been seen to fall. This had been the signal for the Germans to step up the pressure on the road with heavy mortar fire. Ski troops drawing sledges with machine guns strapped to them were to be seen fanning out on either flank.

The CO jumped into a car and drove to the crossroads at Maere and told Captain Carey commanding A Company to get back to Sparbu as soon as they could. Two platoons of A Company were brought back to Sparbu then started away to the east on foot. By this time the Germans were in the outskirts of the village. One platoon of A Company was not so fortunate. The Germans surrounded their position and a number of men were killed before the rest were captured. This may have saved the rest of the battalion because the Germans thought that they were trying to escape to the north and therefore continued their advance in that direction.

The first leg of the journey involved marching east to Fiskness, a distance of about eight miles. The road was wide enough for one lorry. The ditches on either side were filled with snow and the surface of the road consisted of several inches of slush on top of potholes and ice. One by one such lorries as there were either broke their axles or slithered into the ditch and were abandoned with much of the heavy kit. Although George flew over several times, the Germans did not seem to be aware of the intention of the KOYLI.

At Fiskness the battalion caught up with B Company and a runner reported that C Company would follow on. The battalion then marched north to Henning. The next obstacle would be getting across the turbulent River Ogna which flows into the fjord at Steinkjer and it would be swollen by the spring thaw. At this point those who believed in Divine Providence had their beliefs amply confirmed. Colonel Hibbert had actually been taken salmon fishing by his father on the river Ogna thirty years previously. His father had been serving on one of His Majesty's ships paying a courtesy visit to Trondheim. The colonel remembered that there was an old wooden bridge some six miles up the river from Steinkjer. A further stroke of luck had been when the KOYLI had fallen in with a Norwegian called Mathieson who had tried to report for duty at Trondheim and had barely escaped by heading north on skis. Although only holding the rank of private soldier in the Norwegian Reserve, in civilian life he was the son of a well-known Oslo ship owner and spoke perfect English. He never left Colonel Hibbert's side. He was able to confirm that the bridge did indeed still exist although nobody knew whether the Germans held it or whether the Norwegians had blown it up.

Colonel Hibbert was in doubt as to whether he could reasonably expect his men to move that night. Regimental Quartermaster Sergeant Wallace, holder of a First World War Distinguished Conduct Medal however assured him that there was nothing a Yorkshireman could not do if he had to. All kit therefore, with the exception of rifles, Bren guns and some ammunition, was destroyed. C Company joined them at 21.00 and the battalion formed up for the march through the hills. The wounded were warmly wrapped up in blankets and strapped on sledges drawn by horses requisitioned from the farms. For the men at the head of the column treading down the snow made for heavy going and the men that followed had to follow a rough and slippery path in single file. Progress averaged about one and a half miles per hour and the file grew longer and longer. The wind blew more and more icily yet nobody fell out. Suddenly as they wound down the steep side of a valley the bridge appeared.

The dark woods on either side constituted a perfect place for an ambush so a fighting patrol was sent out. It crossed the bridge and ten minutes later, which seemed like eternity, two runners appeared. There were no enemy in sight. At the next village there was a short hold-up while Mathieson tried to convince some Norwegian soldiers that the column was British and not German. At last the men were able to crowd into barns and farm buildings and were asleep in the hay within minutes. Four hours later they were on the march again. The third stroke of good fortune, call it what you will, was the German decision not to proceed beyond their capability. This meant that until adequate reinforcements arrived they would not advance beyond Steinkjer. Thus the next bridge at Suynnan was found to be intact with 18 miles to go to Namenslied. The telephone system was still found to be working and Brigade Headquarters was contacted. Lorries arrived and by stages the battalion was lifted back to Namsos.

Chapter 20

Evacuation of the Central Valley

It was General Paget's view that with proper air support and adequate artillery he could have held on to Central Norway. General Carton de Wiart had already expressed his scepticism. It was really the lack of adequate aircraft which was the deciding factor. The vulnerability of lines of supply dependent on ships was obvious. The Chiefs of Staff ordered plans to be drawn up by General Massy and his staff, who was still in the UK, in collaboration with the inter-services planning organization for the evacuation of Central Norway. These were considered by the Chiefs of Staff on 27 April and General Ironside signed the order.

The next morning General Paget accompanied by his principal staff officer Lieutenant Colonel D. Clarke travelled to the Norwegian headquarters, a farm some 12 miles south of Dombaas. They brought a personal message from General Ironside but this in no way altered the distasteful nature of their mission. Colonel Clarke described the scene as General Paget broke the news: 'There was silence and quietly General Ruge said, "So Norway must go the way of Czechoslovakia and Poland". Then he looked up and said, "But why? Why withdraw when your troops are still unbeaten."'

He repeated that he had staked all his hopes on British aid. Then he walked out into the field. It should be borne in mind that the Norwegians could have refused to co-operate or provide transport which would have made it very much more difficult for the British. When Ruge came back into the room he had regained his composure for he said: 'These things are not for us to decide general... we are soldiers... tell me what help I can give you to carry out your orders.'

The British planned to evacuate the troops in the Central Valley through the port of Aandalsnes on the night of 30 April and 1 May and the troops in the north through Namsos on the nights of 1 and 2 May. First the royal party had to be evacuated. On the night of 29 April the cruiser HMS *Glasgow* together with two destroyers under Captain Pegram put into Molde. The quay was ablaze as was most of the little town. King Haakon and his entourage had to be ferried aboard by a local tug. In the royal party were the Crown Prince, the Norwegian ministers, the British, French and Danish envoys besides the staffs of the legations. In addition there was Norway's stock of gold: 23 tons of bullion. At the king's insistence, the royal party and the government were conveyed to Tromso in the far north. The following night the *Tatar*, a destroyer, put into Molde to pick up Captain Denny and his base staff together with General Ruge and his staff. Ruge thought he was bound for North Norway but when he learned otherwise, with his foot on the gangplank, he adamantly refused to board.

The question arose as to what extent the Royal Air Force and the Fleet Air Arm could cover the evacuation. Fighter cover over Aandalsnes and Molde was out of range except for short patrols by the two-engine Blenheim light bomber. The RAF was able to mount a series of light bombing attacks on the main German bases at Fornebu [Oslo], Aalborg [north Denmark] and Stavanger, and these were stepped up the day before the evacuation was due to begin. On 24 April the aircraft carriers *Ark Royal* and *Glorious* under Vice Admiral Wells were off the Norwegian coast and Vaernes airport was attacked by thirty-four aircraft. Further attacks on Vaernes were made on 28 and 30 April and 1 May. The basic problem was that at that stage of the war only torpedo or Skua dive bombers were carried on aircraft carriers, whereas what was desperately needed was fighter cover. Was it all worth it? It is estimated that twenty enemy aircraft were destroyed, but the Fleet Air Arm lost fifteen aircraft. Moreover the aircraft carriers themselves were vulnerable, requiring an escort of no less than two cruisers and six destroyers.

While the Green Howards had been holding the Germans at Otta, General Paget was considering the problem of disengagement. At 18.00 on 28 April he ordered the KOYLI to move eight miles south from Dombaas to form a rearguard. The Germans stuck to their routine of closing down the fighting in the evening which gave the British the opportunity to run a train down the line and pick up the Green Howards. The Royal Engineers then blew up the road bridge in the narrow Rosti Gorge which, it was estimated, would give the British twenty-four hours respite.

General Paget had given General Ruge an undertaking that he would not abandon the Norwegians: some 4,000 troops in all. The Germans in Trondheim were by this time linked up to the troops advancing up the eastern valley from Oslo. This would put them in a position to advance south from Trondheim to Dombaas and the Norwegians were posted to defend this route. Bearing in mind that withdrawal for all intents and purposes could only be made at night, the Norwegians were able to pass through the British positions on the night of the 29 April.

The majority of British troops were disposed about the woods round Dombaas and the story becomes one of the withdrawal of individual units down to Aandalsnes. Let us therefore retrace the fortunes of the hapless 148 Brigade. In the action at Tretten Bridge the 1st/8th Sherwood Foresters had lost four officers and twenty-one men as well as a number of wounded. When darkness fell the survivors tried to get away over the hills as the Germans controlled the main road. Several officers and seventy-five men of mixed units under Captain Beckwith, moving at night above the tree line, got fifty miles north before being captured. The Foresters were split up into four parties and made their way either on foot or in lorries to Aandalsnes. The survivors got aboard the *Arethusa*, the *Galatea* and the cruiser *Belfast*, reaching Scotland on 5 May. Captain Hallam was awarded the Military Cross for his leadership.

After the rearguard by 148 Brigade put up by the Leicesters a mile north of Tretten, the remnants were picked up by Norwegian buses. Only six officers and about 150 men eventually reached Aandalsnes. Jo Kynoch's account tells us what the Regimental history does not about the march down to Aandalsnes. The railway line was temporarily out of action.

'At about 8pm on 29 April, the Leicesters assembled at Dombaas station and prepared to face the 60-odd mile march along the railway track. The ballast between the sleepers became gravelly... my long stride meant four steps on the sleepers and the fifth on the gravel... around midnight some of my colleagues began to crack up... It had been almost a week since we had any food... It started at first with a lone voice somewhere at the rear of the column, then several voices could be heard shouting and screaming at the major "the bloody man's a maniac, I'm not going any further". I looked behind and saw some of them tearing their overcoats and helmets off and throwing them down on the side of the track... At 2am there was another uproar... Major Gorman made his way to the back. "I see some of you are without your greatcoats and steel helmets and even your best friend, your rifle." "What bloody good are rifles to a beaten army," a voice wanted to know." "We are not a beaten army" the major snorted. Shortly after the major relented and the men collapsed into a hay barn for the rest of the night.'

On arrival at Otta the York and Lancasters had been ordered to prolong the right of the line held by the Green Howards. Throughout 28 April they were bombed and machine gunned from the air, but they were well dug in and casualties were relatively light. When night fell the battalion was withdrawn and entrained for Dombaas. Here they spent the day in the woods and as soon as it got dark they were put on a train for Aandalsnes. By this time a regular occurrence would be that the railway line would be damaged by bombs during the day but repaired by the Norwegians at night. Having reached the small lake at Lesjaskong at the top of the pass between the Gudbrandsdal and the Romsdal, luck for the York and Lancasters finally ran out, and they had to detrain and continue their journey on foot.

It fell to the 1st Battalion KOYLI to fight the final rearguard. The 27 April had been spent sleeping and reorganizing in the woods outside Dombaas. Although the night was intensely cold they were fortunate in having plenty of 'compo' rations i.e. tinned meat and vegetables together with cheese, biscuits and plenty of tea. General Paget had undertaken to evacuate the Norwegians first so that they could be shipped to North Norway. On the other hand the KOYLI were ordered to move forward three miles and hold the enemy up for forty-eight hours. In the event they were ordered to pull back that very evening.

This posed a problem because A Company and a platoon of B Company had been deployed on the far bank of the river. They could not cross the river because the ice was breaking up and the water level was rising. This meant that the only way for them to withdraw was to advance towards the enemy and cross by a bridge further down the river. This they managed in the nick of time thanks to the Germans being unaware that British troops were in the vicinity. The experience of D Company was rather different. Many regular soldiers before the war had served on the North West frontier of India and the one thing they understood was the art of ambush. On came the Germans marching up the road in column. D Company waited until they were within 150 yards before opening fire and practically the whole of the leading platoon was shot down. For over an hour the Germans tried to break through and suffered a number of casualties including the crew of an 81mm mortar.

Major Cass, then commanding the KOYLI, had anticipated that the Germans would try to outflank the position and he had therefore deployed both A Company and HQ Company in depth. Both companies became heavily engaged and it was most encouraging that they should have had the support of four Norwegian field guns despite their vintage. C Company of the Green Howards had been placed in the rear in case the Germans tried to cross the river higher up. This was indeed attempted in portable rubber boats, but C Company had no difficulty in sinking the boats and a number of the enemy were drowned.

The Green Howards were sent off to Aandalsnes by lorry. Meanwhile the railway line had been pronounced serviceable and by backing a train out of a tunnel the remaining troops were boarded as soon as it was dark. By this time small groups of Germans were installed on the surrounding hills but all that they could see were the sparks from the engine as it drew down the line. Despite sporadic fire there were no casualties. At Lesja, the scene of the brief RAF debacle a few weeks earlier, the train stopped to pick up 400 Norwegians and some of 15 Brigade's anti-tank personnel. The heavily laden train crawled on for a further 15 miles with the men, huddled in open trucks or windowless carriages, trying to keep warm. Suddenly there was a tremendous jolt and the train came to a halt. There were two engines; both were derailed and one had turned over. The first coach was also derailed and had telescoped killing eight men and injuring thirty. Apparently the repairs to the line over a bomb crater had not proved strong enough to take the weight of the train.

Amidst the chaos of the crash, the cries of the injured and the hiss of escaping steam, the troops were somehow formed up. About 18 miles further on at Verma was a railway tunnel and it was decided to march the men there and take refuge in the tunnel. Some lorries were eventually organized to pick up the injured. The rest of the men, marching, stumbling over the potholes and craters in the roads, finally reached the tunnel about 09.00. The tunnel is 800m long; the walls were coated in slimy soot and the light did not penetrate far from either end. The men somehow found room to sit and doze and to sleep fitfully despite the fact that on several occasions the Germans tried to bomb the entrance to the tunnel. Although they were aware that they were sharing the tunnel with an ammunition train, the men's spirits began to recover.

Meanwhile the general and his staff had not been inactive. There was a further train in the tunnel and in the evening the driver started to get up steam. This meant that the men had to evacuate the tunnel. A complicated manoeuvre was necessary whereby the train had to be run a half mile back up the track to Verma station before coming down the line on a lower track. At this point the Norwegian engine driver said that he could not get up enough steam to get the train up the hill. This posed a bit of a problem for the British but they found that by posting two burly Yorkshire men on the footplate with fixed bayonets the engine driver could be induced to change his mind. The train ran back for half a mile and when it returned the men scrambled aboard and the train moved off for Aandalsnes.

Throughout the day the enemy had been drawing nearer and nearer. A party of Royal Marines had been sent up the line to the scene of the crash. After several brushes with the enemy they were forced to retire to the head of the Verma gorge. At 18.00 news was received that the enemy were through the Royal Marines position. Immediately a company of KOYLI and a platoon of Green Howards were sent up the gorge to act as a rearguard and the Germans were halted. The embarkation of troops from Aandalsnes was planned for two nights. Admiral Edward-Collins arrived on the evening of 30 April with four cruisers and six destroyers, followed by Admiral Layton on 1 May with two cruisers and five destroyers.

Admiral Edward-Collins entered Romsdalfjord at 2145 just as it was getting dark. Destroyers started to ferry men to the cruiser *Sheffield* anchored in the harbour. The men of 148 Brigade continued their march to Aandalsnes and had been dispersed around the woods. As they came aboard they were deadbeat and ravenously hungry, otherwise discipline was generally good. The *Galatea* and *Arethusa* then went alongside the stone quay and took off the rest, some 1,800 men in all.

The next day, 1 May, the two anti-aircraft ships in the harbour were forced to put to sea while awaiting the night operation. By this time the Germans were well aware of what was going on and Admiral Layton's force suffered several air attacks as they steamed in. One destroyer called in at Aalesund to evacuate British personnel and the destroyer *Diana* put in to Molde to collect General Ruge and his staff who had agreed to go north to join the king. By midnight two destroyers had ferried 1,300 men to the cruisers *Manchester* and *Birmingham*. The admiral thought that most of the men had been embarked so he withdrew seawards taking General Paget and his staff with him.

Two anti-aircraft vessels, the *Calcutta* and the *Auckland* were left behind to bring off stragglers and the rearguards. The crew of the *Calcutta* were considerably surprised when 750 men trooped aboard which just about put her down to the Plimsoll line if not above it. The *Auckland* then nosed into the stone quay and the rearguard of 23 officers and 218 men boarded in just seven minutes flat. Not one soldier was left behind and by 02.00 on 2 May the campaign in the Central Valley was over.

ı

Chapter 21

'Impossible' the Navy do not know the meaning of the word

The successful evacuation of Central Norway had depended entirely upon the Royal Navy. A brief resumé of the conditions under which the Navy had been operating might therefore be appropriate. Rear Admiral Vivian's 20th Cruiser Squadron had been given the task of defending the anchorages at Aandalsnes and Namsos. Part of his squadron was made up of C Class anti-aircraft cruisers. Their 6-inch guns had been removed and replaced by eight 4-inch high angle anti-aircraft guns. In support was a flotilla of sloops under Captain Poland. Smaller than a destroyer, the sloop had been developed during the First World War as an anti-submarine vessel. The latest version, the *Black Swan* class was equipped with six 4-inch high angle guns. A weak point in the Navy's anti-aircraft armament proved to be the 2-pdr pom pom guns which were slow and unwieldy. What was really needed were rapid firing smaller calibre weapons. Only later in the war were the Swiss design 20mm Oerlikon and, best of all, the Swedish design 40mm Bofors gun firing explosive shells generally adopted.

For three days off Aandalsnes the sloop *Black Swan* had suffered almost continuous air attack during the hours of daylight. She had to keep on the move almost constantly and had used up most of her ammunition. In one day alone she fired off no less than 2,000 rounds of 4-inch and 4,000 rounds of pom-pom ammunition and it was gratifying that five enemy aircraft were seen to crash. But the recoil mechanism on the pom-pom guns was beginning to jam, so on 21 April she was relieved by the *Curacao*. No provision had been made to enable navy ships to replenish their anti-aircraft ammunition and they had to return to Britain. The *Black Swan*'s respite was brief for on 26 April she was back on station.

The next day at about 16.00 a flight of Stuka dive bombers appeared and circled round the *Black Swan*. One of the Stukas attacked on the starboard bow, that is to say ahead, and from the right and a bomb struck on the quarterdeck towards the stern. Luckily the bomb was primed with a delayed action fuse and it passed through the wardroom, then through a magazine full of ammunition and out through the hull between the propellers, before exploding. The only casualty was one man with a broken ankle. There was however considerable damage to the hull below the water line. One of the features of any warship is that there are watertight doors above the water line between the transverse partitions or bulkheads which divide up the vessel which enable the pumps to control flooding. As she limped back to England it was found that if she kept up a certain speed water would be sucked out of the flooded compartment faster than it seeped in.

The experience of the sloop *Bittern* off Namsos was not quite so fortunate. On 30 April Stukas in formation varying from three to nine aircraft kept up an almost continuous attack. By late afternoon two Stukas had been shot down and the *Bittern* remained unscathed. Late in the afternoon three Stukas attacked on the port bow, that is from the left. The third then crossed over, wheeled round and attacked from astern. The *Bittern*'s forward guns put up a barrage against the two dive bombers ahead, but the third managed to land a bomb on the quarter deck. This exploded on impact and ignited a box of high explosive demolition charges on the deck. A huge explosion followed.

The captain, Lieutenant Commander R. Mills could see that the stern of the ship had been practically blown off. Again it was the watertight bulkheads which saved the vessel temporarily, but she was on fire and all the fire pumps were out of action. Lieutenant Johnson and Petty Officer Hopgood gallantly plunged into the inferno to release three men trapped in the aft magazine which was full of ammunition, before deliberately flooding it. There was nothing for it but to give the order 'abandon ship'. Fortunately the destroyer *Janus* was able to nose along the *Bittern*'s bows and all the crew were taken off. The *Janus* was then ordered to sink the *Bittern* with a torpedo.

The most vulnerable ships of all were the anti-submarine patrol trawlers manned by men of the Royal Naval Patrol Service, usually former fishermen. The officers were for the most part drawn from the Merchant Navy or trawler skippers with a retired Royal Navy Commander in charge of four boats. Armament consisted of a single 20mm Oerlikon gun and several Lewis heavy machine guns. The latter fired the same .303 solid bullet as the standard infantry rifle, a most effective weapon in trench warfare but by naval standards a mere pea shooter. The armed trawlers were soft targets for the Stuka and out of twenty-nine vessels sent to Norway, in the brief campaign, no less than eleven were sunk or driven ashore.

The main function of the trawlers was to guard the entrance to the fjords from U-boats. However they also proved invaluable 'maids of all work' ferrying troops and stores from the larger vessels to the shore. It would have been pointless to expect unarmed Norwegian vessels to risk themselves in the daylight hours. The one Norwegian vessel which took part, the torpedo boat *Trygg*, was sunk. Working largely at night, one of the greatest problems for the crews was lack of sleep.

The story of the armed trawler *Arab*, commanded by Lieutenant Commander Stannard, illustrates what conditions were like. The *Arab* arrived off Namsos at 02.00 on 28 April and was immediately put on to ferrying stores. The next morning was spent fighting a fire on the pier. Then the *Saumur*, a French transport, fouled her propeller and the *Arab* was ordered to hold her out in the fjord. That night, the second without sleep for the crew, was spent ferrying 850 French troops aboard one of the transports. The only partial shelter during the day was afforded by anchoring under the cliffs. The following day the *Bittern* arrived and the *Arab* was ordered to take up a position 400 yards to the west. Thus when the following morning the Stukas dived on the *Bittern* out of the morning sun, they would flatten out at the bottom of their dive over the *Arab*. This enabled Stannard's men to pump the Stukas with Oerlikon shells while they were within a reasonable range and several were brought down.

By this time the crew of the *Arab* were desperately short of sleep. As luck would have it, Stannard found a cave halfway up the cliff in which his crew were able to get some rest in relays. He also set up a gunsight at the top of the cliff for his Lewis machine guns. Two other trawlers, the *Gaul* and the *Aston Villa* took refuge under the cliff, but this did not prevent all three from being damaged by near misses and the occasional hit. The other two trawlers eventually sank and the *Arab* took their crews aboard. The *Arab* was ordered home and with her speed down to three knots [less than 4mph], she set sail for Scotland. This was not however, quite the end of the story. Out in the Norwegian Sea a Heinkel found her and signalled 'steer east or be sunk'. A sailor would not normally have tempted fate with such a forecast. Stannard held his course and his men held their fire. When the bomber was within 800 yards, the *Arab* opened up with everything that she had got and blew the Heinkel out of the sky. In his report Stannard demonstrated the sort of man he was. He was against installing steel shields on his guns because he said the gun crews will shelter behind them instead of concentrating on firing their guns at the enemy. He was awarded the Victoria Cross.

General Carton de Wiart was informed of the withdrawal from Central Norway on the evening of 27 April. The original plan was that the evacuation through Namsos should not take place until the nights of 1 and 2 May. Vice Admiral J. Cunningham commanding 1st Cruiser Squadron, together with the French cruiser *Montcalm* and three large French transports, had sailed from Scapa Flow on 29 April. Quite unexpectedly, on arrival off the Norwegian coast they sailed into thick fog.

The next day, Captain Lord Louis Mountbatten, already earning a reputation for being courageous but foolhardy, proposed that he should take three destroyers into the fjord. On that occasion Lord Mountbatten's own destroyer the *Kelly* was not hit but another destroyer found that its masts were sticking out above the low bank of fog. Thus the Germans could see the target but the British could not see the enemy. A very near miss, which caused some casualties in the *Maori* convinced Lord Mountbatten that discretion would be the better part of valour and he withdrew seawards.

The three French transports, the cruiser *York* and five destroyers entered the fjord on 1 May. Two of the French transports were able to get alongside the stone quay, while the destroyers and trawlers ferried the troops to the bigger ships in the fjord. Carton de Wiart had agreed that the French, who through no fault on their part had hardly fired a shot, should be evacuated first. The 13 Chasseurs Alpins were halfway between Namsos and Steinkjer. They were therefore withdrawn through the British lines, an operation rendered straightforward by the decision of the Germans not to advance beyond Steinkjer.

The next to be withdrawn to Namsos were the KOYLI, while the Hallamshires were left to hold the bridge at Bangsund just south of Namsos. The road east of Namsos to the railway junction at Grong was being held by the 67th Chasseurs Alpins who were likewise withdrawn. The Lincolns, after their epic march of 45 miles had arrived at Namenslied on the evening of Thursday 25 April. There they rested for three days awaiting their turn to be evacuated. The nights were bitterly cold and although they were under cover they had no blankets, but rations were plentiful. During the daytime enemy air patrols were frequent but by this time the British had learnt to keep their heads down in order not to give away their positions. On the evening of 28 April the Lincolns marched by company en route for Namsos to which they were called forward on 2 May. It was with a heavy heart that they had to abandon their arms which they were told would be taken over by the Norwegians.

HMS *Alfridi* managed to come alongside the stone jetty and the battalion marched straight on board. The Lincolns were then transferred to the French auxiliary cruiser *El Kantara*, while lorries went out to collect the 750 men of the York and Lancaster Regiment (The Hallamshires) at Bangsund. The last bridge had been blown at midnight. The *Alfridi* returned to collect the rearguard and the last man got aboard at 03.15. To the *Alfridi*'s guns fell the last melancholy task of destroying the massed transport on the quay. In all some 5,400 men had been evacuated. General Carton de Wiart recorded in his diary that he had thought it impossible to evacuate so many men in one night, but he added, 'the Navy do not know the meaning of the word impossible'.

By this time the Germans were well aware that evacuation was taking place, and the two aircraft carriers which might have provided some air cover, had been withdrawn. As dawn broke the next day the sun began to burn off the fog and between 08.45 and 15.30 the convoy was attacked no less than five times. The Germans adopted steep dive tactics and the French destroyer *Bison* was set on fire. Luckily all personnel were taken off by another vessel without further mishap and the *Bison* was then sunk by Allied gunfire. About 14.00 the *Alfridi* also was hit by two bombs and eventually capsized. This time the lives of about 100 men were lost.

A matter that must finally be aired is the question of the delay by the British in informing the Norwegians of their intentions. The Norwegians were not told until after the meeting with Ruge on 28 April. This caused some feelings of shame among the British commanders and some feelings of resentment on the part of the Norwegians. All that can be said in mitigation is that if you are about to conduct a delicate operation from a vulnerable position, the fewer people who know about it in advance the better. The same was to apply to Dunkirk a month later.

The end in central Norway followed swiftly. General Hvinden Haug signed a capitulation on 3 May. The brave 4th Brigade retreating through the high Valdres valley south of Dombaas surrendered. Colonel Getz, in command north of Trondheim capitulated on 4 May, and the next day the gallant little band holding out in the isolated fort of Hegra raised the white flag.

Chapter 22

The Norway Debate

The collapse of the Allied front in Central Norway and the inevitable British evacuation, precipitated what came to be known as 'The Norway Debate' in the House of Commons. The upshot was the fall of Chamberlain. Everybody seemed to know that it would happen but it was a question of when? Norway was the catalyst. As early as September 1939 John Colville, an extremely able junior civil servant attached to the Prime Minister's Office, wrote in his diary: 'We agreed that it would probably be a good thing if Chamberlain resigned soon and left the conduct of the war to some younger and forceful successor. Unfortunately I can see no Lloyd George on the horizon at present. Winston is a national figure but is rather too old and the younger politicians do not seem to include an outstanding personality. Halifax would be respected, but he has not the drive necessary to keep the country united and enthusiastic.'

Over the last year or two Churchill had made some dazzling speeches, but at other times his speeches fell flat and people would shake their heads and say 'the old boy is past it'. Chamberlain had invited Churchill to resume his old job as First Lord of the Admiralty to some extent because it was much safer to have him on board as a member of the Cabinet than have him a loose cannon on the back benches. During the first six months of the war Churchill had made himself the Parliamentarian best known to the general public by a series of popular broadcasts on Sunday evenings. But in May 1940 it was by no means certain that he would become Prime Minister.

On the afternoon of Tuesday 7 May, Chamberlain had opened the debate on the Norwegian campaign with a tired and defensive speech. Clement Attlee as leader of the small Labour party, and therefore leader of the opposition, although not a great orator followed with a much sharper speech concluding, 'It is not Norway alone, Norway comes as the culmination of many other discontents. People are saying that those mainly responsible for the conduct of affairs, meaning Chamberlain and his two staunchest allies Sir John Simon and Samuel Hoare, are men who have had an almost uninterrupted career of failure. Norway followed Czechoslovakia and Poland. Everywhere the story is too late.'

Churchill's former second in command during his brief sojourn in the trenches, Sir Archibald Sinclair, now leader of what was left of the old Liberal Party, spoke in a similar vein. One of the most colourful participants was Sir Roger Keyes, the hero of Zeebrugge, who entered the Chamber resplendent in his uniform as an Admiral of the Fleet. Not noted for his eloquence he nevertheless said: 'I have great admiration and appreciation for my right honourable friend the First Lord of the Admiralty. I am longing to see proper use made of his great abilities.' The point was not lost on the House.

When Leo Amery rose there were not many members in the Chamber as most were at dinner. Clement Davies, a Liberal member, and well known as an anti-Chamberlain conspirator passed behind Amery and whispered, 'Keep going and I will rustle up an audience for you'. Chamberlain thought that he could rely on Amery as a colleague and fellow Birmingham MP of many years standing. Indeed at one time Amery had been a dedicated supporter of the great Jo Chamberlain's campaign for Imperial Preference. Amery recorded in his diary that he had looked up a quotation from Oliver Cromwell's speech when he had closed down the Long Parliament. 'I only kept it by in case the spirit should move me to use it....It was not until after eight that I got up in a House of barely a dozen members. However they streamed in pretty rapidly....and I found myself going on at an increasing crescendo of applause... I cast prudence to the winds and ended full out with my Cromwellian injunction to the Long Parliament: "You have sat too long here for any good you have been doing. Depart I say, and let us be done with you. In God's name go."'

The debate continued on the Wednesday afternoon. Herbert Morrison, the tough leader of the London County Council opened for the opposition. He let it be known that Labour would call for a division, thus making the debate into a vote of censure. This provoked the Prime Minister into making a fundamental mistake. He appealed to partisan support at a time when everybody was calling for a coalition government that would pull the parties together. In a short intervention that lasted one minute Chamberlain said: 'I do not seek to evade criticism, but I say this to my friends in the House, and I have friends in the House, I accept the challenge... At least we shall see who is with us and who is against us, and I call on my friends to support me in the lobby tonight.'

Lloyd George then made the best speech that he had made for many years and the last major contribution that he was to ever make. 'It is not a question of who are the Prime Minister's friends... It is a far bigger issue... He [the PM] has appealed for sacrifice. The nation is prepared for every sacrifice so long as it has leadership... I say solemnly that the Prime Minister should give an example of sacrifice because there is nothing which can contribute more to victory in this war than that he should sacrifice the seals of office.'

A privy councillor can intervene at any point and Churchill rose to say: 'I take complete responsibility for everything that has been done by the Admiralty and I take my full share of the burden.' Lloyd George then retorted 'the right honourable gentleman must not allow himself to be converted into an air-raid shelter to keep the splinters from hitting his colleagues.'

It fell to Winston Churchill to wind up the debate for the government. Harold Nicolson, a Tory and former appeaser recorded in his diary, 'Winston has an almost impossible task. On the one hand he has to defend the Services, on the other he has to be loyal to the Prime Minister... He managed with the extraordinary force of his personality to do both...while demonstrating that he really has nothing to do with this confused and timid gang.'

Churchill, of course, had to vote with the government but some surprising people voted against such as Nancy Astor, and Quintin Hogg, later known as Lord Hailsham, both previously strong appeasers. A number of younger MPs were in uniform. While serving in this country they had the right to attend the Commons if required by the Whips. An example was John Profumo, then the baby of the House. When he asked for permission the Guard's adjutant said, 'All you want to go up to London for is to visit a brothel'. In the event Profumo managed to vote against the government and take his pleasure.

In total only forty-one Conservative MPs voted against the government but 60 members, mainly Conservative, abstained. The Conservative majority fell from 213 to 81, which in normal times would have been an ample mandate for the Conservative government to have continued in office. After the result was declared, Chamberlain left the house looking pale. Later that evening, he summoned Churchill to his room and told him that he did not think that he could go on. At the time he was not aware of the cancer that would kill him just six months later.

A majority of MPs wanted a coalition government like Lloyd George's administration in the First World War. R.A. Butler known to all as 'Rab' records in his memoirs: 'on the evening of 8 May while the debate on the Norwegian campaign was still raging, Hugh Dalton came to see me. He told me that the Labour Party would enter a government under Halifax but not under Chamberlain or in the company of Simon.' In any event the Conservative Party would make the final choice owing to its massive majority. The Prime Minister's Parliamentary Private Secretary Alec Douglas-Home, still only in his twenties, had been to see Butler before the debate on Norway. 'He urged me to talk to Halifax and persuade him to become Prime Minister', Rab recalls.

Thursday 9 May was a day of intense politicking among various groups. In the morning Halifax returned to the Foreign Office from a conversation with the Prime Minister. Chamberlain had pressed him strongly to accept the succession and he felt that he could do the job, but the thought had given him a strong stomachache. Rab concluded: 'I saw that in truth Edward did not really want the premiership.'

In Churchill's memoirs *The Gathering Storm* the famous two minutes silence is described as taking place at a meeting on the Friday morning. To historians this seems to be an extraordinary quirk of memory. Butler records that the meeting took place at 4.30 on the Thursday afternoon. 'As the bearer of a message, I happened to be in the Cabinet room when the three men Chamberlain, Churchill and Halifax came in accompanied by David Margesson, the Chief Whip. Winston immediately said to me in good spirit; 'there is no place for you here, your turn will come later'.

John Colville records that on many subsequent occasions he heard Winston give an account of what happened: when Chamberlain had summoned Lord Halifax and himself to the Cabinet Room, he looked at him sharply and said: 'Can you see any reason, Winston, why in these days a peer should not be Prime Minister?' Two of Churchill's supporters, Lord Beaverbrook and Brendan Bracken had warned Churchill that if the subject of Halifax's candidature should come up, his best course would be to keep his mouth shut. Colville's account continues: 'Winston saw a trap in this question. If he raised no objection Chamberlain would turn to Lord Halifax and say: 'Well since Winston agrees I am sure that if the King asks me, I should suggest his sending for you.' Therefore Churchill turned his back and gazed out on Horse Guards Parade without giving any reply.

In Churchill's memoirs he says: 'As I remained silent a very long pause ensued. It certainly seemed longer than the two minutes which one observes in commemoration of Armistice Day.' Colville continues: 'There was an awkward pause after which Halifax himself volunteered the suggestion that if the King were to ask Mr Chamberlain's opinions about his successor he should propose Mr Churchill.'

On Friday morning the Germans launched their long awaited offensive on the Western Front. In view of the sudden military crisis, Chamberlain thought that he should stay on temporarily. In the intense politicking that had arisen over the last forty-eight hours a further key figure emerged: Sir Kingsley Wood. He was a self-made City solicitor and a close personal friend of Chamberlain's. With a Cabinet post as Lord Privy Seal he would walk in St James Park with Chamberlain on most mornings. Kingsley Wood told his friend that frankly the unleashing of the onslaught made a change in leadership even more imperative.

There remained one more piece in the jigsaw to put into place – viz the position of the Labour Party. At 18.15 on Thursday Attlee and his deputy Arthur Greenwood came to see Chamberlain. Churchill described how Attlee and Greenwood sat on one side of the table and Chamberlain, Halifax and himself on the other. The Labour Party was about to hold its Whitsun Conference at Bournemouth. Such are the rule-driven procedures of the Labour Party that it was not before 17.00 on Friday that Attlee telephoned Downing Street to say that Labour would serve in a coalition government but not under Chamberlain. The latter then left for the

Palace to tender his resignation and Churchill was sent for. By six o'clock that evening George VI had invited Churchill to form a government.

As Churchill drove back from the Palace with his personal bodyguard, Inspector Thompson, Churchill was silent. Thompson then ventured to say: 'I only wish the position had come your way in better times for you have an enormous task.' Tears came into Churchill's eyes and he replied: 'God alone knows how great it is. I hope that it is not too late. I am very much afraid that it is. We can only do our best.'

Churchill immediately asked Chamberlain to be leader of the House and Halifax to remain as Foreign Secretary. He then effectively appointed Anthony Eden as his right hand man by giving him the War Office. Sir Archibald Sinclair the leader of the Liberal Party took the Air Ministry. Clement Attlee became the Lord Privy Seal and A.V. Alexander who had served as First Lord under Macdonald got the Admiralty. Other significant appointments were Kingsley Wood as Chancellor of the Exchequer; Ernest Bevin, the dominant Trades Union leader of his day, was appointed to the Ministry of Labour to get the unions behind the government and Lord Beaverbrook, the Press tycoon, was given the Ministry of Air Production. Churchill did not get to bed until 03.00 on the Sunday morning when he records: 'I was conscious of a profound sense of relief. At last I had the authority to give directions over the whole scene. I felt as if I were walking with destiny and that all my past life had been but a preparation for this hour and for this trial.'

People soon woke up to the fact that things were going to be different when Parliament was summoned to meet at 14.30 the very next day on what would otherwise have been sacrosanct: Whit Monday. Churchill then went down to the House and made a short statement in effect aimed at the general public through the papers. It was the bugle call for which the British people had been waiting.

'I have nothing to offer but blood, toil, tears and sweat. You ask what is our policy? I will say it is to wage war, by sea, land and air with all our might and with all the strength that God can give us; to wage war against a monstrous tyranny, never surpassed in the dark lamentable catalogue of human crime. That is our policy. You ask what is our aim? I can answer in one word: it is victory, victory at all costs, victory in spite of terror, victory however long and hard the road may be, for without victory there is no survival. Let that be realised; no survival for the British Empire, no survival for all that the British Empire has stood for, no survival for the urge and impulse of the ages that mankind will move forward towards its goal. But I take up my task with buoyancy and hope. I feel sure that our cause will not be suffered to fail among men. At this time I feel entitled to claim the aid of all and I say, come then, let us go forward together with our united strength.'

Chapter 23

'Rough Winds Do Shake the Darling Buds of May'

While the British had been locked in a furious battle of words, the Germans were waging a more deadly battle with tanks and guns across the Channel. No apologies are made for further digression as it is the sequence of events which took place during the first month of the Churchill administration that decided the outcome of the Norwegian campaign. As the fall of France became daily more probable the Norwegian campaign became less and less relevant. Eventually complete withdrawal and the concentration of all forces on home defence became the most obvious option. For the next few weeks all that the politicians could do was to react to each new disaster as the drama unfolded.

Allied strategy was based upon the assumption that the Germans would launch their main offensive through Belgium in the north as they had done in 1914, and this turned out to be correct. But whereas Count Schlieffen's plan in 1914 had provided that the German army should wheel left and advance on Paris, this time it would be different. A brilliant staff officer and one of the greatest German commanders on the eastern front General von Manstein devised a plan known as *Sichelschnit*, [the cut of the scythe]. This provided for a breakthrough in the centre with a curving movement west which would cut off the British and French forces to the north from the main body of the French army.

It is surprising that Allied intelligence was not more aware of German intentions. The disposition of the German forces indicates quite clearly what the German General Staff's priorities were. Army Group B, commanded by General von Bock consisted of twenty-eight divisions of which only three were armoured. Bocks' command extended from the north of Holland down to Liege in Belgium. Army Group C, under General von Leeb, faced the Maginot line from Luxemburg to the Swiss border with seventeen divisions, none of which was armoured. This was sufficient to keep substantial French forces detained in their concrete fortifications and inactive during the next few crucial weeks. Army Group A, commanded by General von Rundstedt, the most illustrious of all German commanders in the Second World War, was in the centre with forty-four divisions of which seven were armoured. The famous Panzer or armoured divisions were largely responsible for the speed of the German victory on the western front. Each consisted of 328 tanks and five motorized infantry battalions in close support, but it is a myth to suppose that most German troops rode around in tanks or trucks. The bulk of the German army travelled by train and ultimately by foot.

The Allied forces on the western front were by no means inferior in numbers but there were serious deficiencies in equipment and training and there was imperfect unified command. The massive German and French armies were largely composed of conscripts and reservists. The Dutch army was tiny, but the Belgian army, which had put up such a great fight in the 1914/1918 War was bigger than the British Expeditionary Force. To begin with the I Corps had three divisions and II Corps only two divisions, while there were two further divisions in reserve.

The Blitzkrieg or lightning attack started on the morning of 10 May with the hordes of Army Group A emerging from the forests of the Ardennes which the pundits had thought to have been virtually impassable for columns of armour. Simultaneously Bock's Army Group B crossed the Dutch border and paratroops seized key airports round Rotterdam. Within a couple of days panzer units had linked up with them. French and British units raced north to the Belgian frontier to support the Dutch. This is exactly what the Germans wanted them to do because it weakened the line in the centre. The Germans did not intend to come on heavy with the Dutch. After all neutral Holland had been hand in glove with the Germans in the First World War and was to give the Germans less trouble than any other occupied territory in the Second. The German commander had threatened to bomb Rotterdam and negotiations for a ceasefire were in progress. Unfortunately there was a mix up of orders and a substantial force of bombers reduced the centre of Rotterdam to rubble in just three hours. It was clear to the Dutch what would happen to Amsterdam shortly so they sued for peace. Holland collapsed in just four days, but it did give time for the Royal Family to escape to London and Dutch naval and merchant ships made an invaluable contribution to the Allied cause.

Belgian forces had been put on a war footing in 1939 and general mobilization brought numbers up to 900,000, but they were short of artillery and not supported by either tanks or aircraft. The Belgian army had taken up a position on the Albert canal facing north-east and the River Meuse facing east. There had been little co-operation with either the French or the British, so fearful were they of antagonizing the Germans. While Belgian strategy was to try and hold the Germans until the Allies came up, by the 12 May they had been forced back to the River Dyle just east of Brussels.

Thus three days into the German offensive the dispositions on the Allied front were: the French Seventh Army was on the north Belgian coast, the Belgian army lay between Brussels and Antwerp. The BEF was south of Brussels. The French First Army was positioned around Namur and the French Ninth Army faced the Ardennes. Finally to the south the French Second Army manned the Maginot line where they were to remain more or less idle for the rest of the campaign. The BEF thus faced General Bock's Army Group B, but to begin with most of the pressure was on the flanks. The French and the Belgians to the north were driven back, but the main German thrust was to the south through the Ardennes by General Rundstedt's Army Group A with its two brilliant Panzer generals, Heinz Guderian and Erwin Rommel.

The crucial day was 13 May when German engineers managed to construct pontoon bridges across the Meuse and tanks were able to cross over to the west bank. On 14 May the French Ninth Army front was breached and the next day the Germans penetrated the line held by the French First Army. General Billotte, commander of the French First Army and now overall commander of the BEF and the Belgian army ordered a withdrawal as far as a line of the River Escaut (Scheldt), to be phased over three nights. On 19 May General Guderian's panzer units broke through the French Ninth Army front and reached Peronne on the Somme. Despite an attempted attack by a French armoured division from the south-east commanded by General De Gaulle, there were no more French troops between the Germans and the sea.

The War Cabinet, that is Churchill, sent the CIGS Lord Ironside over to Lord Gort's headquarters on 20 May urging him to break through the 50-mile panzer corridor to the south. Gort refused and Ironside could clearly see that the BEF was not strong enough. Gort did however mount a limited counter-attack south-west with two brigades supported by tanks in the Arras area which temporarily checked Rommel's panzer division. Marshal Weygand had now taken over as Commander-in-Chief of the French Army. The 73-year-old Marshal was considerably more energetic than his predecessor General Gamelin, but his attempts to mount an offensive to cut north through the panzer corridor also came to nothing.

The Germans themselves were astounded at the speed of their own advance. Not only Hitler but also his generals had in mind the repulse of the German army on the Marne, almost at the gates of Paris, in 1914. On the morning of 24 May Hitler travelled to General Rundstedt's headquarters. The latter agreed with Hitler that it was more important to switch the panzer divisions to the south of the panzer corridor to face the main body of the French army rather than incur losses trying to wipe out the BEF. From 24 May onwards a halt was called to the German Army Group A's advance from the Boulogne area south of Dunkirk.

General Blanchard recognized that the Dunkirk bridgehead was the only hope for the remaining French and British forces in the north and a phased withdrawal was ordered. On 25 May Lord Gort ordered all British troops north of the panzer corridor to concentrate on Dunkirk. The destruction of the Dunkirk bridgehead was left to von Bock's Army Group B, minus the panzer divisions, which put the Allied forces on a much more equal footing with the Germans. General Bock had reproached the Führer saying 'when we finally reach Dunkirk the British will be gone'. It has been suggested that Hitler wanted a negotiated peace with the British, but surely if the BEF had surrendered to the Germans it could only have strengthened the German hand. Hermann Goering merely said that he hoped that 'the Tommies' could swim as the Luftwaffe would destroy any rescue fleet.

From 19 May onwards the Joint Services Committee had considered the question of evacuation but it was not until 19.00 on 26 May that the Admiralty signalled Vice Admiral B.H. Ramsay, flag officer commanding Dover, that Operation Dynamo was to begin. Unfortunately when the British intention to evacuate was communicated to the Belgians they naturally and quite justifiably reasoned: why should we carry on fighting just to enable the British to get away. For three days the Belgians had borne the brunt of the fighting with Army Group B, but on 27 May King Leopold requested a ceasefire. Thus the whole of the northern flank of the BEF and that of the French Seventh Army was exposed.

Back in England frenetic meetings had taken place from 20 May onwards and it was decided that Admiral Ramsay should have control of all sea movement. The naval vessels placed at Ramsay's disposal were thirty-nine destroyers, thirty-eight minesweepers, sixty-one minesweeping craft, eighteen anti-submarine trawlers, six corvettes and seventy-six miscellaneous craft. Civilian vessels included thirty-six pre-war ferries from cross-Channel and Irish sea routes together with a veritable armada of fishing boats and smaller craft. The main port was to be Dover, but we should never forget the Admiralty small boat pool of yachts, river craft and motorboats operating out of Ramsgate. A valuable addition were forty-three Dutch shallow draft motor vessels known as Schyts and many Belgian craft. The grand total came to over 900 vessels. Each one had to be issued with navigational instructions, charts, fuel and provisions besides being fitted into a schedule of when and where to sail.

Captain Tennant, twelve officers and 120 ratings, were sent in to organize embarkation. The task was horrendous. The whole of the sizeable inner port was inaccessible on account of blazing warehouses, damaged quays and damaged vessels. The gently shelving but sandy beaches meant that only very small vessels drawing 1 to 1.5m could take men off. On the first day only 7,669 men were brought back to England. Even today when you sail into Dunkirk harbour, the wooden lattice mole extending out into the sea on the east side of the outer harbour has a distinctly temporary look about it. In the evening of the first day, 27 May, Captain Tennant took a desperate gamble and signalled a destroyer to come alongside the east mole. A destroyer can take aboard about 900 men.

The following day 17,804 men were brought back to the UK but the price was the loss of the *Queen of the Channel*, a large ferry. On 29 May, Ramsey stepped up the number of ships to: seven ferries, three hospital ships and two more destroyers allocated to the east mole. The result was that 33,500 men were lifted from the mole and 13,700 taken off the beaches. The cost was two destroyers sunk and seven damaged. By the morning of 29 May the BEF was deployed round the perimeter of Dunkirk and nowhere had the Germans broken through.

On 30 May 53,823 men were brought home but there were problems. Freshening wind caused some surf on the beaches and the Luftwaffe was stepping up the attacks. Squadrons of Stukas dived on the ships. On 31 May the surf abated and 22,942 men were lifted from the beaches and 45,072 men from the harbour. The first day of June proved sunny with clear skies and brought the Luftwaffe's heaviest attacks. Six destroyers were sunk or damaged and several large ferries were sunk including the *Isle of Guernsey* carrying 490 wounded men. In all thirty-one vessels were sunk but 64,429 men were got away.

Criticism has been levelled at the RAF but the constraining factor was the retention in the UK of the minimum aircraft considered necessary for home defence. Nevertheless Fighter Command flew 2,739 sorties within the month and 132 enemy aircraft were shot down. But the price of fighting away from home with slender resources had to be paid and the British lost 145 fighter aircraft.

There were other factors to be taken into account. The shortest route was 39 miles along the French coast, but shore based artillery fire made this route increasingly hazardous. Two other routes lay north of the Goodwin sands; one 55 miles from the south of Dunkirk while the safer route north was 87 miles.

Parity between French and British troops was early agreed upon. The irony was that many French troops were transported to ports in France only to be marched off into captivity when France finally capitulated. On 2 June Ramsay was forced to suspend daylight sailings, nevertheless by midnight a further 26,256 men were evacuated. But the strain was beginning to tell on the crews and a few civilian ships refused to sail. At the same time some ships set up new records, the *Medway Queen* paddle steamer made seven trips. It was agreed with the French Admiral, commanding no less than sixty-three vessels, that the operation should be closed down at midnight on 4 June.

Nine German divisions were hammering at the gates of Dunkirk. The harbour, the main beaches and the sand dunes on the eastern side were subject to continuous bombing and artillery fire. In general discipline was good and despite all ranks being tired and short of food, there were few cases of drunkenness, looting or insubordination. A few British troops were left behind but it should never be forgotten that the main rearguard was French. On the last night 26,175 men were taken off. The last ship to leave at 04.30 on 5 June was HMS *Shikari* one of the Navy's oldest destroyers crammed with French soldiers.

The grand total came to 366,162 men but the cost had been great: six destroyers sunk, fourteen damaged by bombs and twelve by collision; nine substantial ferries lost and many smaller vessels. Countless acts of heroism went unrecorded. The club burgee of a yacht from the Little Ship Club was found on Dunkirk beach; a cockle-fishing boat which had never been out of sight of the Essex coast was blown to pieces by a mine.

Some 150,000 British troops remained to the south of the panzer corridor, most were successfully evacuated, but not all. The 51st Highland Division went into captivity at St Valery on the coast of Normandy. General Rundstedt launched his offensive to the south on 5 June. On 14 June General Weygand advised the French government to seek an armistice and on 17 June Marshal Petain, a mere ghost of the former defender of Verdun, broadcast to the nation. Back in England the spirits of the people and the government had been considerably lifted by the deliverance at Dunkirk and the calm sea was attributed by many to Divine Providence.

At the same time Churchill sternly reminded the House of Commons: 'We must be very careful not to assign to this deliverance the attributes of victory. Wars are not won by evacuation'.

Unknown to the British public a political drama had been played out behind closed doors. Churchill's position as Prime Minister was by no means secure. On 25 May Halifax, in his capacity as Foreign Secretary, had a conversation with Senior Bastianini, the Italian Ambassador. On the face of it this meeting was designed to keep Italy out of the war. She was still neutral. In effect Lord Halifax, his minion Rab Butler and a number of others, took the view that Mussolini should be employed to act as a mediator to secure peace.

According to Halifax, Churchill said on 27 May that if Hitler were prepared to make peace on the terms of restoring Germany's African colonies and over lordship of Central Europe, that was one thing but it was unlikely. Churchill's fundamental position was that it would be better for Britain to go down fighting than to enter into another false and humiliating peace. In the War Cabinet there were originally six men to which Churchill co-opted one more – Sir Archibald Sinclair. He was leader of the old Liberal Party which only had twenty-five seats. The real point was that he was an old friend of Churchill's having served with him in the trenches and was a staunch anti-appeaser. Attlee had a distinguished war record and could be counted on not to be seduced by talk of a spurious peace. Arthur Greenwood (Labour), a tough Yorkshireman, made it quite clear that he followed Churchill's line. The key figure was Chamberlain. Churchill handled him with great care and respect. On the first of his desperate trips to talk to the French government he had asked Chamberlain 'to mind the shop.' Chamberlain was a man of immense moral integrity who displayed towards Churchill the same loyalty Churchill had shown him when he was in office.

The sequence of events was as follows: on Sunday 26 May the Cabinet met at 17.00 and Churchill said it would be best not to decide anything until we saw how much of the army got away. On Monday at the morning session the Cabinet decided to evacuate Norway altogether. Matters came to a head when the Cabinet met in the afternoon. Halifax wrote in his diary: 'I thought that Winston talked the most frightful rot and after bearing it for some time I said exactly what I thought of him adding if that really were his view, our ways must part.' At this point Churchill saw that he had to keep Halifax on board. Churchill realized that perhaps he had been too overbearing and during the break for tea Churchill and Halifax took a turn round the garden at No. 10. Halifax appeared to be mollified. At the Cabinet meeting the next afternoon Churchill said that the French were trying to get us onto the slippery slope of peace negotiations. Halifax said that we might get better terms before France went under. Chamberlain said that the alternative to fighting on involved a considerable gamble.

Churchill often acted on political instinct and on the evening of 28 May he called a meeting in the House of Commons of the whole of his administration, some seventy MPs of all parties. As he records: 'I had not seen many of my colleagues outside the War Cabinet except individually and thought it right to have a meeting.' Hugh Dalton, a prominent socialist gave a vivid account of what Churchill said largely corroborated by Leo Amery. 'It is idle to think that if we tried to make peace now, we should get better terms from Germany than if we went on and fought it out. The Germans would demand our fleet - that would be called disarmament. We should become a slave state, though a British government which would be Hitler's puppet, would be set up. If this long island story of ours is to end at last, let it end only when each one of us lies choking in his own blood upon the ground.' Churchill toned down this account in his own memoirs. He did not expect what followed: 'there then occurred a demonstration. About twenty-five politicians of different points of view before the war surprised me. Quite a number seemed to jump up from the table and came running to my chair, shouting and patting me on the back.'

Greatly encouraged by this and strengthened by the more encouraging reports from Dunkirk, Churchill met the War Cabinet again at 19.00. Chamberlain moved away from Halifax, and the latter conceded that Mussolini should not be approached. From that moment Churchill sensed that he had the Tory Parliamentary Party behind him and that night he sent a message to the French government urging them to fight on.

See Fig. 5 The Western Front 1940 – p.xii.

Chapter 24

The German Drive to the North

After the heady stuff of a change of government and the launch of the German offensive in France, a return to the Norway scene is perforce a bit mundane, but the sequence of events is of importance. Whereas the Norwegian campaign was of little relevance to the campaign in France, the development of the latter came to determine the complete withdrawal from Norway.

From Trondheim to Narvik the distance is about 360 miles but the distance overland is at least three times as long with a single-track road twisting and turning through the mountains and along the narrow strips of flat land on the shore of the fjords. In 1940 the single track railway from the junction at Grong near Namsos only ran for several hundred miles as far as Mosjoen. It was extended over the high pass across the Arctic Circle and down to Fauske later in the war at the cost of the lives of 1,500 slave labourers, mainly Russians. The best port before Narvik is reached is at Bodo. This was comfortably within striking distance of the airport at Vaernes and when on 4 May two flying boats flew from Scotland to Bodo, they were destroyed within two hours of landing by several Heinkel 111 light bombers.

In point of fact the road to the north was supremely defensible. A couple of properly equipped divisions with artillery and adequate air cover could have probably held the Germans. In the circumstances the best that the planning staff could come up with was the concept of 'the independent company'. These were supposed to be light, mobile guerrilla units. Romantic though the idea may be, guerrillas, commandos or Chindits do not win campaigns. There were to be five companies each consisting of about 270 men. The officers were all regulars, some of them ex-Indian Army. Each company was divided into three platoons commanded by an officer and their equipment included Alpine rucksacks, Arctic boots and sheepskin coats. The first of the independent companies was landed at Mo at the head of the Randsfjord and the rest at Bodo which was to be their

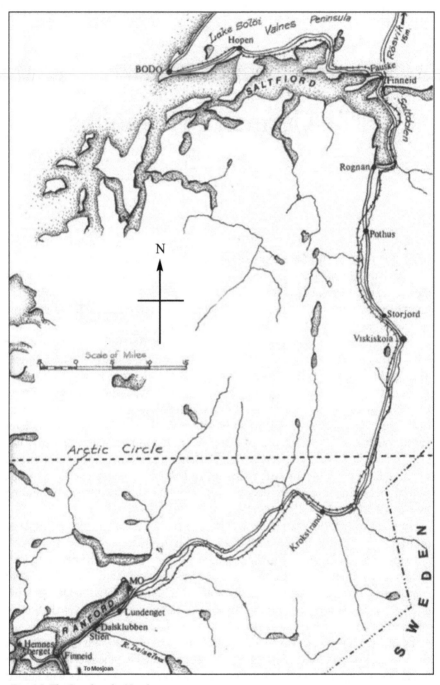

Fig. 16. The Road to the North

base. Lieutenant Colonel C. Gubbins was placed in command of what was given the code name Scissorforce.

Both General Carton de Wiart and General Audet had been dubious about the prospects for a fighting retreat north from Grong. But there was a Norwegian force in the field under Colonel Getz retreating up from the south and a Norwegian battalion had been moved down by railway to support them. It was therefore agreed that a party of 100 Chasseurs Alpins and a section of British light anti-aircraft guns should be sent by sea from Namsos to Mosjoen.

On the night of 8/9 May, No. 4 Independent Company was moved to Mosjoan and No. 5 Company moved 10 miles south to link up with about 400 retreating Norwegians. Two platoons of about 100 men were placed on the flank of the Norwegians and one on the railway line at the river bridge, which was about to be blown. The following day in the early morning a body of about fifty of the enemy on bicycles came down the road. As previously noted Indian army officers know how to mount an ambush. When the British opened fire, very few of the enemy escaped alive. Nevertheless by midday the pressure was so great that Colonel Gubbins was forced to order a retirement to Mosjoen.

What happened next has been described by one Norwegian historian as a coup as audacious as the invasion of Norway itself. A party of about 300 German troops embarked at Trondheim on the coastal steamer *Nord Norge*, manned by destroyer personnel. Although agents reported the movement to the British Naval HQ at Harstad, by the time the cruiser HMS *Calcutta* and the destroyer *Zulu* could enter Ranfjord, they were 40 miles behind the *Nord Norge*.

Two Dornier seaplanes preceded the *Nord Norge* and landed forty men to the west of Hemnesberget. By 19.00 the *Nord Norge* had discharged her cargo at the little port which lies about 15 miles to the seaward of Mo. All the British warships could do was to sink the empty ferry ship. A platoon of No. 1 Independent Company put up a brisk fight but was forced to retreat, which enabled the Germans to cut the Mosjoen/Mo Road at Finneid. The Norwegians, to their credit, counter-attacked and were able to get away to the north, but the British at Mosjoen had to be lifted by destroyer and taken back to Bodo.

Much has been made of the fact that the Germans employed special mountain troops whereas such units did not exist in the British Army. There were Austrian ski troops attached to both German formations in south Norway and to General Dietl's force at Narvik but only after the evacuation of Mosjoen was a specialized division brought into action. Despite the imminent offensive in the west, the Führer wanted the Norwegian campaign cleared up as soon as possible. The 2nd Mountain Division, commanded by General Feuerstein was therefore diverted from the western front. This consisted of five mountain infantry battalions together with three troops of mountain artillery and this further improved the odds of the Germans succeeding in the north.

The importance of stemming the German advance from the south was fully appreciated by the staff in Harstad. One of the last acts of General Mackesy before handing over to General Auchinleck on 9 May was to put 24 Guards Brigade under notice to move south. On the morning of 13 May the scattered units of 24 Guards Brigade converged on Skaanland, a fishing village on the mainland opposite Harstad. The plan was for the battalions to sail at four hour intervals: the Scots Guards first in two destroyers; the Irish Guards on the transport ship *Chobry* and the South Wales Borderers in the cruiser *Effingham*. It took from 17.00 to 03.00 the next morning to ferry troops and equipment to the *Chobry* a modern Polish motor vessel. No doubt the Germans were kept fully informed by their agents ashore and their reconnaissance planes. The *Chobry* remained at anchor the whole of the next day, a sitting duck for the German bombers which tried to bomb her three times without success. As Colonel Faulkner, the Irish Guards CO commented 'one bomb would have gone through her like butter'.

The Navy considered it far too hazardous for the *Chobry* to sail through the narrow Leads because in many places there was too little room to manoeuvre against air attack. She therefore sailed out into the Atlantic and turned south outside the Lofoten Islands. Shortly after midnight, with the sun barely below the horizon, as she turned into Vestfjord towards Bodo three Heinkels appeared overhead. At least two bombs hit the ship and what followed is best described by some of the men that were there.

'The cabins collapsed like a pack of cards, the lights went out and the whole of the top decks amidships were immediately ablaze...the fire divided the ship in two halves with the result that most of the men had to go forward and most of the officers aft. The men filed up from their mess decks many in full kit carrying their rifles. At the sound of Regimental Sergeant Major Stack's familiar voice the companies formed up...as the flames reached the ammunition boxes stowed on the decks the men were formed into lines and began heaving the mortar bombs and ammunition cases overboard, but there was still much ammunition down in the hold...the bombs had landed near the senior officer's cabin and the second or third had killed the commanding officer. Rescue parties searched the burning wreckage and brought the wounded up on deck. Some of the lifeboats aft were launched by the Polish crew and the wounded were lowered into them. About twenty isolated men had to jump into the sea and fortunately were quickly picked up by escorting vessels. Captain Fitzgerald was having a shower. Both he and his batmen were trapped and only escaped by squeezing through a porthole into the sea... the lifeboats forward could not be lowered as the electric winches had no power and the hand winches were jammed. There was nothing to do but wait for the escorting destroyer to come alongside. Not a man moved until given the order and Father Cavanagh started to recite the Rosary. As HMS *Wolverine* came alongside there was no disorder, gang planks and ropes were put in place and 694 men transferred to the destroyer in 16 minutes.'

The whole incident was reminiscent of the legendary discipline of the South Wales Borderers on the *Birkenhead*, a nineteenth century troopship wrecked on the south-west African coast.

The battalion came ashore somewhat unceremoniously in Harstad, some wrapped in blankets and others in naval greatcoats – and what did they do? They formed up as if on parade. Then over the next few days began the task of re-equipment. The ordnance depot was perilously short of Bren guns and there were no mortars. Rifles and steel helmets had to be purloined from a Pioneer Company.

More or less at the same time, by a similarly capricious decree of the god of war on 17 May, the South Wales Borderers were temporarily put out of action, though in a less cruel manner. The cruiser *Effingham*, carrying not only the Borderers but also the Guards Brigade Headquarters, left Harstad on 17 May. The captain, fearing air attack, tried to take a short cut. By the greatest of misfortune the *Effingham* ran onto an uncharted shoal at 20 knots a few miles short of her destination, Bodo. There she stuck fast and later sank. Again the troops had to be lifted back to Harstad by destroyer minus much valuable stores and equipment.

On the morning of 11 May, the Scots Guards embarked on 'puffers', the indispensable Norwegian fishing vessels, which ferried them to the cruiser *Enterprise*. They were accompanied by a destroyer the *Hesperus*, a sloop and a small merchantman carrying a troop of four 25-pdr field guns. The Guards were also to be supported by a party of Royal Engineers and three Bofors AA guns. Their orders were to hold Mo at all costs, but this meant sailing south to enter the narrow Ranfjord and then a considerable way inland past the Hemnesberget peninsula. Fortunately the little convoy was not bombed until shortly after they had landed at Mo.

The battalion then marched some 7 miles south to a good defensive position at Stien where a swollen river debouched into the fjord. The weakness lay on the left which was thickly wooded and where the ground rose steeply. The nights of 12/13, 13/14, and 14/15 were miserable. The men were tired from the march and from digging in or building barricades. There were no sleeping bags or hot food. Open fires were forbidden in order not to give their positions away to aerial reconnaissance. If they had been trained and equipped for fighting in the snow, like the Finnish Army, they would have been initiated into the art of

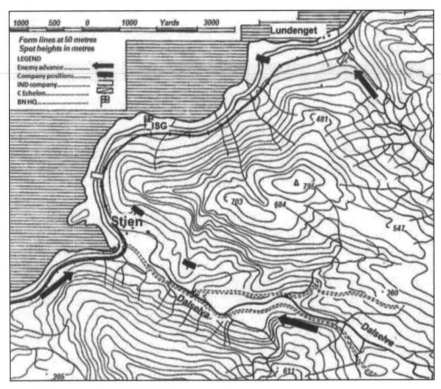

Fig. 17. Action at Stien 17-18th May

building wigwams round fir trees with fir branches and equipped with portable wood-burning stoves.

On 15 May the hopelessly outnumbered Independent Companies were ordered back to Mo. Lieutenant Colonel T. Trappes-Lomax commanding the Scots Guards prudently ordered B Company to move back to a position north of Mo in case the Germans moved round the top of the fjord and attacked from the rear. Evidence of enemy activity on the other side of the fjord was provided by a seaplane which a lucky shot from a Bofors gun brought down.

At midnight the bridge over the river at Stien was blown with 1,000lbs of gelignite and later the wooden bridge was demolished. The following afternoon 17 May, the Germans, numbering some 1,750, started to move forward from Finneid. Initially they tried attacking along the fjordside. Small arms fire grew in intensity and later mortar fire. At 18.00 it was reported that 150 parachutists had landed about 7 miles to the south-east and were making their way over the high ground towards Lundenget, a hamlet on the fjordside to the rear of the Stien position.

At this time of the year there are no real hours of darkness and by 22.30 the Germans were attacking down the river. Each time there was a threat the Guardsmen had to leave their positions to meet it. No. 16 platoon bore the brunt of it. Guardsman Bryson inflicted heavy casualties on the enemy and on two occasions went out into the open to rescue wounded men for which he was awarded the Distinguished Conduct Medal. By midnight the left flank was virtually surrounded. Two hours later the battalion was ordered to withdraw. There had been 80 casualties but only three men were killed which was ascribed to the volume of enemy fire rather than its accuracy.

HQ Company provided the rearguard and the battalion fell back through B Company's reserve position. Meanwhile Lieutenant Colonel Gubbins had been advanced to acting brigadier in command of all troops in the Bodo / Mo area. After conferring with General Auchinleck on the telephone, he gave the order to retire north of Mo, then after the British and Norwegians had passed through, the two bridges over the River Rana north of Mo were blown up. In this necessarily condensed summary only certain incidents can be selected. For example Captain Ellinger, a Dane serving in the Norwegian army attached himself with his machine guns to the Independent Companies and played a big part in facilitating the withdrawal of the companies from Finneid. Similarly a Swedish volunteer, Captain Count Lewerhaupt, was largely instrumental in helping B Company to get back. The company had been cut off and was only able to rejoin the battalion several days later by crossing two mountain ranges in deep snow and a large river.

The final stage of the Scots Guards' retreat was dominated by consideration of two defensible positions: one at Krokstrand south of the virtual mountain pass, which happens to be almost exactly on the Arctic Circle, and Viskiskoia north of it. Early on 20 May a message was received from General Auchinleck to make a stand at Krokstrand: 'You have now reached a good position for defence... I rely on the Scots Guards to stop the enemy.' Colonel Trappes-Lomax, the man on the spot, could see that it was not as good as it might appear on the map. Behind him was a single track road running for about 20 miles over a bare pass with no tree cover, between banks of snow some 8ft deep. Trappes Lomax realized that if the battalion were forced to traverse the snow-belt, which looked almost certain, transport for food, ammunition and other equipment would be essential. Thus when the Norwegians crossed the snow-belt on the night of 19/20 May each carried a Scots Guard driver to make sure that the Norwegian lorries came back.

Three defensive lines were drawn up at Krokstrand. The enemy did not attack until 21 May in the evening when they easily outflanked the first line. The main position where the bridge had been demolished was only held for a few hours before it was enfiladed from the higher ground. Then for some reason the enemy attacks slackened. Perhaps they thought that the British would resist longer. This may have been because a corporal had brought down a reconnaissance aircraft with a Bren gun. If he had missed he would have been reprimanded severely for endangering his fellow troops by giving the position away. Also Captain Ellinger and his machine guns had destroyed a 12-man cycle patrol which may have made the enemy more cautious. That night the battalion was able to slink away over the high plateau in small parties and take up a new position at Viskiskoia. The cost was nevertheless considerable. The men lost most of their kit and were utterly exhausted after the 23-mile trek.

On 23 May the Scots Guards were deployed to cover the demolished bridge over the Saltdal river while No. 3 Independent Company had marched up from Rognan, the fishing village lower down the river, towards the open sea. At this point an incident occurred which does little credit to two distinguished soldiers. General Auchinleck later was the commander in the Western Desert who effectively stopped Rommel, while Gubbins ended up as a major general. Suddenly Colonel Trappes-Lomax received a message that he was to report back to Harstad to explain why he had given up the Krokstrand position. 'What's that for' one of his brother officers observed, 'saving the battalion?' Command devolved onto Major Graham, but the effect of withdrawing a popular and competent CO in the middle of a battle was bound to demoralize all ranks.

The following afternoon the Germans attacked. By this time the British had no artillery support and the Guards' supply of 2-inch mortar ammunition had run out. By 16.00 the Independent Company had been driven back, and the enemy was soon in possession of the high ground on the right. The whole position was thus enfiladed.

After the disaster of the *Chobry,* literally 'a soviet' of Irish Guards officers had drawn up its own command structure. There were no officers fit for active service above the rank of captain and there were only four of these. Captain McGildowny took over as CO with Captain Gordon Watson MC as adjutant. Four companies were commanded by senior lieutenants. Nevertheless by the afternoon of 20 May the battalion was reequipped and able to embark on two destroyers the *Walker* and the *Fieldrake*. As they left Harstad the town was being bombed and a tanker full of high octane fuel was on fire. They then had to sail well out to sea to avoid the British minefield.

The two destroyers carrying 1, 2 and 3 Companies were far better suited than the *Chobry*, with their steel decks, albeit not thick enough to withstand a direct hit from a bomb, but they carried anti-aircraft guns which would be sufficient to keep aircraft above a certain height. HQ Company and No. 4 Company travelled in puffers with Norwegian crews along an inshore route. Even with local knowledge one puffer hit a rock and had to be towed into Bodo. The Irish Guards spent the night in the ruins of Bodo and the next day puffers

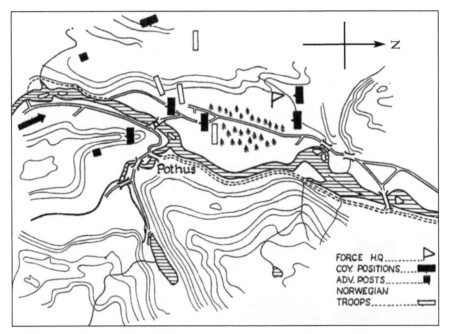

FORCE H.Q.............▷
COY. POSITIONS.....■
ADV. POSTS...........■
NORWEGIAN
TROOPS.............⬭

Fig. 18. Action at Pothus 25 May 1940

conveyed them up the Saltdalfjord which runs for 30 miles inland to Fauske. All British forces in the area were then amalgamated into Stockforce commanded by Lieutenant Colonel Stockwell under the general direction of Brigadier Gubbins. Stockforce included part of No. 2 Independent Company and some small Norwegian units together with a troop of 25-pdr guns from 166 Field Battery. Meanwhile the Scots Guards continued down the fjord to Rognan where they were able to embark.

Even today there is a gap in the road from Fauske to Rognan which has to be traversed by ferry. The village of Pothus lies some 10 miles further up the Saltdal and this afforded a good defensive position for the brigade. On the eastern side of the river opposite the village is a thickly wooded razor-backed ridge jutting out from the mountains. On the north side of the ridge is a turbulent tributary running into the main Saltern River. A rough track crosses the tributary by a light suspension bridge and continues down the eastern side of the river till it crosses over the Saltern River by a light bridge 3 miles further down. On the western bank, the main road crosses the Saltern River from east to west by an iron girder bridge. The road then runs down to Rognan.

The Germans could outflank the position either by working through the rough wooded ground on the west bank or crossing the mountains on the east side. Captain McGildowny placed No. 1 Company at the end of the ridge on the east side with a patrol up on the ridge itself. No. 3 Company was to defend the west bank while No.4 Company was higher up in the woods on the west bank. No. 2 Company and the men of the Independent Company were held in reserve with battalion HQ. Some Norwegian machine gunners were placed up on the flank of No. 4 Company.

The plan was that the Scots Guards, having passed through, the main girder bridge would be blown. As and when No. 1 Company would be forced to retire from the ridge, the suspension bridge would also be blown. It proved to be a perfect late spring day on 24 May. The sun beat down on the guardsmen in shirt sleeves as they dug themselves in, all the while plagued by ants and swarms of midges. The night was as cold as the day had been hot. At midnight the Scots Guards, which could have been expected to exchange banter with the Irish Guards, tramped through their position in silence and then continued down the fjord to Rognan where they embarked. The main bridge was then blown up.

Early the next morning the leading German scouts appeared on bicycles and the Norwegian machine gunners opened fire. After this there was silence for several hours while the Germans brought up their infantry and support weapons. As the men were breakfasting on biscuits and water, parties of Germans began climbing up the ridge and working their way parallel to the river. The guardsmen responded with small arms fire but the rocky scrub gave the enemy excellent cover. The small troop of 25-pdrs and the Norwegian mortars put up a creditable performance but they could not compete with the artillery and mortar fire which the Germans were able to bring to bear on the two forward companies. When the German infantry reached the top of the ridge they rushed forward hurling stick grenades and the riflemen were hard put to beat them back. The platoon on the far left reported that the enemy higher up on the ridge were already moving round the flank.

In the late afternoon No. 1 Company was withdrawn from the ridge but by the time that they got down to the river, the lower bridge had already been blown. They therefore carried on downstream looking for somewhere to ford. Eventually the men took off their rifle slings and knotted them together. Guardsman Murphy then stripped and plunged into the river, but was swept down some hundred yards before he got a foothold on the other side. Captain Eugster managed to anchor himself on a bank in the middle of the river to help the men across while Platoon Sergeant Major Thomas threw any man who hesitated into the water.

What had not been foreseen was the speed with which the Alpine troops were able to scale the mountain on the left flank. In order to deal with them Colonel Stockwell dispatched No. 2 Company. Meanwhile No. 4 Company up in the woods on the right was in contact with the enemy. The Germans, true to form, dug in opposite them and then sent patrols round the flank. In one case figures in Norwegian peasant dress appeared among the trees. It is hardly surprising that Guardsman Tracy should strike up a conversation, from a safe distance, with what appeared to be two large blonde ladies, but when one of the subalterns moved to investigate more closely, the ladies in question opened fire with light automatics.

During the night German engineers built a pontoon bridge half a mile south of the main Pothus bridge and from the steady stream of troops crossing over, it was not difficult to deduce that the main German assault would be on the west bank of the river. A general order to withdraw was then given at 19.00. The main problem was how to disengage from the enemy. Fortunately this was partly solved by the appearance of a single Gloster Gladiator fighter, one of only two operating out of Bodo, which proceeded to shoot down three Heinkel bombers in succession. Deprived of air superiority for a few hours and the ability to see what exactly the British were up to, the Germans failed to press home their advantage.

By midnight the bulk of the battalion, less HQ Company which was providing the rearguard, and a number of stragglers, had been shipped on puffers from Rognan to Finneid a few miles short of Fauske. A further problem was that No. 2 Company was still high up on the mountainside, several hours distant by messenger. Earlier in the evening a Norwegian interpreter had found them and then led them over mountain tracks, many miles round the head of Saltdalfjord and eventually down to Fauske.

The Irish Guards took up a temporary position a few miles short of Bodo but were then ordered back to Bodo itself. Here they got their first showers and hot meals for days. By this time, 27 May, the War Cabinet had taken the decision to withdraw from Norway altogether. Just ten days after the Irish Guards had landed in Norway a message was received at midnight on 30 May: 'Destroyers *Firedrake* and *Fame* at the quay – five minutes to get aboard.' The battalion landed at Harstad the next morning and within 24 hours embarked on the ill-fated liner HMS *Lancastria* about to join a convoy bound for home. Tragedy struck the *Lancastria*'s next assignment, evacuating British and Allied personnel after the Fall of France. On June 17, off St Nazaire, she was sunk by Ju88 bombers with the loss of more than 4,000 lives.

Chapter 25

Harstad

It is now necessary to retrace our steps to the first British landings in the Narvik area. The early days were bedevilled by a divided leadership. Naval forces were commanded by an Admiral of the Fleet no less, The Earl of Cork and Orrery, the military forces by Major General Mackesy. The admiral had been a typical Churchill appointment, an aristocratic Irishman noted for his dashing leadership in the First World War and his irascible disposition. Mackesy was an engineer and, as one might expect, cautious and methodical. Never were two commanders more different in temperament. The admiral and the general met for the first time aboard ship on 15 April only to discover that even the instructions that they had received were different. Cork had been told that he had to take Narvik as soon as possible. Admiral Whitworth had signalled on 14 April after the naval victory on the previous day that the enemy forces in Narvik were thought to number 1,500 to 2,000 and believed to be thoroughly demoralized.

Lord Cork had wanted the cruiser *Southampton* to meet him with a view to landing with 350 Scots Guards and 200 Marines at Narvik itself. Two of Whitworth's destroyers had reconnoitred and concluded that a landing on the Rombaksfjord side of the Narvik peninsula with the support of naval guns would have been feasible. General Mackesy did not agree. The shoreline of rocks and small beaches provided excellent ground for siting machine guns which would have been invisible from the sea. All army officers had been schooled in the bitter memories of the Gallipoli landings. Not only Mackesy's staff but also a number of naval officers including Captain Maund, later admiral, of the Naval Staff were of the same opinion. Indeed the stiff fight put up by Dietl's men in the final assault on Narvik some weeks later rather confirms that Mackesy had been right.

Both Mackesy and Cork went on a reconnaissance in the cruiser *Aurora*. By this time Lord Cork had modified his views. He was short of stature and had tried making his way through 4ft of snow and found that without snow shoes it was virtually impossible. On 20 April Mackesy cabled the CIGS to the effect that any attempt before the thaw would involve the destruction of the 24 Guards Brigade which by this time had become available.

The next issue between Mackesy and Cork concerned the decision whether or not to bombard Narvik. Mackesy's instructions were clearly designed to avoid civilian casualties as far as possible. Mackesy argued that a bombardment of the town could prejudice Anglo-Norwegian relations. For some days Tromso radio had been urging Norwegian civilians to leave the town and Mayor Broch and his staff had got numbers away. In the end it was decided that the area of bombardment should be restricted to the port and railway and that a landing should only be made if the Germans surrendered.

As a result of almost continuous heavy snowfall the bombardment was postponed until 24 April. It lasted for three hours in the course of which the *Warspite* fired 150 rounds from her 15-inch guns. The buildings along the quayside were completely destroyed but civilian casualties were mercifully light. By all accounts the Germans were seriously shaken but did not surrender. Whether the machine-gun posts on the hillsides or along the shore, which were co-ordinated to fire along fixed lines, were seriously affected, we shall never know because no British troops landed.

At least on 21 April the command structure was simplified with the appointment of Lord Cork as supreme commander. In point of fact the German forces were dangerously weak but there was a glimmer of hope for them. General Dietl realised that with the collapse of the Allied expedition in Central Norway, if he could hang on long enough, succour would arrive from the south. The first thing that General Dietl had done within days of landing had been to launch a surprise attack near Bjornfjell. This had overwhelmed the Norwegian garrison troops who had escaped from Narvik on 9th April. Bjornfjell is the last little town before the railway line crosses over into Sweden. Thus the Germans had secured the whole of the railway line running from Narvik to the Swedish border and it was Bjornfjell that Dietl now made his main base.

Early on the Germans opened negotiations with the Swedes with a view to bringing in supplies by rail. The official line of the Swedes was that they would not permit ammunition or troops to be conveyed over Swedish railways. They were prepared to allow such things as clothing, ski equipment and medical supplies. Several hundred specialists dressed in various outfits, such as nurses, came in over the next few weeks.

When Mackesy had first arrived at Harstad he made a cautious approach to the Norwegian authorities and ascertained that there were no Germans in the immediate area. The cruiser *Southampton* then crossed over to the mainland and two companies of Scots Guards were put ashore at Salangenfjord. This put the Scots Guards 20 miles from Fossbakken and the main road from Narvik to Tromso, the capital of the north. Contact was thus made with the patrols of

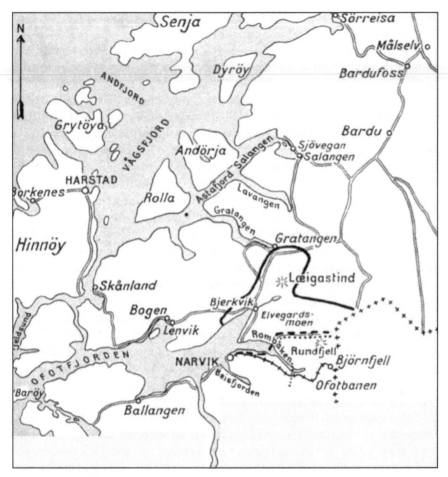

Fig. 19. Harstad/Narvik

General Carl Fleischer, the Norwegian commander. On the morning of 15 April three transports escorted by the battleship *Valiant* and nine destroyers arrived off Harstad. The 1st battalion Irish Guards and the rest of the 1st battalion Scots Guards disembarked together with brigade headquarters and a battery of Royal Artillery.

Predictably air raids soon started and relations with the local population of about 4,000, who were not flattered by the selection of their little town as a base, were strained by the fact that no heavy anti-aircraft guns arrived for a week. To what extent the Germans were able to infiltrate spies over the few weeks is debatable. British servicemen were convinced of their presence. The daily air raids usually took place in the morning and the bombs were nearly all

174

aimed at the ships lying at anchor. Raids did not normally last for long, about a quarter of an hour. All the while naval ships put up a massive barrage straddling the silver dots of the aircraft with little white puffs of smoke, but rarely bringing any aircraft down. Above the noise of the barrage the bombs made the loudest noise of all, sending up great plumes of white spray. Some of the largely wooden buildings in Harstad were destroyed and most of the shops were boarded up. However, military staff could buy the things they wanted at the British canteen such as sweet jams, unsubtle sauces, cigarettes and whisky and gin in abundance.

For three days chaos reigned in Harstad. On 16 April the 2nd battalion South Wales Borderers came ashore and the number of troops was doubled by all the trappings of a divisional headquarters: base staff, signal units, engineers and even a railway construction company. Captain Dix who landed with a unit from the Royal Ordnance Corps recalled that his first and lasting impression was that every quay and warehouse stank of fish. Cargoes landed had to be sorted and despatched to the unit concerned which might well be in one of the neighbouring villages. Transport was desperately short and the troops were expected to manhandle three kitbags with seventeen items of clothing, the scale for a winter garrison. Much of the clothing and equipment was simply burned six weeks later.

Harstad anchorage could only accommodate six vessels at a time. To anchor more than a few hundred yards offshore was out of the question as the centre of the fjords is far too deep. The larger ships at anchor depended upon a fleet of some 120 Norwegian fishing vessels, powered by paraffin engines, to fetch and carry from the shore. Needless to say the Norwegian captains and crew were richly rewarded for their services. Meanwhile the Royal Navy developed their own base at a village on the mainland called Skaanland some 15 miles to the south. Submarines were not the menace that they might have been for the reason already explained. The Navy sank two of them in the first week. Aircraft were a much greater hazard as they concentrated their attentions on ships rather than shore targets. A cruiser on a bad day could expect five air raids and destroyers were under orders to keep constantly under way. In eight weeks the Harstad/Narvik area suffered 140 air raids.

The final total of Allied troops in the area amounted to about 30,000 giving the Allies a comfortable majority over General Dietl's forces bottled up in Narvik. A significant number of these were units of the French Army. The 5th Demi-Brigade of Chasseurs Alpins which had virtually lost all its equipment at Namsos had been sent back to Scotland with General Audet and the rest of Carton de Wiart's men. The latter's second in command, Brigadier General Bethouart was sent to Harstad to command all French units. He had under his command three brigades as follows:

175

27th Demi Brigade, Chasseurs Alpins, consisting of the 6th, the 12th and 14th battalions
13th Demi Brigade of the Foreign Legion consisting of the 1st and 2nd battalions
The Polish Brigade known as the Chasseurs du Nord consisting of the 1st and 2nd Demi Brigades each with two battalions.

In addition there were:

The 342nd Independent Tank Co; The 2nd Independent Group of Colonial Artillery and the 14th Anti-Tank Company from the 13th Demi Brigade.

When the Germans had invaded Poland in 1939 few members of the Polish Army ever thought that they would end up serving in the French Army. When the Russians, seeking to safeguard their western front, had moved into Poland on the 17 September it was only a matter of weeks before the Poles were forced to sue for peace. In a sense Hitler was putting the clock back to the Europe that he had known as a boy when Poland had been divided between the three great powers: Germany, Russia and the Austro-Hungarian Empire. For months after the collapse there was a steady stream of soldiers over the short Polish/Rumanian border on their way to carry on the fight in France. A number of Polish Air Force planes had managed to fly to France and later a number of Polish pilots were to serve with great distinction in the Battle of Britain. In addition there was a small navy and a few destroyers, seven submarines and a number of merchant vessels which had managed to get away through Danish waters to either Britain or France. General Sikorski set up his headquarters in Brittany where entirely Polish units were recruited, equipped and trained to serve with the French Army. The Polish Army in France was as rigorously trained by professionals as any other army. There had always been a large Polish migrant community working in France and young Poles living in France flocked to the Polish colours.

When it came to the unfamiliar nature of large scale amphibious operations, as with Norway, the French and the Poles experienced the same sort of problems as the British. To begin with a force had been assembled to go to Finland. The organization was marginally better off than had been the British experience especially since the force for Finland had not been disbanded. Nevertheless equipment belonging to a unit was loaded onto one ship and the men onto another. The mules, essential transport in many French units, were loaded on to one ship and the fodder for the animals on to another. Machine guns were loaded on to one ship and the ammunition on to another.

Embarkation had started on 21 April in three large liners: *Le Chenonceau, Le Colombie*, and *Le Mexique*. The French civic authorities had given the Poles a send off as only the French know how. A dinner was laid on in the hotel de ville for the officers and trestle tables in the market place for the men. The square was decked with French and Polish flags, the bands played and many were the barrels of cider and Calvados consumed with singing and dancing until dawn. In one respect the voyage to Norway differed from the earlier British experience, the weather was calmer. Five boring days were spent at anchor in the Clyde with no shore leave. Early on 1 May the French ships left Greenock and once at sea joined the larger convoy of eleven ships escorted by twelve French and English destroyers.

The men were kept busy with parades on deck, weapons drill, lectures and answering such questions as: will we see polar bears? On the night of 3 May the convoy crossed the Arctic Circle and the Poles were told that they were to land at Tromso. Entering the bleak labyrinth of fjords, they saw at first the desolate snow bound mountains and later the isolated farmhouses painted with the traditional red ochre. On arrival off Tromso, the tiny capital of the north, they found that not only did the King of Norway and his government occupy most of the buildings but that there had been a muddle and they were redirected to Harstad.

On the quay at Harstad, they were met by Major Paris, chief of staff to General Bethouart commanding the First French Light Division to which the Polish Brigade was to be attached. Harstad was already bursting at the seams and allocating billets in the neighbourhood was a minor nightmare for the staff. One Polish battalion was transported to Borkenes, a little fishing village on the seaward side of Hanoi Island. The men had landed with little more than their rifles and knapsacks and it took at least a week to sort out which machine guns, mortars and a whole host of items of equipment, belonged to which unit.

On Thursday 16 May, the Poles started their move to Ballangen on the southern bank of the Ofotfjord. The skippers on the puffers were enormously hospitable. The 17 May happened to be Norway's National Day, the rum flowed and the sailors sang sea shanties and the Norwegian National Anthem.

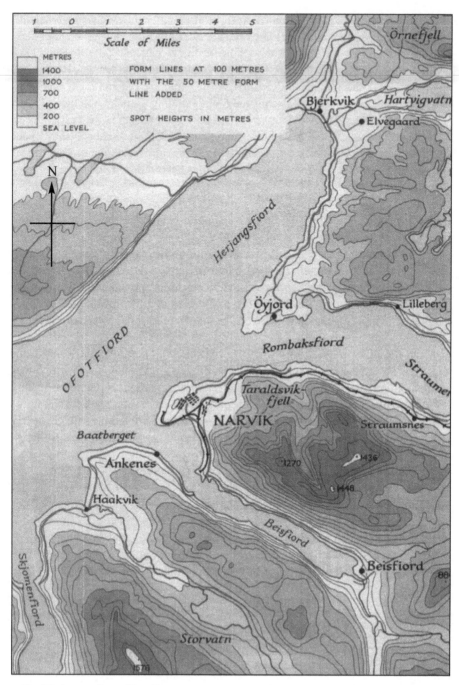

Fig. 20. Approaches to Narvik

Chapter 26

Bjerkvik and the Capture of Narvik

On 28 April General Bethouart had arrived at Harstad from Namsos. A graduate of the military college at St Cyr, he had always been interested in mountain warfare. He shortly crossed over to the mainland and made contact with General Fleischer. The main assault on Narvik was to become a largely Franco-Norwegian affair supported by the Polish brigade under General Bohusz-Szyszko. The expedition remained entirely reliant on the Royal Navy.

Both Churchill and Ironside, the dominant figures on the Military Co-ordinating Committee considered, unfairly as it turned out, that General Mackesy had been unduly dilatory. At the same time it was decided to build up the strength of the Allied forces in the north of Norway to corps level. On 5 May instructions were issued by the Secretary of State for War to Lieutenant General Claude Auchinleck to assume command of British and French troops in North Norway but that there should be no interference with Lord Cork's plans, largely drawn up by Mackesy, for the capture of Narvik. The instructions also spoke of the object as being to preserve a part of Norway as a seat of government for the Norwegian king and people. His first orders from the Chief of Staff were to report on the area to be held and the means required. In conjunction with Lord Cork, General Auchinleck reported that they would require: four cruisers and six destroyers, seventeen infantry battalions, 200 anti-aircraft guns, seven batteries of field artillery and howitzers, together with some armoured units. In the light of the deteriorating situation in France, the Chiefs of Staff telegraphed that reinforcements would have to be severely limited. Auchinleck then replied that he could not answer for the consequences.

For the Allies the position had been greatly simplified by the evacuation from Namsos. Mackesy's hand had been strengthened in the first week of May by the arrival of the following reinforcements:

1. Two battalions of the French Foreign Legion.
2. Two battalions of Chasseurs Alpins.

3. Four battalions of the Polish Brigade.
4. Field battery No. 203 Royal Artillery with twelve 25-pdr field guns.
5. The French had their own 75mm field guns and some light tanks. They were later joined by a battery of colonial artillery.
6. Four auxiliary landing craft.
7. In total the British finally provided 130 anti-aircraft guns.

No French or British units had ever fought north of the Arctic Circle. Indeed the natural habitat of the French Foreign Legion was either the Atlas Mountains or the Sahara Desert. They even brought their mules with them. One Legionnaire described his first impression of a fjordside village as 'a few scattered houses in a desert of snow and silence'.

What further improved the outlook for the Allies in the north was the arrival of some air support. A small force of fighter planes came into operation, although nothing like enough and there were no bombers. The landing ground at Bodo had been temporarily brought into use, but the German advance from the south had been so rapid that it had to be abandoned. A site near the naval headquarters at Skaanland just south of Harstad was developed, but after clearing the snow and herculean efforts to put the runway in order, the ground still turned out to be too soft. A flight of Hurricanes from No. 26 Squadron was flown in from the aircraft carrier HMS *Glorious* on 26 May, but three of the eleven tipped onto their noses on landing to the despair of the pilots and the visible distress of the men who had worked so hard to get the runway ready. As a consequence the squadron was diverted to the airfield at Bardufoss which had been in operation for several days.

The first thing that had to be done at Bardufoss was to extend the runway to 1,400m. A local labour force had come forward and General Fleischer put a reserve battalion to work manually as there was only one bulldozer. Eventually the airfield was equipped with 8 heavy and 12 light anti-aircraft guns. A company of Chasseurs Alpins was assigned to protect the airfield from possible attack by paratroops. The first aircraft for Bardufoss had taken off from the aircraft carrier *Furious* at 06.00 on 21 May. They were Gladiator biplanes of the reorganised No. 263 squadron which had been so badly mauled at Lesjaskog in the Gudbrandsdal. It was a miracle that they had made the short flight from the aircraft carrier. The weather was foul, visibility was poor, and the pilots had been issued with naval charts. These give the depth of the seas but do not give the heights of the mountains. As it was two Gladiators were wrecked on mountainsides.

Group Captain M. Moore had under his command 263 Squadron of Gladiators commanded by Squadron Leader J. Donaldson and No. 46 Squadron of Hurricanes commanded by Squadron Leader K. Cross. From 22 May until 7

June there was always some Allied air activity which was enormously encouraging to the troops on the ground. RAF sorties numbered from ten when the weather was really bad to a peak of ninety-five on the day on which Narvik fell. In total the Gladiators claimed twenty-six enemy aircraft and the Hurricanes eleven, but the cost was high. No less than twenty RAF planes were lost. There were in addition six naval amphibian aircraft at Harstad and there was usually an aircraft carrier patrolling the coast. Finally we must not forget the sterling work of the anti-aircraft crews. It was largely boring, invariably cold and often lonely. Nevertheless it was warm work when there was a raid and the guns brought down a total of twenty-three enemy aircraft.

General Bethouart was against Lord Cork's idea of a direct assault on Narvik and the plan eventually hammered out was substantially as conceived by General Mackesy. First there should be a combined sea and land attack on the little town of Bjerkvik on the northern shore of the Ofotfjord. The Norwegian ski troops on the left and the Chasseurs Alpins on the right should attack Bjerkvik from the north. The Poles at Bogen were to advance along the shore of the Ofotfjord from the west while the Royal Navy were to land the French Foreign Legion at Bjerkvik and Elvegaard.

The Norwegians would continue to push from the north and would attempt to cross the Kulberg plateau up in the mountains. On the southern shore the British and the Poles would advance from the small port of Ballangen to the Ankenes peninsula which overlooked Narvik from the south. The final assault on Narvik was planned to be launched from the Oyjord peninsula across the Rombaksfjord to the northern shore of the peninsula on which Narvik stands.

After the bombardment on 24 April, General Dietl had withdrawn his headquarters from Narvik and moved further inland along the railway line towards the Swedish border. For the time being he regarded the Norwegians in the north under General Fleischer's command as the main threat to his position. He therefore deployed two battalions of his mountain troops 17 or so miles north-east of Narvik. He then posted a company on the Ankenes peninsula and the remainder of his mountain troops around Narvik. Dietl was fortunate in that he was able to arm the 2,000 or so sailors from the destroyers which had been sunk, with arms captured from the Norwegian base at Elvegaardsmoen. These were at best amateur soldiers so he placed them mainly along the railway line.

With the Royal Navy controlling Ofotfjord, the only way in which German supplies and reinforcements could be brought in was by air. On 14 April the first ten JU52 transport planes landed on the ice of Hartvig Lake. But a J52 could only bring in a ton of supplies at a time. A battery of mountain artillery was brought in, but once the thaw set in, Lake Hartvig just east of Bjerkvik could no longer be used. Thereafter supplies had to be dropped on the mountainside by parachute. General Falkenhorst made available what he could bearing in mind the constraints placed upon him by the OKW whose priority was the Western Front. In point of fact a total of 1,100 men were brought in, half of them being paratroops.

Earlier the Norwegians had withdrawn to Fossbaken on the road north to Tromso after General Dietl had made a surprise attack on the Norwegian position at Bjornfjell due east of Narvik. It is perhaps to be regretted that to begin with, while Mackesy was developing his strategy, General Fleischer was operating independently. The Norwegians then brought in fresh troops from the north, which brought their strength up to four battalions and they proposed making a frontal attack on the German position at Lapphaug which is the highest point on the road from Fossbaken to Gratangen. The Scots Guards were fitted out with white camouflage coats and snow shoes. As they say in the Guards 'the impossible we achieve, miracles take a bit longer'. On this occasion General Fleischer was not expecting any miracles because he placed them in reserve.

The attack started on 24 April, but in those latitudes the weather can turn and frustrate the best laid plans. A snowstorm blew up and lasted for two days. It took the Norwegians eight hours to cover a mere two miles and then, when they did at last attack the enemy in an entrenched position, they were repulsed. The Norwegians on the right were able to make much more rapid progress and to make their way down the road to Gratangen where the battalion could get shelter for the night. By the morning of the next day the Norwegians up on the mountain were still separated from them. What made the Germans such formidable foes was that if they detected a weakness, they would rarely fail to act on it. The Germans at Lapphaug moved forward and surrounded the Norwegians at Gratangen where they opened up with a murderous burst of machine gun fire. A party of Norwegians managed to break out of the position but about 100 men were either killed or wounded and 150 taken prisoner. One effect that this action had was that General Dietl decided to shorten his defensive line and to withdrew from the Lapphaug/Gratangen area altogether.

After the setback on 25 April, General Fleischer reorganized his forces into two brigades. The 6th Brigade on the left consisted of three battalions and one mountain battery under Colonel Loken. Stuck up in the mountains, where sometimes the snow was 9ft deep, they slowly pressed the German outposts back towards the Swedish border. Both sides suffered equally from biting winds, sudden snowstorms and freezing nights in the white wilderness. On the right the 7th Norwegian Brigade consisted of two battalions of infantry and one mountain battery plus a motorized battery commanded by Colonel Faye. They worked in close cooperation with the French who provided two companies together with a mortar section for the advance from Elvenes to Bjerkvik.

By 10 May French ski troops had secured the top of the 3,000ft mountain lying on the west side of the pass. The Norwegians were slightly ahead on the east side, but the Germans hung on to the road stubbornly. In ten days the French and Norwegians had not progressed much more than 5 miles. On the left the Norwegian 6th Brigade moved forward again on 12 May and after two days fighting reached the edge of the Kuberg plateau. As one Norwegian staff officer described it: 'Our push had to be made through narrow valley passages between mountain tops of up to 3,000ft. The Germans had climbed up and established themselves on the summits and in order to go forward we had to climb up and get them.'

The capture of Bjerkvik at the head of Ofotfjord was seen as the essential condition before Narvik could be taken. Once that had been achieved the plan was to advance along the shore to Oyjord at the northern entrance to Rombaksfjord. The force for the landing at Bjerkvik consisted of two battalions of French Foreign Legion numbering some 1,600 men. General Bethouart and Lord Cork were to direct operations from the bridge of the cruiser *Effingham* (she ran aground and was lost a week later). Massive covering fire would be provided by the battleship *Resolution* which had replaced the *Warspite*. In addition there were the cruiser *Aurora* and five destroyers. A French mortar battery was even mounted on the foc'sle of the *Havelock*. Ten French light tanks were carried in the hold of the battleship and the infantry were carried in the cruiser and destroyers. Four landing craft spearheaded the landing with 120 assault troops. This minor armada was covered by aircraft operating from HMS *Ark Royal*.

Promptly at midnight on 12 May the bombardment began. Houses were set ablaze and the church blew up. Plainly it had been used as an ammunition dump. Norwegian sources had informed the French that the civilian population had been evacuated. Captain Lapie serving with the Legion described what it was like: 'the noise of the guns, the flames, the smoke spreading over the snow and the mountains and falling to the sea, the mighty ships... At the end of an hour's bombardment a sudden silence fell and then we saw that the sea was dotted with small boats full of men... A boat made an attempt to land, but failed and as pre-arranged moved away to the left. Another boat making for the wharf on the right, from seaward, also moved away to the left of the target area. The gigantic form of Boyer-Resses, the Commandant of the 1st Battalion could be seen standing up in the boat bawling orders regardless of the bullets spattering the water.'

The second echelon followed and soon the Legionnaires had consolidated themselves on the high ground to the west of the little town. There was some difficulty in unloading the tanks on to tenders. Eventually five tanks made it to the shore. The fields were by this time largely clear of snow and the tanks were described as 'frisking about like young puppies'. It was the tanks which effectively silenced the German machine-gun posts. Nevertheless the Austrian ski troops put up a stiff resistance, spraying the streets with small arms fire and it took at least two hours to clear the town. As a corporal in the Foreign Legion recalled 'a frightful butchery ensued in the course of which we slaughtered more civilians than Germans. Machine guns riddled the doors and windows with their crossfire, then the infantrymen rushed forward hurling grenades... With rifle in hand I was to scour a dreadful calvary strewn with mangled corpses, cradles overturned on dead babies, and the wounded moaning in pools of blood.' The civilian population had not been evacuated.

At 09.00 the staff went ashore and the first thing that they saw was a column of troops marching in close formation along the road from the west. They were the Polish troops who had been put ashore in the bay of Bogen and who had marched 20 miles overnight with their machine guns slung on their backs. To the considerable chagrin of the Poles they were too late for the fight. Further to the east the 2nd Battalion Foreign Legion, supported by two tanks, landed at Elvegaard. The Germans put up strong resistance in the village itself and the Legionnaires had to fight building by building. Support fire from the cruiser *Effingham* was of great assistance. The Legionnaires then marched up to the former Norwegian base at Elvegaardsmoen which they reached at 07.30 the next morning.

It took three hours of close quarter fighting to clear the enemy and when at last they were successful they found 100 heavy machine guns together with ammunition and tons of stores. Beyond the camp the battalion came up against a rocky eminence with three German machine-gun posts. A tank destroyed two of them but the third kept firing. The Legion, perhaps the most famous mercenary regiment in the world, had been reluctant to take refugees after the Spanish Civil War. Most French officers were rightist and deeply prejudiced against the 'Reds' but when it came to actual combat this is how Captain Lapie described the Spaniards: 'thirsting to get at the fascists, three young Spaniards sprang from rock to rock like tigers. Two were cut down only yards from the remaining machine gun. The third smashed the heads of the machine gunners with the butt of his rifle and then heaved the bodies over the cliff.'

In the field hospital at Elvegaardsmoen the French doctors soon struck up a rapport with the German doctors and both attended to caring for the wounded regardless of whether friend or foe. When the German bombers returned the next day, despite the clear Red Cross markings on the roof, the hospital received a direct hit and doctors, nurses and patients alike were killed.

Up on the mountain plateau there was still a gap between the Norwegian 6th and 7th Brigades which enabled the enemy to escape from the net that was tightening round them and to withdraw to a shorter line in the mountains towards the Swedish border. A motto of the Foreign Legion is 'a Legionnaire must keep on keeping on'. Accordingly as soon as the Germans had withdrawn

184

into the mountains, a Legion motorcycle section set off along the shore of the fjord. With no enemy in sight they reached the tip of the Oyjord peninsula from whence they could look across the Rombaksfjord to Narvik, only a mile distant.

On 29 April the South Wales Borderers and the Chasseurs Alpins, which were able to provide ski troops, landed on the Ankenes peninsula at a little village called Haakvik. General Dietl was perilously short of troops with which to oppose the Allied build up and the landing was unopposed. From Haakvik the Borderers advanced along the coast road, now reasonably free from snow, to within a mile and a half of the village of Ankenes. From there it was only a mile and a half across the Beisford from Narvik. They were thus within artillery range of Narvik itself. The Borderers were able to dig in opposite Ankenes and it was here that Brigadier Fraser was slightly wounded while on reconnaissance. The French Alpine troops struck inland from Haakvik and advanced along the spine of the Ankenes peninsula as far as Lake Storvatern. This move covered the flank of the Borderers.

The next German strongpoint was the village at Beisfjord at the head of the fjord. On 1 May German patrols approached the French at lake Storvatern and the next day a stronger party of about 100 men counterattacked towards Haakvik. Fortunately the attack was beaten back with considerable losses to the enemy but only because the cruiser *Aurora* was able to come inshore and bring her big guns into play. The initiative then passed to the Chasseurs. Two companies supported by ski troops succeeded in taking the three main high points north of Lake Storvatern. It was then decided to make no attempt to take Beisfjord village until the final assault on Narvik. On 14 May the South Wales Borders were withdrawn and shipped to Bodo but not before suffering their first few casualties. Their place was taken by 2nd Polish Battalion which was ferried in two days later. Thus the only British troops left on the Ankenes peninsula were the Royal Artillery 25-pdr gun crews and some anti-aircraft guns.

The plan was that the Polish Brigade should take over from the British on the Ankenes peninsula south of Narvik where the officer commanding 2nd South Wales Borderers was operating with one battalion of Chasseurs Alpins and one company of Irish Guards at Haakvik, to the west of Ankenes. To the east of the immediate environs of Ankenes, the Chasseurs Alpins had taken much of the ridge running almost to the Swedish border. On the morning of 17 May there had been a brisk German counter-attack against the Chasseurs Alpins before the Poles arrived and this was only repelled with the support of the battery of British 25-pdr guns under French command. On landing at Haakvik, General Bohusz-Szyszko took command of all troops operating south of Narvik. Tall with craggy, granite-like features, he was a veteran of Pilsudski's army which had driven out the Russians after the First World War and also of the all too brief campaign in September 1939.

Commanding the troops on the coast between Haakvik and Ankenes was Colonel Dec. He was everything that you would imagine a Polish cavalry officer to be. He was highly strung, with an unmatched reputation for heroism earned in the Polish campaign. The Poles listened respectfully to the phlegmatic British major who briefed them. Without taking his pipe out of his mouth the major tried to explain to the Poles that the Germans were entrenched on the mountain side in a series of well concealed machine-gun positions capable of firing on interlocking fixed lines. His understatement 'it's inadvisable to go up there, you might get hurt!' was completely lost on the Poles.

Regardless of the British warning Colonel Dec decided upon immediate action. He would take the mountain. Lieutenant Szaszkiewicz did succeed in getting to the top with four machine-guns and took up one of the positions formerly occupied by the Germans. It was not long before he found himself pinned down by an accurate enfilading fire. At midday a runner was able to get down to Colonel Dec's headquarters and explained the position, whereupon Colonel Dec ordered the men to retire. That night, thanks to a mist, the Poles got back at a total cost of nine lives and forty wounded.

General Bethouart had decided that the main attack on Ankenes should be co-ordinated with the landing at Narvik from the north. At midnight on 27 May the assault on Ankenes began. As one observer put it: 'from behind the boles of pine trees, from every dugout, from a hundred hideouts in the snow from behind rocks, the word went out that every Pole loves to hear "attack"'. Machine guns opened up to give the infantry covering fire and, while most of the fleet's guns were concentrated on the northern shore of Narvik, a British Royal Artillery battery gave Colonel Dec valuable support.

The main thrust was by Colonel Dec's men along the shore towards Ankenes with part of the force advancing over the spur of the mountain. General Bohusz-Szyszko established his own command post up on the mountain overlooking Ankenes. It was known that this is where most of the German resistance would be encountered. Moreover the Germans were more heavily armed than the Allied infantry. At Ankenes there were twelve sub machine-guns for every German company plus two heavy machine guns and four heavy mortars. All German NCOs were armed with tommy guns (light automatics). The Poles advancing along the shore were halted after 200 yards by a withering fire. Scaling the ridge Captain Zamoyski rallied his men and reached the summit. His then decimated company moved down towards Ankenes, but at this point the Germans emerged from their concealed foxholes and started firing into their backs. Thus although the Poles were in the outskirts of Ankenes, the Germans still controlled the heights.

Then came the German counter-attack and for a while both General Bohusz-Szyszko's outpost and the forward Polish units were out of radio contact with the Polish HQ at Haakvik. Eventually the general got back to his HQ and was able to direct the fire from several British destroyers onto the German mountainside positions. Meanwhile the reserve battalion at Ballangen had been summoned. This is reminiscent of some of the British actions in the Central Valley. Why were not all forces concentrated on the *point d'appui* before the attack started? That is the technique later used by Monty: 'you don't attack until the figures suggest that there is an overwhelming probability that you are going to win'.

The Germans were defeated as much as anything by the action of Colonel Chlusiewicz up in the mountains. Tall, heavily built, methodical, a veteran of the old Tsarist army, he was reputed to be the worst bridge player in the brigade. His orders were to advance east through the mountains towards the head of the Beisfjord and cut the German line of retreat along the shore of the Beisfjord. Granted that his part of the front was less strongly defended, he advanced cautiously. He was able to draw on the support of a first class battery of French colonial artillery. He took one mountain top after another until he could look down on Beisfjord. It was this menace to their line of retreat which caused the Germans to withdraw from Ankenes. Several boatloads of Germans tried to escape across the fjord to the Narvik side but their boats were sunk by artillery fire.

When Colonel Dec's men finally entered Ankenes the houses were little more than piles of red splintered timber with broken tables and chairs, beds and cupboards lying all over the place. Mercifully the civilian population had moved out. The action had cost Colonel Dec's men dear: two officers and fifty men dead and 100 more wounded. On the other hand Colonel Chlusiewicz's casualties were light. That evening the chaplain of the brigade officiated at the burial of the dead with the bitterly ironical words, 'You are the first in this war to have won an Allied battle... one day you will be able to return to a liberated and free Poland.'

The final assault on Narvik had been postponed until 27 May in order to get the longed for air support from Bardufoss. The general plan was that the attack should come from three directions. The 13th Demi Brigade of the Foreign Legion would cross the Rombaksfjord in landing craft and land at Orneset beach just to the east of Narvik itself. A second echelon would land slightly nearer to Narvik at Taraldsvik. South of Narvik across the Beisfjord, the Polish brigade would keep up the pressure, advancing round the top of the fjord. On the northern bank of Rombaksfjord a battalion of Chasseurs Alpins supported by Norwegian ski troops would advance eastwards towards Dietl's main base now up in the mountains.

The landing on the north side was preceded by a bombardment at 23.40 with a destroyer and a cruiser and artillery sited on the north bank of Rombaksfjord.

Both Cork and Bethouart were on the bridge of the cruiser *Cairo* from where General Bethouart was able to direct the fire. A German sailor described how hundreds of shells crashed without interruption along the railway line, exploded with a thunderous roar in front of tunnel entrances and huge rocks came hurtling down the slopes. In the wake of the bombardment the 1st Battalion, Foreign Legion landed at 00.15 without encountering much opposition. Needless to say, not everything went according to plan. The Germans regrouped along the railway line high above the beach so that the attackers had to scale the cliffs at Orneset under heavy machine gun and mortar fire. Eventually they reached the railway line and a Norwegian battalion landed from fishing boats on Orneset beach and passed through the French positions.

When the French and the Norwegian battalions were put ashore at 04.00 it was already broad daylight, but air and naval support was hamstrung by a seafog at Bardufoss. No flights by Hurricanes or Gladiators were possible for several hours. The fog however had not affected Trondheim airport. Stukas carrying extra fuel tanks and Messerschmidt 110 twin-engine fighter bombers were unopposed for several hours. Two bombs hit the flagship *Cairo* and thirty men, mainly from the anti-aircraft crew, were killed or wounded. Only one vessel, a puffer, was lost. She was carrying ammunition and simply blew up. Until some air support was restored the cruiser and destroyers had to withdraw to the wider waters of the Ofotfjord. It was not until 06.00 that British Hurricanes appeared over the battlefield.

The Germans seized the opportunity to counter-attack along the railway line. This threatened the flank of the Norwegians who fell back almost as far as Orneset beach. The Germans were thus able to dominate the beach with mortars and heavy machine guns which prevented landing craft with the second battalion of Norwegians from landing at Orneset. General Bethouart's chief of staff was killed when 150 yards from the shore. Another beach at Taraldsvik slightly nearer to Narvik had to be used.

There then ensued a critical half-hour until the German counter-attack began to falter. Then on the cliffs above Orneset a cry rang out: *'A moi La Legion'*. Despite a mortal head wound, Captain de Guittaud rallied his men. In his company there were sixty casualties. Twenty out of thirty-five Legionnaires were killed in one section. The Germans then withdrew east along the railway line, but such was the cover afforded by rocks and the scrub already in leaf that it was not until late afternoon that the hillside was cleared. Hill 457 was found to be littered with shell craters and corpses.

Major Haussel, left in charge of the garrison in Narvik, realised that with only 150 mountain troops and 250 sailors he could not hold off a final assault for long. The only line of retreat was along the southern fjordside to Beisfjord still in German hands. Shortly before 07.00 on 28 May the major gave the order to retire and the last German troops were away from the town by midday. General Bethouart courteously suggested to General Fleischer, who had joined him, that the Norwegians should be the first to enter Narvik.

North-east of the Rombaksfjord Norwegian ski troops and the battalion of Chasseurs Alpins continued to press the Germans back for several days. The weather had changed. The entry in Captain Lapie's field service book is poetic: 'Spring began to appear, pale green leaves peeped from the old dark branches. Waterfalls, freed from their canopy of snow and ice, tumbled down to the stream. Only their song echoed in the woods; no birds could be heard. This silence, this death of nature was one of the most extraordinary things experienced in our progress across the mountains.'

Chapter 27

The Beginning of the End

Towards the end of April when the outlook for the Allies in Central Norway had looked bleak, ex-Prime Minister Mowinckel, who had joined the coalition government on the outbreak of the Norwegian war, had a conversation with the Swedish Foreign Minister in Stockholm. What became known as the Mowinckel plan was that North Norway should become neutralized. It was probably suggested by the Swedes, but British diplomats thought that the suggestion had emanated from Berlin. The only beneficiaries as far as the British could see would be the Germans. The plan entailed the occupation of Narvik by Swedish troops. The majority of the Norwegian government were not keen on the idea as Norway had only managed to break free from union with Sweden thirty-three years previously. The proposal therefore came to nothing.

As late as 19 May Churchill, by then Prime Minister, could tell the Foreign Secretary that the most important reason for maintaining forces in Norway was to keep a superior German force away from the main point of decision – 'Norway is paying a good dividend now'. But by the evening of 20 May he was advocating the abandonment of the Narvik theatre. On 23 May the Chiefs of Staff summarized the arguments:

- The Norwegians in the north under General Fleischer had neither the numbers nor material for effective resistance.
- We could spare no more aircraft.
- We had only one and a half divisions in Norway. By June 15, the Germans would have seven divisions totalling 107,000 men.
- There was already talk of invasion. At present about half the Home Fleet's destroyer force was involved in the Norway theatre which might be required nearer home.

Thus by the evening of 24 May, the Defence Committee had decided upon a complete withdrawal from Norway. The effect on the strategic decisions taken by General Auchinleck was that up to 24 May the aim was to stop the Germans

190

advancing up the road from Trondheim. Thereafter it was to cover the taking of Narvik, a prestige move, and to mask the subsequent general evacuation.

It had been a horrendous week for the British government. The telegram ordering Lord Cork to evacuate his forces from Norway more or less coincided with the order to put Operation Dynamo, the evacuation from Dunkirk, into operation. The telegram to Lord Cork was received on the night of 24/25 May. The order to start the evacuation from Dunkirk was issued on 26 May. The almost certain collapse of France which would follow and the need for troops, and above all ships, with which to repel a possible invasion was the justification for closing down the Norwegian campaign.

The delicate question of informing the Norwegians arose. The British government had agreed that the storming of Narvik should go ahead. The British and the Norwegians desperately needed a success; the Poles wanted vengeance; in the hour of France's agony, the French wanted a victory and General Bethouart was the man to deliver it. Although it meant keeping French troops away from France he agreed to go ahead. Later he added: 'I am operating with Norwegian troops whom for reasons of *honneur*, I will not abandon on the battlefield.' Narvik was taken on 28 May but the Norwegians, although they had their suspicions, were not informed about the evacuation until 1 June. In so far as the Germans were concerned the secrecy was fully justified for they remained unaware of the evacuation until the last day or two. This enabled the Allies to quietly slip away, a tricky operation to say the least.

There were five sectors to consider: first, the British and Norwegian troops operating in the south in the vicinity of Bodo; second, the Norwegians fighting to the north-east of Narvik; third, the French, the Norwegians and the Poles fighting in the vicinity of Narvik; fourth, the considerable base staff at Harstad and its environs and fifth, the Norwegian king and government at Tromso.

First let us turn to the situation in the south. After the Scots Guards had passed through the Irish Guards' position at Pothus, transport took them down to Rognan where they were treated to a most welcome hot breakfast. They were then transported by puffers down the fjord to the village of Hopen about 10 miles short of Bodo. Here they were billeted over a wide area, some of the young soldiers sleeping for up to fifteen hours [see Fig. 16].

When the Irish Guards got away from Pothus, they were transported by truck to Rognan and puffer to Fauske on the far side of the Saltdalfjord. The Norwegians fully appreciated that Fauske was the best place to stop the Germans from advancing north to Rosvik or west to Bodo. Fleischer therefore sent an extra battalion to Fauske. Norwegian suspicions were first aroused when the South Wales Borderers at Bodo were not brought forward. They were even more dismayed when the Irish Guards were ordered back to Hopen.

On reaching Finneid the Germans divided their force in two. Part advanced cautiously through Fauske towards Bodo which they expected to be heavily defended. The other part advanced north towards Rosvik where today, but not then, a ferry crosses over the next fjord. Beyond is wild country, stretching for some 50 miles, in those days traversed only by rough tracks along fjordsides or over mountain passes to Narvik.

Part of the Norwegian force had little option but to withdraw west towards Bodo. The rest withdrew north to Rosvik. Norwegian Divisional HQ then informed their troops on the ground that the British would be evacuating Bodo. The Norwegians at that point had not been told that the British were evacuating Norway altogether. They were told that Bodo would not be evacuated for three days and this enabled them to withdraw to Rosvik. But the Germans were hot on their heels and one rearguard company lost a number of men taken prisoner, the rest were then transported by puffer to the Lofoten Islands.

First thing on the morning of 27 May, German bombers attacked the airfield at Bodo and the two Gladiators remaining operational were destroyed on the ground. That evening a stronger force of bombers flying in relays virtually destroyed the little town. Ironically as it turned out, the main jetty was left intact. Setting fire to the majority of houses, which were constructed of wood, was not difficult. Some of the more significant buildings were constructed of stone such as the hospital where a number of wounded Scots Guards lay. They were evacuated thanks in no small measure to the courageous conduct of the Norwegian nurses. Four fifths of the buildings in Bodo were destroyed; the radio station was shattered but not the broadcasting equipment. The station continued to thunder out Edvard Grieg's famous hymn of death, 'The mighty host of saints we see as a thousand mountains clad in snow'.

The Scots Guards had been ordered back to a position between Soloi Lake and the Saltdalfjord. Meanwhile B Company had been left at Hopen as a rearguard. By the evening of 30 May the Germans had moved up and at 18.30 the bridge was blown. During the evening a considerable engagement developed with heavy mortar and machine gun fire. The Germans were seen to have suffered a number of casualties. Nevertheless by 02.00 the next morning they were clearly making ground on the flank. Finally, with covering fire from a South Wales Borderer Bren gun, B Company was withdrawn.

Early the next night the withdrawal of the Scots Guards together with the South Wales Borderers took place. As for the enemy, all that was seen was a cycle patrol. Everything in the way of kit and stores and transport had to be destroyed and by midnight the last man had embarked on the destroyers *Echo* and *Delight*.

The last vessel to leave Bodo was the so-called *Raven* commanded by the colourful Sir Geoffrey Raven. In fact she was a small Norwegian steamship pressed into service as a sort of Q-ship – a warship in disguise. Manned by naval ratings and Irish Guardsmen her armament consisted of one Bofors and one Oerlikon gun. Both anti-aircraft guns were carefully concealed. Otherwise her sole armament was an assortment of heavy machine guns. She had been patrolling south of Bodo but on 3 June she was back at Rosvik where she attacked some German vessels trying to cross the fjord. Her last assignment was to blow up some oil tanks north of Bodo. Having set them ablaze she then encountered a much more heavily armed German corvette. The intrepid Sir Geoffrey immediately sailed into the attack and the corvette, thinking that HMS *Raven* must be part of a flotilla, turned tail and fled.

The distance from Rosvik on the Bodo peninsula to Narvik is about 85 miles but there were no proper roads and the tracks that ran over the mountains and along the fjordsides were deep in snow in winter and sludge in the spring. Nevertheless General Dietl's main hope of relief was from this quarter. German strategy was based on an elite force of mountain troops undertaking a march from Rosvik with severely limited equipment to Narvik. It was known as Operation Büffel. A group of so-called German scientists, officially supposed to be studying the environment but in fact acting as fifth column, had actually surveyed the route before hostilities had broken out and a system of airborne supply points had been worked out. It was estimated that this would take a fortnight and by the time that Narvik fell, the German relief force had got almost half way, a considerable achievement.

While Dietl's men, short of food and ammunition, were in no position to counter-attack on land the Germans were able to step up the scale of air attack. On 29 May the Luftwaffe launched redoubled attacks on shipping and on 2 June successive groups of bombers escorted by ME110 twin engine fighter bombers, carrying extra fuel tanks, raided Harstad and the Skaanland naval base. Narvik was also heavily bombed and most of the centre, what is the today the business quarter, was destroyed by high explosive and incendiary bombs. The RAF's primary task was to defend shipping at Harstad and Skaanland. There were simply not enough fighters to patrol Narvik as well. In the course of several days fighters from Bardufoss fought twenty-four actions and shot down nine enemy aircraft.

On the Narvik front, General Dietl was genuinely surprised that the Allies did not seem to be pressing their advantage, which would have meant pushing his forces over the Swedish border into at least temporary internment. Supported by fire from destroyers, the Foreign Legion pursued the Germans along the Rombaksfjord. The Germans, retreating along the railway line, demolished the tunnels as they went. The Poles, driving the Germans north-east towards the railway line, met up with the French on 2 June.

The Germans held three mountain strong points: the Rundfjell which adjoins the Swedish frontier to the north, the Bjornfjell where the railway crosses the Swedish border and the Haugfjell which lies to the west of the Rundfjell and the Bjornfjell. The Norwegian position on the Kuberg plateau was separated from the Germans by a chain of lakes and morasses which the thaw had made into a formidable obstacle. Three Norwegian battalions were preparing for a direct attack on the Rundfjell. Once this had been accomplished, the plan was to attack across the lakes with, it was hoped, Allied artillery support.

While pushing forward on the north flank, the Norwegians had taken over most of the French line north of the Rombaksfjord and the final offensive was scheduled for 8 June. There was therefore some dismay on the part of the Norwegians when General Bethouart cancelled the encircling movement planned from the south. Understandably it was with considerable anger that the Norwegians learned on 1 June that the Allies intended to leave Norway altogether.

The position of Sir Cecil Dormer at Tromso was not an enviable one. Unable to come clean with the Norwegians as to British intentions he had to endure some harsh criticisms. President Carl Hambro said at one point that the Norwegians felt that they could no longer trust the British. On 1 June Lord Cork decided to put an end to the duplicity and instructed Sir Cecil to tell the Norwegians that the British were leaving. King Haakon, and the Crown Prince and the Norwegian government were at first reluctant to leave. This might have had a serious effect on the allegiance of the crews of about 1,000 Norwegian ships, especially the modern tankers, on hire to the British. In the end the king and the crown prince together with most of the members of the government, while maintaining that they were the only legitimate Norwegian government, agreed to go into exile in Britain.

It was decided that General Fleischer should go with the government in order to command such free Norwegian forces as could be got away. General Ruge, on the other hand characteristically said that he could not abandon his men twice. He elected to stay behind and to go into a German prison camp. Fortunately he lived to enjoy a hero's welcome on his return in 1945. The time gained before the Germans found out what was going on enabled General Ruge to organize an orderly withdrawal and the Norwegian forces were able to demobilize in the back areas. Thus most of them avoided deportation to Germany. A preliminary armistice came into effect at midnight on 9/10 June.

The crucial problem for the Admiralty and the organizers of the evacuation was naval escort. Lord Cork had asked for fifteen destroyers. In the event only eleven were forthcoming. This was due to the heavy losses of destroyers at Dunkirk and the continuing evacuation of France. In point of fact the naval forces at Cork's disposal were:

1. The aircraft carrier *Ark Royal* with a three destroyer escort.
2. The aircraft carrier *Glorious* with a two destroyer escort.
3. This left six destroyers which were required for the actual embarkation.

Early on a few store ships were directed to Tromso to load stores and diplomatic and other personnel. This sailed with an escort of armed trawlers, providing protection against submarines only. Of great importance was the cruiser HMS *Devonshire* which took off King Haakon, the Crown Prince, the government and the Norwegian gold reserves. She sailed alone far out into the Norwegian Sea before heading south.

A slow convoy consisting of eight merchantmen with an escort of one destroyer, one sloop and ten armed trawlers was the first to sail. Fortunately the Germans remained ignorant of what was going on, for as we have seen, armed trawlers remained vulnerable to air attack. A second slow convoy was despatched on 7 June. Fifteen troopships consisting of pre-war liners and ferries were sent to two rendezvous, about 180 miles from the Norwegian coast. There they passed under command of Rear Admiral Vivian on his flagship the cruiser *Coventry*. From the rendezvous, the troopships came in two at a time, with submarine protection, to the sheltered waters of the Vaagsfjord. The troops and equipment were then ferried aboard by destroyers and puffers which collected the men from various quays up and down the shore. Although there is no real darkness at that time of the year, as much embarkation as possible was carried out at night.

The priorities were: men first, light AA guns plus ammunition second, then 25-pdr field guns. The heavy AA guns kept firing to the last if intrusive enemy aircraft appeared. This meant that a number of heavy AA guns had to be immobilized by damaging the breech blocks and abandoned. Huge quantities of stores had to be destroyed and all transport was lost. The Irish Guards drivers, with tears in their eyes were ordered to drive their immaculate vehicles into the fjord.

The troopships sailed in two convoys:

Group 1 consisted of six liners, the *Monarch of Bermuda*, the *Batory* and the *Sobieski*, both Polish ships together with the *Franconia*, the *Lancastria* and the *Georgia*. These left the rendezvous with 15,000 men on 7 June.

Group 2 consisted of four large and three small merchantmen which embarked about 10,000 men on 7 and 8 June. The second convoy finally left the rendezvous on 9 June escorted by the cruisers *Southampton* and *Coventry* and five destroyers. The second convoy also had the protection of the *Ark Royal* with her patrolling aircraft and screen of three destroyers. The *Southampton* was the last to leave with the troops of the rearguard, together with Lord Cork and Generals Auchinleck and Bethouart aboard.

As previously explained, owing to faulty torpedo firing mechanisms, Admiral Doenitz had withdrawn his submarines. It might have been a very different story if he had not. Protection from air attack was better than expected. The three days of evacuation were mercifully clouded and overcast. Nevertheless the aircraft based at Bardufoss were on almost continuous patrol. On 2 June, the aircraft carrier *Glorious* joined the *Ark Royal* and besides bombing some German shore installations, their Skua fighter aircraft helped to keep the Luftwaffe away.

Although Admiral Forbes at Scapa Flow made arrangements for an escort force to meet the returning convoys, to begin with their only escort was HMS *Vindictive*, an elderly cruiser. No destroyers could be spared as they were all needed to embark the remaining troops. If by any chance German surface ships of any size had fallen in with them it would have been rather like Sir Francis Drake intercepting a Spanish treasure fleet.

Chapter 28

Operation Juno

The Norwegian Sea, although a large area, is not as vast as a casual glance at the Mercator projection in most atlases would suggest. Thus the distance from the Norwegian coast to the coast of Greenland is about 1,000 miles, about as far as the distance from the North Cape to the southern tip of Norway. The distance from Norway to Iceland is only 700 miles, comparable to the length of Britain. German warships intending to break out into the north Atlantic shipping lanes had to cross the line: Orkneys, Shetlands, Faroes and Iceland, which was constantly patrolled by the Northern Patrol. After the battles of Narvik, German surface ships had not menaced Allied supply lanes and this may well have led to a degree of complacency in British naval circles. In fact the Germans were by no means defeated at sea and at the very point of the British evacuation of North Norway they were planning their final coup code named Operation Juno.

At the headquarters of the Kriegsmarine on the Tirpitz Embankment in Berlin, Grand Admiral Raeder, Chief of the Naval Staff, had worked out a strategy with Admiral Saalwachter of Group Command West based at Wilhelmshaven. Broadly speaking the plan was for a sortie of surface ships to attack transports and warships in the Harstad area. It was emphasised to Vice Admiral Günther Marschall, appointed to command the task force, that his main objective was to bring relief to General Dietl. It was added, almost as an afterthought, that worthwhile targets at sea might also be attacked.

On 4 June Vice Admiral Marschall, flying his flag aboard the battleship *Gneisenau,* together with her sister ship *Scharnhorst* sailed from Kiel. They were accompanied by the heavy cruiser *Admiral Hipper,* barely repaired from the damage inflicted by HMS *Glowworm,* together with four destroyers. On the night of 6/7 June they made rendezvous about 500 miles west of Tromso, well to the north of Harstad, with the tanker *Dithmarschen* which enabled the destroyer escort to refuel.

On 5 June Sir Charles Forbes, commanding the Home Fleet at Scapa Flow had received a report from the Q-ship *Prunella,* an armed merchant vessel designed to lure submarines. She was in a position 200 miles north-east of the Faroes as part of the Northern Patrol. She reported two unidentified warships hull down which appeared to be heading for the Faroes/Iceland gap. It might possibly have been two of Marschall's ships, but if that were the case they would have had to turn north fairly soon because they would have had 500 miles to go to reach the rendezvous.

Neither British naval intelligence nor Coastal Command had any idea that a German force was at sea. Nevertheless Admiral Forbes proceeded to make the same sort of mistake that he had made two months before when he left the entrance to Narvikfjord uncovered. Despite the fact that his resources were stretched to the limit by the almost simultaneous evacuation from Dunkirk, he sent the battleship *Renown* and the battle cruiser *Repulse* together with two cruisers and five destroyers off to the Faroes/Iceland gap under the command of Admiral Whitworth. If there was one general principle that became established later in the war it was that if you want to intercept either surface ships or U-boats, the place to look for them is where your own convoys are. It was futile to think that if you despatch a strong force to an area where you believe the enemy to be, you may strike lucky and find them.

All that Forbes had left himself with at Scapa Flow was his own flagship the *Rodney* and one other battleship the *Valiant*. Group 1 of the homebound convoy had already sailed on 7 June. The best that Forbes could do was to sail to meet them. He weighed anchor just after midnight on 8 June which meant that Group 1 had been without an adequate escort against surface ships for the first leg of the homebound passage. He remained with Group 1 until just past the Faroe Islands, then on the evening of 10 June he turned back to meet Group 2.

Admiral Marschall intended to attack shipping in the Harstad area on 9 June but first he had to complete refuelling his destroyers and more importantly he wanted to evaluate the intelligence available. At 20.00 on 7 June he called a conference on his flagship, the *Gneisenau*, a somewhat novel event at a remote and desolate spot far out in the Norwegian Sea. Earlier in the day there had been reports of two groups of Allied ships, one of which was a convoy of seven ships, all on a westerly course. Marschall and his staff had concluded that they were empties. The main hard evidence came in from two U-boats on about the same latitude as Harstad. They reported three groups, one included two aircraft carriers while two cruisers and destroyers were escorting two large steamships; all of them were heading west.

Present at the conference were two rear admirals in addition to Marschall and the two captains commanding the battleships. One of the popular misconceptions about the Germans in those days was that German society and the armed forces in particular were hidebound by rigidity and excessive deference to rank. This is belied by the fact that it was the youngest officer in the room Lieutenant Kohler who piped up with a question, 'Could it be that the British are pulling out?'

About 22.30 Marschall was handed a wireless flash; a reconnaissance aircraft had reached Harstad, but only a gunboat had fired on it. Where was the rest of the British fleet? As Marschall noted in his diary: 'the unusually strong security force leads me to suppose that the surprising westward movement may mean that the British are evacuating Norway. Several signals were exchanged with Navy Group West, but it was still insisted that Marschall should attack Harstad. Marschall decided to disregard Navy Group West's orders. Fanning out into a wide spaced screen and steering a south-easterly course the Germans came down like a wolf on the fold.'

Shortly before 06.00 on 8 June the first victims were the British trawler *Juniper* and the empty Norwegian tanker *Oil Pioneer* which had been sent on ahead. The *Gneisenau*'s medium calibre guns set the oil tanker ablaze and a torpedo from a destroyer finished her off. The Germans were adept at jamming British radios and neither vessel succeeded in sending out a successful call for help. Twenty-five men from the tanker and only four from the trawler were picked up. Scouting planes from the *Scharnhorst* sighted HMS *Orama* and the *Atlantis* to the north and the *Admiral Hipper* was sent to intercept them. The hospital ship *Atlantis* was allowed to proceed on her way unmolested provided that she sent out no wireless signal. In her company was the empty troopship *Orama* which, being surplus to requirements, had been sent on ahead. Several salvoes from the *Admiral Hipper* sent her to the bottom, but not before 274 men had been picked up, including some German prisoners.

Aboard the *Scharnhorst* was a section of the B Dienst, the German code breaking service. They reported radio intercepts from two aircraft carriers, the *Ark Royal* and the *Glorious* to the north. Having spent several fruitless hours more on a course to intercept the convoys Marschall turned north to where he knew the aircraft carriers to be. At the same time he detached the *Admiral Hipper* and the destroyer escort towards Trondheim as shortage of fuel would not have enabled them to continue north for long. At 15.45 a midshipman in the crow's nest of the *Gneisenau* thought that he saw a thin line of smoke on the starboard bow; a powerful lens on a range finder confirmed a mast. The German battleships turned 70 degrees to the east and soon the *Scharnhorst*'s chief gunnery officer reported: 'Thick funnel and mast with turret, probably also flight deck'. In fact it was the 22,500 ton aircraft carrier *Glorious* commanded by Captain Guy D'Oyly-Hughes accompanied by two destroyers, the *Acastar*, commanded by Commander Glasfurd, and the *Ardent*, commanded by Lieutenant Commander Barker.

The RAF personnel at Bardufoss had been some of the last Allied units to leave. Early on the morning of 8 June eight Hurricanes and ten Gladiators had landed on the flight deck of the *Glorious* successfully. There had been some reluctance to allow them to even try, especially as none of the RAF aircraft had hooks with which to engage the arrester wires on the deck. Nevertheless they made it without mishap, their pilots absolutely dead beat.

There has been much discussion subsequently as to why Lord Cork had allowed the *Glorious* to go on ahead of the main convoy. One reason was that she was short of fuel and indeed when spotted by the enemy she was steaming at 17 knots on only twelve out of her eighteen boilers. The captain of the *Glorious* has also come in for criticism. Although he could fly he was a submarine expert with little previous experience on aircraft carriers. Also, although generally popular with the men, his ship was not a happy one. As one of his Fleet Air Arm officers described him: 'DH was a very vain man and would not admit his ignorance on air matters, he tried to enforce his views by bullying and bluster.'

The historian Correlli Barnett expresses another view, 'His dangerously unrealistic orders for air operations earlier in the Norway campaign had brought him into conflict with Commander Heath RN. Hughes had put the latter ashore at Scapa to await a court martial and it is thought that Hughes had persuaded Lord Cork to let him take the carrier on ahead to pursue the charge against Heath.'

At 1615 the *Glorious* sighted the enemy and increased her speed. In theory she could have outrun the battleships. Not a single aircraft on the *Glorious* was fully armed and ready for take-off. There were aircraft on the hanger deck and these were at ten minutes notice to fly. It was necessary therefore to lift them up to the flight deck. Part of the trouble was that the extra RAF planes were cluttering up the flight deck. Moreover in order for torpedo planes to take off it would have been necessary to turn the ship into the south-westerly wind which was the very direction from which the enemy were approaching.

The first salvo was fired from Anton and Bruno the triple 28cm (11-inch) guns of the forward gun turrets aboard the *Scharnhorst*. The opening range was enormous 26km (about 13 miles) nevertheless at 16.38 the *Scharnhorst* scored her first hit. In the course of the action the *Scharnhorst* fired a total of 212 rounds. At one point four of the Swordfish torpedo planes on the *Glorious* had been hoisted on to the flight deck, but before the aircraft carrier could turn into the wind a fire in the upper hanger prevented them from taking off. At 17.00 a salvo hit the bridge and Captain D'Oyly-Hughes was killed. The *Glorious* developed a list and the aircraft on the deck slid into the sea. A heavy shell then hit the deck aft and the order to abandon ship was given. She continued on an erratic course for twenty minutes then sank.

At the start of the action, the *Acasta* and the *Ardent* had immediately responded by putting down a smoke screen which impeded the German gunnery officers from observing the fall of the shot. Marschall later paid tribute to the daring and the skill of the two British destroyers. By constant changes of course and speed, by laying down smoke screens and then darting out of the smoke to fire their own torpedoes, the German ships were compelled to keep changing course. The *Ardent* fired two four-tube salvoes which forced the battleships to take avoiding action, but she herself was sunk shortly before the carrier.

At 17.30 the *Acasta*, although seriously damaged, broke the cover of the smoke screen and crossed the bows of the *Scharnhorst* from port to starboard (left to right). At a range of about 14km (13,000 yds), she turned and headed for the battleship. As she did, she fired a four-tube salvo of torpedoes. The *Scharnhorst* turned to starboard to comb the torpedoes and after some minutes it was deemed safe to turn back on her original course. Meanwhile the destroyer was speeding back and the *Scharnhorst* engaged her with her portside guns. Nine minutes later the *Scharnhorst* suffered a violent blow on her starboard quarter – the side opposite to that on which she was engaging the *Acasta*. A torpedo had torn a hole 12 x 4 metres wide just below the after triple gun turret. Within seconds sea water flooded the compartment below and 48 crewmen were killed. It took more than one torpedo to sink a German battleship because of the watertight bulkheads.

The *Acasta* sank shortly afterwards and only one crewman survived, Leading Seaman Carter. A shortened version of his account of what happened reads as follows:

'We were stealing away from the enemy making smoke...the captain then passed a message to all positions. "You may think that we are running away from the enemy. We are not. Our chummy ship [*Ardent*] has been sunk, the *Glorious* is sinking, the least we can do is to make a show." We then came out of the smoke screen, altered course to starboard firing our torpedoes from the port side. I fired my torpedoes from my tubes aft, the forward tubes fired theirs. I'll never forget the cheer that went up. On the port side a yellow flash and a great column of smoke and water shot up from the enemy ship. We went back into our smokescreen and altered course, but this time when we poked our nose out, the enemy let us have it. At last the captain gave orders to abandon ship... I will always remember the Surgeon Lieutenant Stammers. Before I jumped over the side I saw him still attending the wounded, a hopeless task. When I was in the water I saw the captain leaning over the bridge, take a cigarette from a case and light it. We shouted to come on our raft. He waived and shouted, "Goodbye and good luck".'

Admiral Marschall did not know at the time whether any British signals had been successfully transmitted. On the *Scharnhorst* one of the engines had been damaged and her speed was down to 20 knots. His first duty therefore was to get his damaged ship back to the nearest safe port at Trondheim. Marschall could not afford to delay and therefore did not stop to pick up survivors. The first that the British even knew that the German battleships were at sea was at 09.00 the following morning [9 June], when the warship *Valiant* met the *Atlantis*. The *Valiant* was on her way north to meet the last convoy. An hour later her signal relaying the hospital ship's account was confirmed by the cruiser *Devonshire*. Admiral Cunningham on his way back from Tromso on the *Devonshire* had received a garbled message from the *Glorious* mentioning two pocket battleships. At the time he had been only 100 miles to the west, which is about three hours steaming time from the *Glorious*. In view of the political importance of his passengers, the King of Norway and the government he decided not to break radio silence.

The first the Admiralty knew of the disaster was a broadcast emanating from HQ German Armed Forces naming the *Scharnhorst* and the *Gneisenau* and telling the world of their successes. The loss of life was horrendous: 1,515 men, the greater part being drowned. On the Arctic convoys it used to be reckoned that a man only lasted about five minutes in the icy water. In the Channel in summer men may last several hours before hypothermia sets in. The chill penetrates the marrow of the bones and numbs the brain. Many men succeeded in clambering aboard the Carley life floats but soaked, they then had to endure three Arctic nights without food, water or shelter.

The irony is that a British cruiser passed within five miles of the scene of the battle but did not see anything. Likewise two RAF planes passed overhead in ignorance of the tragedy below. Not until 03.00 on the morning of 11 June did a Norwegian cargo vessel, the *Borgund* pick up three officers and thirty-five ratings from the *Glorious*. These included Leading Seaman Carter from the destroyer. The survivors were landed in the Faroes. All the RAF pilots who had fought so gallantly and would have been invaluable in the Battle of Britain a few months later, were lost. Another Norwegian vessel picked up five men from the *Glorious* and landed them in Norway. They were the only five survivors out of 39 men who had climbed aboard the same life raft two days earlier. Finally, two men were picked up by a German seaplane.

Admiral Forbes at Scapa Flow took action as soon as he heard that the German battleships were at sea, although he did not then know about the *Glorious*. The *Valiant* put on speed to the north. The *Repulse* with two cruisers and three destroyers was ordered to join the convoys south east of Iceland. Forbes with the *Rodney* and *Renown* and two destroyers left Scapa at midday on 9 June when the serious menace was past. One empty transport which went to Harstad by mistake and two smaller Norwegian ships were sunk by enemy aircraft. Otherwise all ships made it back to Scotland.

On 10 June the *Gneisenau* and the *Admiral Hipper* once more put to sea but by this time the birds had flown and the next morning Marschall returned to Trondheim. On returning to the Fatherland, Marschall received little thanks from Grand Admiral Raeder, who took the view that by acting on his own initiative rather than obeying his orders to the letter, he had missed the main convoys. He was relieved of his command which may have saved his life because the next fleet commander, Admiral Lütjens, went down on the *Bismarck* the following year.

The RAF carried out two attacks on Trondheim. On 11 June twelve RAF aircraft attacked shipping in the anchorage but no hits were effective. On 13 June fifteen Skuas left the *Ark Royal* and a 500lb bomb hit the *Scharnhorst* but failed to explode. Eight Skuas were lost with nothing to show for it. More successful was the submarine *Clyde* on patrol which put a torpedo into the *Gneisenau* as she left Trondheim ten days later. Thus while the Germans must be credited with a very considerable naval victory, both the battleships *Scharnhorst* and *Gneisenau* were put in dock for repairs and effectively out of action for the rest of the critical summer of 1940. The real heroes were the two destroyer captains of the *Ardent* and the *Acasta* whose self-sacrifice probably saved the vulnerable convoys on their way back to Britain.

Chapter 29

A Leader to Match a Leader

General Carton de Wiart said in retrospect that the Norwegian campaign had been one for which the textbook does not provide. The expedition was not unique except in so far as British troops had never before campaigned above the Arctic Circle. It was not a dress rehearsal for the German offensive in France. It was part of Hitler's offensive in the west in which the Germans took the initiative and which they never lost. All the Allies could do was to react one step behind at each stage.

For the British reader the campaign makes more encouraging reading if it is regarded as a naval rather than a military campaign. Whereas only a few British brigades were involved in the fighting on land, half the Home Fleet was in involved in the fighting at sea. At the same time there were disturbing features. All three Victoria Crosses awarded for the campaign went to naval officers demonstrating that the fighting spirit of the Royal Navy remained as England would expect. On the other hand shortcomings in naval intelligence and planning became apparent and the senior sailors, worthy and competent though they undoubtedly were, perhaps lacked the Nelson touch.

Historians should never leave out of their assessment the interventions of Dame Fortune. It was an incredible stroke of luck for the British that there was something wrong with the percussion mechanism on the latest German torpedoes which reduced the U-boat to temporary impotence. In the open sea a warship could take evasive action if it spotted torpedoes in time, by combing the salvo. In the narrow confines of the fjords a warship, especially a large one like the *Warspite*, had neither the room nor the speed to manoeuvre.

It was an amazing stroke of good fortune for the Germans that their fleet evaded the units of the Royal Navy on the first day of the invasion. Not only were Stavanger and Bergen occupied almost without firing a shot, but also the German squadron which took Narvik found the entry to the fjord empty while a substantial squadron of the Home Fleet was out in the Norwegian Sea chasing shadows. In point of fact the Narvik part of the German plan was foolhardy from the start and the Germans paid the price several days later. Dame Fortune can nevertheless at times be even-handed. Who could have predicted that an isolated battery commander at the entrance to Oslofjord would sink one of Germany's brand new heavy cruisers on the first morning of the invasion?

From a strategic point of view the loss of almost half of their destroyers, the loss of three cruisers and serious damage to Germany's only two operational battleships had a greater proportional effect on the German navy than losses caused to British ships. Some other Allied warships were lost. Churchill argued that German naval losses amounted to a victory, but then he even managed to turn Dunkirk into some sort of a triumph. As the table in the Appendix shows, naval losses on both sides were about even. The point is that Napoleon's dictum, 'God is on the side of the big battalions', applied. Thus the loss of ten destroyers to a navy with only twenty-two represents a far higher percentage than the loss of ten destroyers to a navy with ninety. Whether the German navy, had it remained intact, could have altered the outcome of the evacuation of Dunkirk must remain a matter for conjecture.

The besetting sin of the British has always been complacency. The irrational belief in the invincibility of the Royal Navy continued until the Japanese proved to the contrary. The assumption that the Germans could not land a force on the western seaboard of Norway in the face of the Home Fleet on station at Scapa Flow turned out to be all too fallacious. The most important new factor was the impact of air power which was the beginning of a revolution in naval warfare not then fully grasped by the naval establishment.

Conventional thinking before the war held that deck armour would be thick enough to withstand bombs and that anti-aircraft guns could take care of aircraft. In 1940 armour on battleships was thick enough, although when the battleship *Resolution* was most needed to cover the evacuation of North Norway she had been sent home with a bomb hole through three decks. Incidentally in 1944 Bomber Command sank the *Tirpitz* with 10-ton bombs which no ship's armour could have withstood. In 1940 cruisers and destroyers did not enjoy thick enough decks to withstand direct hits from even medium-sized bombs.

One of the most disastrous decisions taken in 1918 had been the transfer of the main responsibility for an air arm from the infant Royal Naval Air Service to the newly created Royal Air Force, although the fleet got its air arm back later. The Fleet Air Arm in 1939 did not have a modern fighter and the single engine Skua dive bomber was not very effective against land targets. In Norway most land targets were almost out of reach of bombers stationed in Scotland. Support from aircraft carriers, so effective later in North Africa and Sicily, had not yet been developed. Britain started the war with only four aircraft carriers and one of these – HMS *Courageous* – had been sunk by a U-boat in 1939.

The effect of German bombers based at airfields in Denmark effectively closed the Skagerrak to the Royal Navy, thus giving the Germans an uninterrupted line of supply from North German ports into Oslofjord. Once the Germans had established themselves in Southern Norway, the Admiralty was forced to withdraw surface ships from the Norwegian coast south of Bergen. The same thing happened after the withdrawal from Central Norway although this simplified the Navy's problems to some extent. The fjords and inland waterways of the Leads were largely out of bounds to British submarines in Southern and Central Norway. British submarines continued to have some success along the coast, for example the *Clyde* seriously damaged the *Gneisenau* off Trondheim in June 1940.

Only when fighter bases were established in Northern Norway was some measure of protection afforded to ships off Harstad and other anchorages. The Stuka dive bomber proved deadly to all ships, but in turn became particularly vulnerable to British fighters later, especially in the Western Desert when Britain reached parity in the air. The main ports for supply of ground forces in Norway, Aandalsnes and Namsos had both been flattened in a couple of days. The problem of providing air cover for supply ships and naval escorts in the North Norwegian theatre was one of the main factors influencing the British government's decision to withdraw from Northern Norway.

It was widely considered that the impact of bombing fighting troops was not so effective. In Norway, and later in the Western Desert, it was found that regular units in well dug in positions could not be dislodged by bombardment from the air alone. This is not to belittle the devastating psychological effect that bombing has on those experiencing bombardment for the first time, especially the territorial units. In Central Norway, damage caused to supply vehicles, roads, trains, and the railway lines and junctions created havoc. The uninterrupted reconnaissance of Allied positions throughout almost twenty hours of daylight put the German ground forces at a huge advantage.

One innovation for which the Germans must be given credit was the use, for the first time, of large-scale air transport. To begin with Oslo surrendered to just six companies of paratroopers. It was the supply and build-up of the Trondheim garrison before the troops advancing from the south arrived which was on a scale hitherto unprecedented. While the initial invasion from the sea had brought in some thousands of troops, over the next few weeks the slow and vulnerable Junkers 52 transport aircraft flew 3,000 sorties bringing in over 29,000 personnel, 259,000 gallons of fuel and 2,376 tons of supplies.

In the field of intelligence the Germans were miles ahead of the British. After the campaign was over, Sir Charles Forbes remarked, 'It is most galling that the enemy should know just where our ships are...whereas we learn where his are when they sink one or more of our ships.' As in so many other fields, the Germans had set out earlier and had been reading British naval signals since 1934. In 1940 there was still an imperfect exchange of intelligence, especially between the RAF and the Navy and when information was passed there were frequently unjustifiable delays. Bletchley Park was still in the development stage and the organization did not have the capacity to translate large quantities of information.

Correlli Barnett, the historian, quotes the example of wireless traffic analysis before Operation Juno. The volume of transmissions over the previous fortnight suggested that the Germans were planning some sort of offensive in the North Sea. On 29 May and 7 June the Naval Section of the Government Code and Cypher School at Bletchley Park repeated these indications to the Operational Intelligence Centre, but the latter failed to pass on the warnings to the Home Fleet. In view of what happened to the aircraft carrier *Glorious* at the hands of the *Scharnhorst* and the *Gneisenau*, why did not Forbes and the Admiralty insist that they should be kept informed as to the whereabouts of those two killers at all times?

The most glaring shortcomings on the Allied side were to be found in the ground forces. The French Army was very properly, largely required in France. The courageous Polish Army had been left to its fate in 1939. The small Norwegian Army was under-funded, under-armed, under-manned, and ill-prepared. The British Army in 1939/1940 was suffering from having been the Cinderella among the armed forces. If Britain had been almost bankrupted by the First World War and had barely recovered from the slump in the 1930s, then one is entitled to ask why did the Germans who had suffered even more, from an economic point of view, manage to rearm so successfully?

In essence the Army was too small to meet its commitments in France and mount a credible expedition to Norway. There was an overall shortage of artillery. The British had an excellent field gun, the ubiquitous 25-pounder, but few batteries could be spared for Norway. Tanks were not much of a factor in Norway, but where they were used by the Germans, the Boys anti-tank rifle proved almost useless, and there were hardly any anti-tank guns available. No British general would have sent an infantry brigade into action without adequate artillery support by choice, but there were few artillery batteries available. Mortar batteries were in scarce supply, partly owing to the German success in torpedoing supply ships or partly the result of the muddle on the original embarkation. Thus all the Germans had to do, as they advanced up the Gudbrandsdal, was to sight their artillery just out of range of effective small arms fire and pulverize the British positions with impunity.

The German infantry was significantly better armed than the British. Each section was armed with several light machine guns as well as sub machine-guns. Thus a German platoon could bring to bear a greater weight of automatic fire than the British, which proved particularly effective in the thickly wooded Norwegian valleys.

There were also deficiencies in other fields, British units were sometimes over laden with clothing, but there was not enough transport to carry the baggage. Most infantry units had been reasonably well equipped with mortars, ammunition and signals equipment when formed up at the assembly points in the UK. What then took place was an unholy muddle. Units were loaded onto one ship and their equipment onto another. In several instances equipment which had been carefully checked aboard by the quartermasters, was then unloaded or transhipped onto another vessel amidst appalling confusion. In one case a unit was put ashore in Central Norway and its equipment sent to North Norway.

The Germans made extensive arrangements to place agents in strategic positions before the invasion. Diplomatic staff all had their part to play. Considerable numbers of businessmen happened to be visiting the country at the time. Thus German forces knew exactly where Norwegian depots were situated and a number were overrun without firing a shot. Much was later made of the use of fifth column in the invasion of France, but it does not seem to have been much of a factor in Norway. It is possible that the sabotage of the railway between Dombaas and Aandalsnes, which derailed a troop train, was an act of sabotage. In the Harstad area a number of people hold that the departure of the *Chobry* with the Irish Guards aboard which was sunk before it reached Bodo was the result of intelligence passed to the Luftwaffe.

It seems quite extraordinary that the telephone lines from one region to another should have remained open. This was of some benefit to the British in Harstad as Norwegian telephone operators developed a coded way of warning of the approach of German bombers. It cut both ways, for the Germans found it useful to be able to tap British conversations and to make their own calls.

In the Twenties the Norwegians had extended the hand of friendship to Wienbarn, numbers of German speaking Austrian children who were starving in parts of the Austro-Hungarian Empire. German Intelligence was later able to recruit numbers of these Norwegian speaking Austrians for their own purposes.

Vidkun Quisling, who headed the puppet Norwegian government, had previously occupied much the same position in Norway as Oswald Mosley had in Britain. Quisling's view was that Bolshevism must be fought with all means available and some regiments of Norwegians were later raised to fight on the Russian front. Generally speaking the majority of Norwegians sympathised with the Western democracies, but once occupied by the Germans, sought to keep out of trouble. Nobody would have welcomed occupation by the heavy-handed Germans. Yet they did not particularly welcome occupation by the British either, especially since they knew that wherever British troops happened to be they would soon attract German bombers and the destruction of their homes. This is not to detract in any way from the courtesy and hospitality, and often self-sacrifice, shown by many Norwegians towards British troops.

British and Norwegian accounts of the campaign vary. General Ruge was dismayed when he saw the paucity and the quality of the troops and their equipment when the first British troops arrived in the Gudbrandsdal. That was hardly the fault of the men of the 149 Territorial Brigade. Meanwhile the Guards were sent to Narvik and were inactive for weeks. What about Chamberlain's statement, 'We are coming in massive force'? When General Paget told General Ruge that the British were pulling out, his immediate response had been, 'Why when you are not beaten?' Colonel Getz at Namsos was particularly bitter that General Carton de Wiart had not mounted a counter-attack with the Norwegian troops and the French Chasseurs Alpins, who had been placed under de Wiart's command but were not used at all. Relations between the Allies and General Fleischer in the North had got off to a poor start. General Mackesy had not immediately worked out a joint strategy with the Norwegians for recapturing Narvik, nor were the Scots Guards immediately placed at General Fleischer's disposal. All that changed when General Bethouart arrived and made immediate contact with the Norwegians.

A glaring flaw in the British system was the lack of a combined operations command. This was particularly noticeable at the embarkation point. The Navy certainly carried out its task of conveying the expeditionary force to and from Norway with skill and dedication, but as the rank and file in the army used to say, 'You can't send half a ship to sea'. You can send half a battalion minus half its equipment into action. The Admiralty must bear the blame for suddenly ordering the cruisers, on which the bulk of the first wave of troops had been loaded, to unload without ceremony their men and equipment which had been so carefully stowed and then to put to sea in pursuit of, as it turned out, a will o' the wisp.

German planning was carried out efficiently and secretly by Captain Kranke [later Admiral] and his staff. Even they were not above an element of inter-service rivalry, such as that between Hermann Goering and Admiral Raeder. Goering was also sensitive about placing units of the German Air Force under army control. In short neither side had developed a fully independent joint service command.

The British were not particularly slow to respond once the Germans had shown their hand, but before that they had been dilatory and had switched from one plan to another. General Paget subsequently pointed out that to begin with there had been no proper appreciation of the information that was available, for example a preliminary reconnaissance would have shown that three infantry brigades could not have been adequately supplied through the port of Aandalsnes, let alone several divisions. Even more lamentable was the failure to acquire new information. The British had no military attaché in Oslo and no intelligence network. The Germans had been collecting information for years.

Even the Royal Navy was not blameless in this respect. More forethought could have been given to Trondheim and Narvik. The latter port had been under consideration for some months.

An assessment of the commanders in the field produces the impression that they did what they could with the resources at their disposal. That phrase 'gross incompetence', so beloved of schoolbook historians does not seem to have applied to any of the commanders involved. General Mackesy came in for considerable criticism for having been right. He refused to throw away men on an assault from the sea on Narvik which might have turned into a second Gallipoli. Other commanders later successfully resisted Churchill's impatience, for example Monty, who refused over a period of three months to launch the El Alamain offensive until it was a near certainty that he would win.

General Paget went on to greater things in the war, but why one is tempted to ask did he not try to deploy a whole brigade in the Gudbrandsdal, instead of adopting holding operations with single battalions? The same could be said about General Auchinleck. When things went wrong as a result of the sinking of the *Chobry* and the *Effingham* running aground, why did he not refuse to move down to the Mosjean Mo area? Later Auchinleck did have the opportunity to demonstrate his ability when he effectively stopped Rommel in the desert.

General Carton de Wiart probably did the right thing by abandoning a near hopeless situation. No one would have accused the one-eyed VC of cowardice but maybe his reactions were getting a bit slow. General Ruge was a universally revered leader but he did not display any exceptional tactical skill on the battlefield. The toughest of the Norwegian commanders turned out to be General Fleischer, a suitable partner for the dashing French General Bethouart.

None of the German generals were tested by adversity except General Dietl. Some writers have suggested that he lacked fibre in abandoning Narvik to his junior officers. This is unfair, by withdrawing the bulk of his force to the Swedish border, he lived to fight another day. He later earned the soubriquet 'The Arctic Fox', one of the most successful German generals in the war against Russia in the far north.

Searching for scapegoats is always invidious. The ultimate blame for the Norwegian debacle must rest upon the organization at most levels, the staff officers, the higher command, above all the politicians – which includes Churchill. Turning to the higher command, the Chief of the Imperial Staff, Lord Ironside, was replaced after the collapse of France. That phrase 'the hardening of the arteries' may well have applied to Ironside, Carton de Wiart, Lord Cork, Lord Gort, Admiral Sir Roger Keyes and all the rest of them swept away by the hurricane in 1940. Perhaps twenty years of imbibing copious drafts of whisky at The United Service Club, known as the 'Senior' and reminiscing about their salad days in the First World War had taken its toll.

A fatal flaw revealed by the Norwegian campaign was the excessive power which the Chiefs of Staff exercised over the commanders in the field. As Professor Kingston Derry points out, there was much intervention by the Military Co-ordinating Committee and even by the War Cabinet with the detailed conduct of the operation. This arose from the fact that the Chiefs of Staff attended both the Co-Ordinating Committee and the War Cabinet meetings. Apart from imposing an almost impossible burden of meetings, the Chiefs of Staff were also in control of what was being done in the field. Bernard Ash records that the Ministerial Committee on Military Co-ordination held twenty-three meetings in the month following the invasion, and the Chiefs of Staff Committee met forty-three times in April. Churchill sent a note to Chamberlain pointing out that the Chiefs of Staff and their deputies together with the three Service Ministers and the Secretary, General Ismay, all had a voice in Norwegian affairs.

As far as interference in the conduct of the campaign is concerned, at the highest level both Winston Churchill and Adolf Hitler outshone all other practitioners. While most ministers used to spend their weekends in the country, for example Halifax generally went up to Yorkshire, Winston on the other hand rarely left his flat at the Admiralty. It was inevitable that the First Lord should spend many hours in the operations room in the company of his admirals and staff. Professor Derry quotes three examples of Admiralty interference within three days: first to modify directions by the cruiser squadrons on 8/9 April; second on 10 April when the First Sea Lord, Admiral Sir Dudley Pound, and Churchill cancelled the attack on Bergen [probably wisely]: third to allow Warburton-Lee to proceed with the destroyer attack on Narvik, without reference to Admiral Whitworth, the man on the spot. This proved to be a costly victory.

When one reads of the interminable Cabinet discussions that took place during the first winter of the war, first about Swedish iron ore, then about intervention in Finland, one gets the impression that Churchill did more than his fair share of the talking. It is true that he stuck to his thesis that we could and should mount an attack on Narvik. A single objective in the north was much more credible than a general invasion of Central Norway. Then he changed his mind and supported the Central Norway project, demonstrating that he was as capable of changing his mind at the last moment as anyone else. This only added to the general confusion and it might have been better if the Allies had stuck to one proposal or the other, but not both.

The Norwegian campaign revealed several flaws in Hitler's temperament. First he tended to lose his nerve when things went wrong and second, he sometimes changed his mind suddenly and unjustifiably. He was plunged into despair on hearing of the destruction of the German destroyers at Narvik and was only dissuaded from ordering Dietl to abandon the town and seek asylum in Sweden by his Chiefs of Staff on the grounds that Dietl had not actually been beaten. According to the historian Cajus Bekker, the Oberkommando der Wehrmacht, effectively Generals Keitel and Jodl together with Hitler, had taken it upon themselves and against Admiral Raeder's advice, to risk the destroyers in the first place. Admiral Raeder in Berlin was guilty of the same sin when he ordered Admiral Marschall to stick to the strategy of attacking vessels off Harstad when Marschall's instinct told him that the British were already pulling out and richer pickings were to be had out in the Norwegian Sea.

Germany gained considerable advantages from the successful occupation of Norway, not the least being the prestige acquired in the eyes of the neutrals like Italy. She acquired air bases within striking distance of Scotland and an extensive coastline giving access to the Atlantic. As a result the vital sea route to Russia later in the war became particularly perilous. On the other hand the occupation of Norway was not entirely to the advantage of the Germans. Norway became a sort of Achilles heel. Hitler was convinced that the Allies would mount their invasion of Europe through Norway. In consequence huge amounts of reichsmarks were expended on coastal defences. Even at the beginning of 1945 there were 350,000 Germans stationed in Norway who otherwise might have been used more profitably elsewhere.

What advantages did Britain get out of it? Let it never be forgotten that over a thousand ships on charter and some 25,000 loyal crewmen made a contribution of inestimable value to the British war effort.

The Norwegian population did not cause the occupying forces much trouble although there was an effective resistance movement. Unfortunately the traditional Prussian military code prescribed that hostages must be taken which led to inevitable reprisals. Nevertheless, as one Polish officer remarked bitterly to a Norwegian after the war 'the German army behaved like angels in your country'. As far as the resistance was concerned just two anecdotes are worth recounting. A Norwegian engineer working on the German heavy water project took his annual fortnight's leave and travelled over to Britain on the 'Shetlands Bus'. He was then able to draw a complete plan of the heavy water plant and was back at his desk on the succeeding Monday morning. The commandos subsequently blew up the plant. In 1944 Lieutenant John Perkins, commanding a motor torpedo boat, brought back three Norwegian spruce trees together with some secret agents. Two trees were flown to King Haakon in London, who insisted that one of them should be placed on display in Trafalgar Square, a tradition that has continued to this day.

Not all Germans thought that the Norwegian campaign had been worthwhile from a military point of view. General Warlimont expressed the view of a number of people on the staff when he wrote: 'If the Allies had been able to establish themselves in Norway, they would have been forced to relinquish their hold once the invasion of France started and it could have been accomplished by us much more cheaply after the campaign.' The leading German historian on the subject, Professor Walther Hubatsch, reached the same conclusion adding: 'Germany undoubtedly had the strength to force the Allies back out of Scandinavia.' He also noted that if the Allies had made the first move, they might have had to contend with the Soviet Union. The Russians coveted the idea of an Atlantic port and might have moved into Northern Norway.

Professor Kingston Derry, author of the excellent official report on the campaign, came to a particularly gloomy conclusion: 'given the political situation in 1939/1940, British intervention in some form was inevitable. Given the paucity of our then resources in men and arms, a more or less calamitous issue from it was likewise inevitable'. One cannot help feeling that these opinions were expressed in the context of the collapse of France. Handled differently, and with proper preparation, defeat in Central Norway might not have been quite so inevitable. The campaign in northern Norway remained credible right up to the moment when the Germans broke through the Allied line in northern France.

What then was significant about the expedition to Norway? It should be borne in mind that the original bone of contention, the supply of Swedish iron ore through the port of Narvik, tended to fade into the background once the Germans got their hands on the Lorraine ore fields, although the Swedish ore was vital, being of much higher quality. Despite the destruction of the harbour and railway at Narvik, the Germans were able to make their first winter shipment of iron ore through Narvik by the end of 1940. We should not conveniently forget that, despite the expression of noble sentiments by the British and the French about going to the aid of a little country, the defence of freedom and so on, both sides were contemplating just such an unprovoked attack throughout the winter of 1939/1940.

As far as Britain was concerned, Norway was the catalyst that brought about one of the most fortuitous changes in government that ever befell this country. It was the failure of the British campaign in Central Norway, a good five weeks before the collapse of France, that brought Churchill to power. It is recorded that in times of peril the Roman Senate used to appoint a dictator for the duration of the crisis. In May 1940 Parliament effectively surrendered its powers to a coalition government led by one stubborn old man who virtually established a dictatorship for the duration of the war. At last Britain had an autocrat to match a dictator, a buccaneer to match an adventurer, an orator to match a demagogue and a leader to match a leader.

Composition of the Commons
in the Thirties

In 1931 only forty-six Labour Members of Parliament were returned as compared with 287 in 1929. A number of heavyweights such as Herbert Morrison and Arthur Henderson lost their seats. Among the Labour leaders only Clement Attlee, Sir Stafford Cripps and the elderly and saintly party leader George Lansbury survived. A consequence of this was that when Lansbury gave up in 1935, Attlee secured the leadership. For a politician to say, 'Never use a word when none will do' is perhaps a bit unusual. Attlee had other qualities. Major Attlee's courage both physical and moral was never in doubt. Harold Macmillan once said about Attlee when he was deputy prime minister in the wartime coalition government that he considered him to be the most effective chairman that he had ever sat under.

By 1935 most of the principal actors in the drama of 1939/40 had been introduced and their differing personalities and background provide an insight into the character of the House. A number of Tory MPs would eventually succeed to peerages, for example one of Chamberlain's parliamentary private secretaries became the fourteenth Earl of Home (later Sir Alec Douglas Home, the Prime Minister).

Edward Wood, better known as Lord Halifax, was educated at Eton and Christchurch College, Oxford where he took a first in Modern History. He had been elected to Parliament before the First World War in which he had served without distinction. He had held several junior ministerial posts and earned a reputation for ability and tact. Surprisingly he was appointed Viceroy of India in the late Twenties. He was deeply Christian, and there are few witty remarks attributed to him and even fewer amusing anecdotes. His very first ministerial post had been as parliamentary private secretary to the Colonial Secretary, none other than Winston Churchill in Lloyd George's post war coalition. The office of PPS is used either to encourage talent or to gag awkward critics. The choice had not been Churchill's and the latter had not even bothered to ask Wood to come and see him. After a fortnight Wood stormed into Churchill's office and demanded to be treated like a gentleman, whereupon Churchill simply smiled and offered him a drink. Ever after that Wood used to say that the way to deal with Churchill was to stand up to him.

The House was by no means the exclusive preserve of privilege. A modest salary for MPs had been introduced in 1913 but financial support either from private sources or trades union sponsorship was essential. John Simon was an example of a politician in the Asquith mould. Born with a first-class brain, he was passed up the ladder by scholarships. The son of a Congregational minister in Manchester, he was educated at Fettes, the Puritanical Scottish public school. At Wadham College, Oxford, the story goes that he agreed with his contemporary F.E. Smith that no political party could encompass two such brilliant minds so they tossed for it. Simon drew the Liberals and Smith the Tories. Both men eventually became Lord Chancellor.

Samuel Hoare represented the moneyed interest; he came from the rich banking family of Gurney Hoare and had been educated at Harrow and Oxford where he took a first in classics and history. His greatest triumph was getting the India Bill through Parliament. At the White Paper stage he answered some 1,500 questions and during the passage of the bill he had to endure a crossfire from Churchill on the one side and Labour, which thought that the bill did not go far enough, on the other.

Hoare's subsequent term of office as Foreign Secretary in Baldwin's government was not so happy. He struck a dubious deal with Pierre Laval, the French foreign minister in December 1935, effectively giving Mussolini a free hand in Abyssinia When the news broke, the level of hostile public opinion took the government by surprise and he was forced to resign. Nevertheless he was back in Chamberlain's cabinet as Home Secretary in 1937. As Lord Privy Seal in Chamberlain's war cabinet he was regarded as one of the big five along with Wood, Simon and Churchill.

The uncritical today tend to regard Neville Chamberlain as a weak man who landed Britain in the war ill prepared. Obstinate perhaps, but not weak, like Macdonald and Churchill and other natural leaders, he was strong-minded and had autocratic tendencies. The Chamberlains were Birmingham manufacturers and the massive engineering company Guest Keen & Nettlefolds was their family business. His father, the great Jo Chamberlain, had dominated Tory politics in Birmingham and should have become Tory Prime Minister had he not been ahead of his time in advocating protection. Neville's elder half-brother Austen had been groomed for stardom. Both brothers had been sent to Rugby School, but whereas Austen went on to Cambridge, Neville had been destined for the family business and served an engineering apprenticeship. Austen had been elected Tory leader of the House in 1921. Unfortunately he was too closely identified with Lloyd George's policy of Home Rule for Ireland and when the coalition government fell, Austen Chamberlain was passed over for Tory leader.

Neville Chamberlain had come to national politics late in life. In 1916 we find him at the age of forty, mayor of Birmingham, the city his father had transformed into a model of civic government. Entering Parliament in 1922, he became briefly Chancellor of the Exchequer in May 1923. In MacDonald's National government he again became Chancellor and continued in that office under Baldwin. He effectively became Baldwin's right-hand man until the latter gave up in May 1937 when he became Prime Minister.

Several luminaries outside the government in the Thirties were to play their part in the drama of 1940. Leo Amery always seemed to pop up at significant times in the life of Winston Churchill. The relationship between the two men always smacked of that between a senior boy and a bumptious junior. When Churchill was a junior boy at Harrow he had been dared to push another small boy into the swimming pool. On learning that his victim was an important figure in the classical sixth, he apologized profusely. He readily pointed out that stature was no bar to intelligence and quoted the example of his own father Lord Randolph Churchill then the *enfant terrible* of the Conservative Party in the House. For twenty years or so Churchill and Amery had sat on opposite sides of the House, Amery, the orthodox high Tory and Churchill, the dazzling young Liberal. In one of the debates on the India Bill Amery used some Latin tag. Churchill, not above a bit of rowdyism, bawled out 'translate'. Amery who was defending the bill, turned on Churchill and said it means 'if one can trip up Sam Hoare the government's bust'. The House collapsed with laughter.

Hore-Belisha was the minister responsible for the War Office in 1938/9. Churchill thought that he had shown considerable courage when he had introduced conscription in the spring of 1939. Blood and guts characters like Lord Gort, VC commanding British forces in France, looked down on him as a too-clever-by-half politician from Manchester. The fact that he was Jewish did not help. The Chief of the Imperial General Staff, General Ironside, recorded in his diary on 2 January 1940 that 'he, Belisha, is incapable of realizing the simplest problem. He does not read the papers sent him and has them read to him a few minutes before he enters the Cabinet'. On 6th January 1940 Belisha resigned and Oliver Stanley took over.

Kingsley Wood exactly falls into Shakespeare's classification of a man who achieved greatness. By ability, chance and some nimble footwork he came to play a crucial part in the drama of 1940. The son of a Wesleyan minister, he qualified as a solicitor and started his own practice in the City. He progressed from membership of the London County Council to MP. Like Chamberlain, with whom he forged a close personal friendship, he had a solid record of achievement as Postmaster General and Minister of Health. A quality he possessed in abundance was energy and one of Chamberlain's more fortuitous appointments was when he appointed him Secretary of State for Air in 1938, a post he held right up to May 1940 when Churchill made him Chancellor of the Exchequer.

Finally mention should be made of a key figure outside Parliament, General Ironside. Unlike Gort he had spent most of the First World War on the Staff. He had distinguished himself in the Boer War and thus by 1940 was one of the oldest generals serving. Standing 7ft, he had a formidable presence and was known as Tiny. He was one of the men whom Churchill cultivated and on a Chartwell weekend between the wars the two men had sat up drinking whisky until five in the morning. He was thought to be just the man to oversee plans for a Scandinavian expedition because, as one of the youngest generals in 1919, he had commanded the Allied expedition to Archangel and knew what winters in the far north were like.

Sources
The Blast of War 1939-45, H. MacMillan, MacMillan & Co, New York, 1967
Britain between the Wars 1918-40, C.L. Mowat, Methuen, London, 1955
The Holy Fox, Andrew Roberts, Weidenfelt & Nicholson, London, 1991
John Simon, *The Times* obituary, April 1955
Samuel Hoare, *The Times* obituary, May 1959
Life of Chamberlain, Keith Fieling, MacMillan, 1947
Leo Amery see Diaries, 1929-45, London, 1988
Hore-Belisha see Nicolson Diaries 1939-45, Ed. N Nicolson, London, 1967
The Ironside Diaries 1937-40, Ed. Macleod & Kelly Constable, 1962
Kingsley Wood, *The Times* obituary, October 1948

Appendix 2

Scandinavia, a Note on its Peoples and History

People tend to talk about the Scandinavians as if they were all one people. While sharing many of the same characteristics and facing many of the same problems, not the least being the winter, each country is different. To some extent this is geologically determined. The Scandinavian peninsula bears the scars of the last ice age. Sweden has hundreds of lakes, Norway fewer lakes but massive fjords in some cases running up to a hundred miles in from the open sea. The Swedish/Norwegian border runs along the central mountainous spine of central Scandinavia, but whereas Norway has a central mountainous region rising to 3,000ft in some places, the Swedish landscape is not dissimilar to the lowlands of Scotland.

The distance from Kristiansand at the southern tip of Norway to Narvik is about 900 miles and from Narvik to the North Cape a further 300 miles. At its widest point Oslo is 250 miles from Bergen. Sweden measures some 1,200 miles from north to south and covers an area about twice the size of Britain. Finland is not mountainous but to say that she is studded with lakes would be an understatement especially on the eastern Karelian side. The distance from north to south is about 900 miles and the distance from the Gulf of Bothnia to the Russian border is about 400 miles.

About a third of Norway and Finland lie above the Arctic Circle, but whereas Northern Sweden and Finland are sparsely inhabited by nomadic Lapps, some reindeer and moose, there are hardy Norwegian fishing villages all the way up to the North Cape. Most of Scandinavia is under snow for six months of the year. In the winter the days are short and the night temperature plummets. As Baedecker might have put it 'any state proposing to engage in armed conflict in those latitudes should only do so with troops trained and equipped for operating in snow. There is often a brilliant but short summer but the land of the midnight sun can be particularly disconcerting if you are being subjected to unopposed air raids'.

For much of the late Middle Ages Denmark was the dominant Scandinavian power holding sway over the ancient kingdom of Norway. This had far reaching consequences for Norwegian society. The Norwegian aristocracy, descended from Viking chieftains, came to be largely absorbed into the common people. Danish officials ruled from centres such as Bergen, the main Hanseatic port originally settled by German merchants. Thus there was much more social equality among Norwegians unlike their two more feudal neighbours. Partly as a consequence of so many small communities being cut off by the high walls of the fjords, Norway never became a great Scandinavian power.

In the seventeenth century the hegemony in Scandinavia passed from Denmark to the Vasa dynasty in Sweden. Gustavus Adolphus intervened with devastating effect in the Protestant cause in the Thirty Years War (1618-1648) and it was not until the late 1600s that the Great Elector of Brandenburg drove the Swedes back across the Baltic. Peter the Great finally defeated Charles XII at the beginning of the eighteenth century and Russia displaced Sweden as the dominant power in the eastern Baltic. The Tsars then assumed the title of Grand Dukes of Finland.

During the Napoleonic Wars, Denmark was absorbed into the continental system and remained an ally of France until 1814. Meanwhile the Swedish dynasty failed and Bernadotte, one of Napoleon's marshals was invited to ascend the Swedish throne. Bernadotte deftly managed to distance himself from his old master after Napoleon's defeat in Russia and, under pressure from the Allies, the King of Denmark was induced to renounce his sovereignty over Norway in favour of Sweden.

Despite Bernadotte's ambition to unite the peoples of the Scandinavian peninsula the trend in the nineteenth century was towards democracy and national self-determination. The Norwegians were able to assert their independence up to a point. In the early nineteenth century a representative assembly met at Eidsvoll and drew up a democratic constitution which remains the basis of the Norwegian constitution today. Partly as a result of pressure exerted by the Allies after 1815 the Norwegians settled for a personal union under the Swedish king while retaining their own democratic assembly. The union with Sweden was never an entirely happy one and in 1905 it was dissolved by mutual consent. The Norwegians then invited a Danish prince to ascend the throne and he assumed the ancient Norwegian name of King Haakon.

The history of the Finns is again different. The pagan Finns were first conquered by the Swedes in the twelfth century. Conversion to Christianity was initiated by Henry, bishop of Uppsala, who is believed to have been an Englishman and became the patron saint of Finland. Gustavus Adolphus introduced the Protestant faith and Finland was elevated into a Grand Duchy. Peter the Great wrested Finland from the Swedes although the matter was not finally settled until 1809 when Finland was ceded to the Russians.

The Emperor Alexander I granted the Finns a free constitution and she became a semi-autonomous state with the Tsar as Grand Duke. Nineteenth century politics in Finland was complicated by rivalry between the Swedish party, representative of large scale Swedish immigration, and the Finnish nationalist party which upheld the Finnish language. At the same time the Russians were pursuing a policy of 'Russification' although repression waxed and waned with the relative liberality of the Tsarist government of the day.

On 15 March 1917, the Tsar abdicated and Kerensky formed a provisional government pledged to carry on the war with Germany. Chaos on the Eastern Front led to the spontaneous upsurge of Workers Soviets all over the Russian Empire including Finland and the Baltic States. The Communist Party came to power in October 1917 and in December 1917 Lenin's government signed an armistice with Germany at Brest Litovsk. The provisional government had declared itself in favour of independence for the nationalities such as the Finns, but the Bolsheviks were only prepared to pay lip service to this undertaking.

In the summer of 1917 the Finnish Diet had met with a Social Democrat majority, and in December the Diet drew up a full-blooded declaration of independence. This was recognized by France and Sweden. Unfortunately there were at the time a number of garrisons of Russian troops in Finland who had not been paid. They organized themselves into bands of Red Guards who ransacked the country.

It was at this point that Baron Mannerheim, a Finnish cavalry general in the Tsarist army, created a small White Army, similar to that appearing in other parts of Russia. It proved insufficient for the task and only the intervention of 12,000 regular German troops under General Von der Goltz enabled Mannerheim to win a decisive victory in April 1918, capturing the ancient fortress of Vyborg. In 1919 Mannerheim organized a corps of 100,000 troops to maintain order, and in June 1919 the Finnish Diet declared a republic. A peace treaty with Russia was signed in October 1919. Thus Finland was conceived in war and, unlike the other Scandinavian countries, retained a credible army throughout the Twenties and Thirties.

Appendix 3

Relative Naval Strength

Hitler consistently complained that other nations were increasing the size of their navies but that under the terms of the treaty of Versailles, the size of the German navy was limited. Partly in order to avoid an arms race, Britain negotiated the Anglo-German Naval Agreement in June 1935. Under the terms of the agreement, the German navy was limited to 35 per cent of the British tonnage in battleships, cruisers and destroyers. The agreement lasted until Hitler invaded Czechoslovakia in the spring of 1939. Only in the case of submarines were the Germans permitted to build 45 per cent of the tonnage of the Royal Navy. The reason for this was that under the dominant thinking in the Thirties, British naval superiority rested on the number of battleships. Britain placed less emphasis on submarines than the Germans. For the latter warfare at sea could not be successfully conducted by surface ships in which she was numerically inferior, but submarines could attack the shipping supply routes upon which Britain and France depended.

Germany did not intend to remain inferior at sea forever. Under Plan Z promulgated in the autumn of 1938 the Germans planned to complete the following by 1948:

1. Six battleships of up to 50,000 tons in addition to the *Bismarck* and the *Tirpitz* which had already been laid down and would be the most modern and up to date in the world. Eight, later increased to twelve heavy cruisers of 20,000 tons.
2. Four aircraft carriers.
3. A large number of light cruisers and 233 U-boats. There were several varieties but Type VII of 500 tons came to be the dominating class, with four bow tubes and one stern tube. They had a surface speed of 16 knots but submerged could only do 7 knots. They had a range of 6,200 miles which meant that they could only remain at sea for about three weeks.

In accordance with Plan Z German naval planners were counting on several more years before embarking on a major war. As things stood in 1940, the

221

Scharnhorst and the *Gneisenau*, both 26,000 tons and each mounting nine 11-inch guns, were the only German battleships operational. The *Bismarck* and her sister ship the *Tirpitz*; both officially 35,000 tons, were each armed with eight 15-inch guns but not yet in commission.

The remaining capital ships were two *Panzerschiffe* or pocket battleships of 10,000 tons each armed with six 11-inch guns. They were specifically designed as long distance raiders. However the philosophy that they could either outrun any ship heavily enough armed to sink them, or outgun any ship fast enough to catch them, had been shown to be fallacious in December 1939 when the pocket battleship *Graf Spee* had been disabled by three British cruisers. The rest of the German navy consisted of two heavy cruisers of 10,000 tons, three light cruisers of 6,000 tons, plus twenty or so destroyers (about 1,800 tons) of various ages.

Ranged against them the Royal Navy could field seven battleships and battle cruisers, four aircraft carriers, fourteen cruisers and sixteen flotillas of destroyers (usually 4-6 vessels). In addition to the Home Fleet there were the ships of the Mediterranean fleet and various other squadrons dispersed over the globe. Only with regard to submarines (the star performers of the Kriegsmarine) was there approximate parity. In September 1939 Britain had fifty-eight submarines operational. Germany had fifty-seven.

In one respect the Germans had the advantage. In 1918 they had scuttled all their capital ships in Scapa Flow, the Home Fleet's main anchorage in the Orkney Islands. Thus all their capital ships were new. The *Gneisenau* had been completed in 1938 and the *Scharnhorst* in 1939. Several British battleships dated from the First World War, for instance that formidable old lady the *Warspite*, although extensively modernized, had been commissioned in 1915.

Before 1939, technological progress between the three main naval powers, Britain, Japan and the United States, and the smaller fleets of Germany, France and Italy, had proceeded on a leapfrogging basis. German submarine technology led the world, but the British were ahead in developing sonar anti-submarine detection equipment (ASDIC).

A major aim of German naval policy was to starve Britain of essential supplies by disrupting her supply lines. The strategy was to make lightning attacks on convoys but avoid loss of surface vessels by withdrawing from general engagements. The cardinal policy of the British was to keep the convoy routes to America open. One of the great virtues of Admiral Sir Dudley Pound, the First Sea Lord, was that, despite the impetuous nature of his political boss, he never lost sight of this priority. Later Churchill admitted that the only thing during the war that had really frightened him was the U-boat peril.

Towards the end of the war heavy capital ships were referred to as 'dinosaurs', but in 1940 they still dominated strategic thinking. Most admirals the world over still thought in terms of deploying battleships like the queen on a chess board. Indeed only surface ships were able to sink the *Bismarck* in the summer of 1941. It was only late in 1941 that the Japanese brought into play more advanced torpedoes launched from the air that the day of the battleship passed.

Sources

The Gathering Storm Vol .I The Second World War, W. Churchill, pub. Houghton Mifflin & Co, Boston, 1948.

Engage the Enemy more closely, Correlli Barnett, pub. Hodder & Stoughton, London, 1991

Appendix 4

The Norwegian Navy

From the start the gallant little Norwegian Navy was operating at a huge disadvantage. Most of the main ports were overrun by the Germans in the first day or two. The Norwegian Navy was operating with no air cover, but without a home port to return to. Early on the two operational coastal defence cruisers the *Eidsvoll* and the *Norge* were sunk at Narvik. Out of nine destroyers, two were undergoing refits in dock. The *Gyller* and the *Odin* were captured in Kristiansand, in the extreme south. The *Garm* and the *Troll* which were operating in Sognefjord were attacked from the air and so damaged that they had to be abandoned. The *Draug* escaped to a British port on 9 April while the *Sleipner* performed sterling service for the British when they landed at Aandalsnes. She was able to sail for Britain on 26 April.

Out of nine submarines, two had been built in 1929 and three in 1913. Several were captured in port and three scuttled by their own crew. The *A2* was depth charged on 9 April and disabled. The *B1* was sunk by its own crew on 12 April, but later refloated and sailed to Britain in May. The *B3* had the misfortune to be damaged by a battery explosion while en route for Britain and had to be scuttled.

The fate of the seventeen torpedo boats, some of them dating from before 1914 was similar. Several of them were involved in sharp action, for example the *Sael* (dating from 1901) was sunk in battle with German E-boats on 18 April. The *Trygg*, operating near Aandalsnes, was bombed and capsized on 25 April. It should be appreciated that minelayers, minesweepers and auxiliary vessels are not capable of operating far from port and despite the service that they were able to render to the British, most of them had to be scuttled or surrendered when the Allies left. The fishing and other civilian craft known as 'puffers' performed invaluable service to the Allies in various fjords and harbours.

Sources
The German Invasion of Norway. G. Haarr.

Appendix 5

Intelligence

Professor Hinsley's post-war official report noted that, 'There was no adequate machinery within the departments of Whitehall for confronting prevailing opinions and lazy assumptions'. Moreover in all three armed services intelligence work was regarded as a backwater into which the unambitious tended to be drawn. Traditionally the Foreign Office has dominated intelligence with reports from embassies and consulates all over the world coming in constantly as a matter of routine. Naval, Military and Air Attaches where they existed, were officially required to make their reports through the Foreign Office. In 1939 Britain did not even have a military attaché in Oslo. Norway and Finland were covered by the attaché in Stockholm.

In the spring of 1940 the volume and detail of material began to gather pace. Inadequacy in the collation and interpretation of these various reports was due to a number of factors. One was the tendency for different agencies to act independently. In many ways naval intelligence was the most comprehensive but even between various naval departments there was rivalry. Thus the Naval Intelligence Division (NID) processed secret intelligence and embassy reports and covered Germany. The Operational Intelligence Centre (OIC) did not receive the same comprehensive spread of material but was responsible for studying the movement of ships and aircraft.

Naval intelligence in 1939 had some way to go to emulate the success of Admiral 'Blinker' Hall's department in the First World War, although with the addition of a few fertile minds like Ian Fleming (of James Bond fame) and other factors it was to achieve unsurpassed glory later in the war. At the beginning of 1940 the Director of Naval Intelligence had not fully succeeded in co-ordinating NID and OIC or eliminating mutual jealousies.

A major source of intelligence was the interception of enemy radio traffic with which the Operational Intelligence Centre at the Admiralty was concerned. Massive strides were being made in monitoring enemy radio traffic, but did not come early enough in 1940 to make much difference to the Norway campaign. Between January and March 1940 the Government Code and Cypher School at Bletchley Park solved fifty Enigma settings in three series, Green, Blue and

Red. This was later done by machine. On 10 April traffic was first intercepted in a new key – Yellow, which had been specially introduced for the Norwegian campaign. It was fairly straightforward and was broken continuously from 15 April.

What took the British agencies by surprise was the sheer volume of cypher traffic which had never before been used tactically. Not only did they not have sufficient trained staff to handle the volume of material, but they did not have the time to collate it. They were swamped by code words. Incidentally the German Navy's 'B' Dienst (B Service) had started to intercept British naval signals as early as 1934. Thus whenever a code was changed it could fairly easily be ascribed to a particular ship or formation. Generally speaking, the Germans were able to read British naval signals throughout the Norwegian campaign. As Admiral Forbes later remarked ruefully, 'the Germans always seemed to know where our ships were, we had to rely largely on physical sightings from ships or aircraft'.

Sources
This section is largely based on *British Intelligence in the Second World War Vol. II* by F.H. Hinsley HMSO 1979/84
Other references:
FO 371/24815-N3602/2/63-N3603/2/63-FO 371/24381-C5895/5/18

Appendix 6

Losses

LOSSES OF WARSHIPS

German		Allied	
Cruiser	1	Aircraft carrier	1
Light cruisers	2	Cruiser	1
Destroyers	10	AA cruiser	1
Training ship	1	Destroyers (1 Polish, 1 French)	9
U-boat	6	Submarines (1 Polish, 1 French)	6
Torpedo boat	1	Sloops	1
		Armed Trawlers	11
		Norwegian vessels (see Appendix IV)	

LOSSES OF AIRCRAFT
(by crashes or enemy action)

German		Allied		
Transport (approx.)	80	Bomber command	27	(in Ist month)
Combat & A A fire	162	Lesjaskog	18	Gladiators
		Skaanland	3	Hurricanes
		Bardufos	8	Gladiators
		Bardufos	8	Hurricanes
		HMS *Glorious*	20	*Fighters
		Trondheim (13 June)	8	Skuas
Total	242	Total	92	

*Not including aircraft already on *Glorious*

LOSSES OF OFFICERS AND MEN

German		Allied	
Killed	1,317	British sailors and airmen	1,515
Wounded	1,604	British soldiers killed/wounded	1,869
		French and Polish soldiers	
		and sailors	530
Lost at sea or missing	1,695	Norwegian soldiers and sailors	1,335
Total	4,616	Total	5,249

Sources
The Campaign in Norway, T. K. Derry, HMSO, 1952
Hitler Strikes North, J. Greene and A. Massignani. Pen & Sword, 2013

N.B. The above figures are derived from sources believed to be correct, but more accurate figures may be available elsewhere.

Appendix 7

Notraship

By a provisional order in council on 22 April, the Norwegian Merchant Marine was brought under the control of the Royal Norwegian Government for the duration of the war. The Norwegian shipowners in London had already set up an organization under the auspices of the British Ministry of Defence called Nortraship (Norwegian Shipping and Trade Mission).

At the time of the German invasion the Norwegian Merchant Marine (ships above 500 tons gross) consisted of 1,172 ships totalling more than 4.4 million tons:

1. 252 vessels totalling almost 2 million tons were tankers.
2. The British Ministry of shipping had already chartered 1.8 million tons or almost 40 per cent of the entire Norwegian tonnage.
3. 160 tankers were already on charter to Britain.

Eventually Nortraship controlled over a thousand vessels grossing over four million tons of which 241 vessels were tankers. It was the largest shipping company in the world employing 25,000 sailors. Freights generated made the Norwegian government in exile completely independent. Only 13 per cent of ships over 500 tons remained under German control.

Sources
Article by Atle Thowsen in *Britain & Norway*, Ed. P. Salmon, HMSO, London

Bibliography

Chapter 1 Disarmament, Pacifism, Rearmament and Appeasement
Britain Between the Wars 1918 - 1940, C.L. Mowat, Methuen & Co Ltd, London, 1955
Britain 1895 - 1951, D. Murphy, G. Goodlad, R. Staton, Collins, London, 2008
The Sparks Fly Upwards, Col. G. Armstrong DSO MC, Gooday, 1991
The Downing Street Diaries 1935 - 1955, Sir John Colville, 1985
Diaries of Sir Alexander Cadogan, D. Dilks, Cassell, 1971
Life of Chamberlain, Keith Fieling, MacMillan, 1947
339 & 389 House of Commons Debates 5s.48.51 Hansard, HMSO
The Amery Diaries 1929 - 1945, L.S. Amery, London, 1983
The Blast of War 1939 - 45, H. MacMillan, 1967

Chapter 2 Churchill at the Admiralty
The Economic Blockade, Vol. 1 W.N. Medlicott, HMSO, 1957
The Second World War Vol. I The Gathering Storm, W.S. Churchill, Cassell, 1948
Grand Strategy Vol. II, J.R.M. Butler, HMSO, 1957
Engage the Enemy More Closely, Correlli Barnett, Hodder & Stoughton, 1991
The Campaign in Norway, T.K. Derry, HMSO, 1952

Chapter 3 Scandinavian Neutrality
Grand Strategy Vol. II Sept 1939/June 1941, J. Butler, HMSO
The Economic Blockade, N. Medlicott, HMSO
British Foreign Policy, Sir L. Woodward, HMSO, 1957
Oxford Companion to the Second World War, Ed. Dear & Ford, OUP, 1995
Insight Guides,
  Denmark, APA Publications, 2000
  Norway, APA Publications, 2003
  Sweden, APA Publications, 2003
  Finland, APA Publications, 2003
Britain & Norway, P. Salmon, HMSO, 1995

Chapter 4 The Winter War
Finland Insight Guides, APA Publications, 2003
Battles for Scandinavia, Ed. J. Elling, Time Life Books Inc, Chicago, 1981
The Gathering Storm, W.S. Churchill, Houghton Mifflin & Co, NY, 1948
British Foreign Policy Vol. I, Sir L Woodward, HMSO, 1957
Oxford Companion to the Second World War, Ed, Dear & Foot, OUP, 1995
The Blast of War, H. MacMillan, MacMillan, 1967

Chapter 5 The Allies Dither
The Campaign in Norway, T.K. Derry, HMSO, 1952
The Second World War Vol. 1, W.S. Churchill, Cassell, 1948
The Ironside Diaries 1937/40, F.M. Lord Ironside, Constable, 1962
Norway 1940, F. Kersaudy, Wm. Collins, 1987
Chiefs of Staff Report, W P (39) 179, HMSO, 1939

Chapter 6 Consequences of the Finnish Collapse
The Campaign in Norway, T.K. Derry, HMSO, 1952
Norway 1940, F. Kersaudy, Wm. Collins, 1987
The Blast of War, H. MacMillan, MacMillan, 1967
Hansard, 19 March 1940

Chapter 7 Weserubung
Die Seestrategie der Weltkrieges, Admiral W. Wegener, Pub. Miller, Berlin, 1929
Hitler m'a dit, H. Rauschning, Ed. France Paris, 1939
Hitler's Naval War, Cajus Bekker, MacDonald London, 1974
Norway 1940, F. Kersaudy, Wm. Collins London, 1987
Tagesbuch Jodl: The World as History, Ed. W Hubatsch, Stuttgart, 1952/54
The War at Sea Vol. I, Captain S. Roskill, HMSO, 1954
The German Northern Theatre of Operation 1940–45, E.F. Ziemke, US Army
The Campaign in Norway, T.K. Derry, HMSO, 1952
Problems of Norwegian Campaign, Prof. Dr W. Hubatsch, Journal of Royal United Service
    Int., 1958
The German Invasion of Norway, G.H. Haarr, Seaforth Publishing, 2011

Chapter 8 The Invasion Fleets
Hitler's Naval War (English translation), Cajus Bekker, MacDonald, London, 1974
The War at Sea 1939–45 Vol. I, Captain S.W. Roskill, HMSO, London, 1954
Engage the Enemy More Closely, Correlli Barnett, Hodder & Stoughton, 1991
The Campaign in Norway, T.K. Derry, HMSO, London, 1952
British Foreign Policy in the Second World War Vol.1, Sir L. Woodward, HMSO, London,
    1970
Narvik, Captain D. Macintyre, Evans Bros., London, 1959
Janes Fighting Ships

Chapter 9 Is it Christmas?
British Intelligence, Professor Hinsley, HMSO
Hitler's Naval War, Cajus Bekker, MacDonald, 1974
The Campaign in Norway, Professor K. Derry, HMSO, 1952
Norway 1940, F. Kersaudy, Collins, 1990
Norway Neutral and Invaded, H. Koht, MacMillan, N. York, 1943
Narvik, Captain D. Macintyre, Evans Bros. Ltd., 1959
The Mountains Wait, T. Broch, Michael Joseph Ltd, 1943

Chapter 10 The Rape of Denmark
The German Northern Theatre of Ops. 1940–45, E.F. Ziemke, Chief Military History Dept.
    of Army, USA
Denmark, Insight Guide 3rd Edition, Apa Publication, 2000
The Oxford Companion to the 2nd World War, Denmark, OUP, 1995

Chapter 11 The First and Second Battle of Narvik
Narvik, Captain D. Macintyre, Evans Bros Ltd., London, 1959
Hitler's Naval War, Cajus Bekker (English translation), MacDonald, London, 1959
Engage the Enemy More Closely, Correlli Barnett, Hodder & Stoughton, 1991
The War at Sea 1939–45 Vol. 1, Captain S. Roskill, HMSO, London, 1954

The Campaign in Norway, T.K. Derry, HMSO, 1952
Supplements to *London Gazette*
First and Second Battles for Narvik Despatches, Rear Admiral Halifax, 25 April 1940,
  HMSO
No. 38005 3 July 1947, HMSO

Chapter 12 The Royal Navy encounters the Luftwaffe
The Rise and Fall of the German Airforce 1939–45, Air Ministry, 1948
Encyclopaedia of World War II, J. Keegan, Bison Books, London, 1977
The Campaign in Norway, AHB /11/117/4 Air Historical Branch, Air Ministry p31-3
The Campaign in Norway, T.K. Derry, HMSO, 1952
Engage the Enemy More Closely, Correlli Barnett, Hodder & Stoughton, 1991
Narvik, Captain Macintyre, Whitefriars Press, 1959

Chapter 13 Submarine Warfare
Memoirs, Admiral Karl Doenitz (trans. Steven Woodward) , Cassell, 1990
Hitler's Naval War, C. Bekker, MacDonald, 1974
Narvik, Captain MacIntyre, Evans Bros. London, 1959
The War at Sea 1939–45, Captain S. Roskill, HMSO, London, 1954

Chapter 14 We are coming as quickly as possible
The Second World War Vol. 1, W.S .Churchill, Cassell, London, 1948
FO 971/24830, Telegram No. 205, HMSO, 12/4/40
CAB 65/12, WM 90 (40), HMSO, 12/4/40
WO 106/1812 Operations to Capture Narvik, DCIGS, HMSO, 11/4/40
The Norwegian Campaign 1940, J.L. Moulton, Eyre Spottiwoode, 1966
The Campaign in Norway, Professor K. Derry, HMSO, 1952
Norway 1940, F. Kersaudy, Wm. Collins, 1987
Norway 1940, Joseph Kynoch, Air Life Publishing, 2002
The Ironside Diaries 1937–1940, F.M. Lord Ironside, Constable, 1962

Chapter 15 The Norwegians Fight
Norway 1940, F. Kersaudy, Collins 1990
The German Northern Theatre of Operations, 1940–1945, E.F. Ziemke, Chief Military
  History Dept of Army, USA
Norway and the War 1939/40, Documents on International Affairs, edited by M. Curtis,
  OUP, 1941
The Norway Campaign 1940, J.L. Moulton, Eyre & Spottiswoode, 1966
I Saw It Happen – Norway, C.J. Hambro, Hodder & Stoughton, 1940

Chapter 16 General Ruge Takes Over
The Norwegian Campaign 1940, J.L. Moulton, Eyre Spottiwoode, 1966
Field Diary, Major General Otto Ruge, Aschentag, 1989
The Campaign in Norway, Professor T.K. Derry, HMSO, 1952
Norway 1940, Bernard Ash, Cassell, 1964
Valdres 1940, Major Andreus Hauge, Fornavsemuseet, 1984

Chapter 17 The Ill-fated 148 Brigade
The Campaign in Norway, Professor T.K. Derry, HMSO, 1952

History of the Sherwood Foresters 1919–1957, Brigadier E.G.C. Beckwith, Wm Clowes & Son, London, 1959
The Royal Leicestershire Regt., Brigadier W. Underhill, (Plymouth), 1958
The Doomed Expedition, Jack Adams, Lee Cooper, London, 1989
War Diaries A11200/5, Archivist Gen. Services, War Office
Norway, War Documents on Intl. Affairs, Ed. M. Curtis, OUP, London, 1941
Norway 1940, J. Kynoch, Air Life Publishing, 2002
Hitler Strikes North, J. Greene & A. Massignani, Pen & Sword 2013

Chapter 18 A Fighting Retreat through the Gudbrandsdal
The German Northern Theatre 1940/45, E.F. Ziemke, US Army
The Campaign in Norway, Professor K. Derry, HMSO, 1952
The York and Lancasters Regt., Major O. Sheffield, Gale & Polden, 1956
The Green Howards, Captain W. Synge, Richmond, 1952
The King's Own Yorkshire Light Infantry, Lt. Col. Hingston, Laird Humphries, 1950
Norway 1940, Bernard Ash, Cassell, 1964
The Norwegian Campaign, General J. Moulton, Eyre & Spottiswoode, 1966
Norway 1940, Francois Kersaudy, Wm. Collins, 1990
The Right of the Line, John Terraine, Wordsworth, 1985
HAB/11/117/4 The Campaign in Norway, Air Historical Branch, 117
The Royal Airforce 1939–45, Richard & Saunders, HMSO 1953

Chapter 19 Trondheim
Narvik, Captain Macintyre, Evans Bros London 1959
Happy Odyssey, Lieut. Gen. Sir A. Carton de Wiart VC, Jonathan Cape 1950
German Northern Theatre Ops 1940–45, E.F. Ziemke, US Army
King's Own Yorkshire Light Infantry, Lt. Col. Hingston, Laird & Humphries 1960
The Royal Lincolnshire Regt. History, ,
The Campaign in Norway, Professor K. Derry, HMSO 1952

Chapter 20 Evacuation of the Central Valley
The Campaign in Norway, T.K. Derry, HMSO 1952
Seven Assignments, Dudley Clarke, Jonathan Cape 1948
Norway 1940, Jo Kynoch, Air Life Publ. 2002
York and Lancaster Regiment, Major G. Sheffield, Gale & Polden 1956
The Green Howards, Capt. Synge, Richmond 1952
King's Own Yorkshire Light Infantry, Lt. Col. Hingston, Laird Humphries 1950
The Norwegian Campaign in 1940, Gen. J.L. Moulton, Eyre & Spottiswoode 1966

Chapter 21 "Impossible, the Navy do not know the meaning of the word."
Narvik, Captain Macintyre, Evans Bros London 1959
The War at Sea Vol.1, Captain S. Roskill, HMSO 1954
The Campaign in Norway, T.K. Derry, HMSO 1952
Happy Odyssey, Lt. General Sir Adrian Carton de Wiart VC, Jonathan Cape 1950
Fra Krigen; Nord Trondelag, Col. Otto B. Getz, Aschehoug Oslo 1940

Chapter 22 The Norway Debate
The Fringes of Power, John Colville, 1939–55
Leo Amery Diaries 1929/45, Ed. J. Barnes, D Nicholson 1980
Harold Nicolson Diaries and Letters 1930–39, Ed. N Nicolson, 1966

The Art of the Possible, R.A. Butler, H Hamilton 1971
The Gathering Storm Vol. 1 2nd WW, W.S. Churchill, Houghton Miflin 1948
Sixty Minutes with Winston Churchill, W.H. Thompson,
House of Commons Debates, Hansard Vol. 360 col.1502, HMSO

Chapter 23 'Rough Winds do shake the Darling Buds of May'
Engage the Enemy More Closely, Correlli Barnett, Penguin Books Ltd
Oxford Companion to WWII, Ed. Dear & Ford , O H P 1995
The Holy Fox (Halifax), Andrew Roberts, Weidenfelt 1991
Why France Fell, Guy Chapman, Holt Rinehart and Winston 1968
The Last Great Frenchman, Charles Williams, John Wiley 1993
Five Days in London May 1940, John Lukacs, Yale 2001
2001 Encyclopaedia of WWII, Ed. John Keegan, Bison Books 1977
"And we shall shock them", D. Fraser, Cassel & Co London 1983
The Reckoning, A. Eden, London 1965

Chapter 24 The German Drive to the North
Campaign in Norway, T.K. Derry, HMSO 1982
The Irish Guards, Major D. Fitzgerald, Gale & Polden 1949
The Scots Guards 1919–1955, D. Erskine, Wm Clowes 1965
Norway 1940, Bernard Ash, Cassel & Co 1964
Norway Campaign 1940, General Molten, Eyre & Spottiswoode 1966

Chapter 25 Harstad
The Campaign in Norway, T.K. Derry, HMSO 1952
Norway 1940, F. Kersaudy, Wm. Collins 1987
Norway Campaign 1940, General Molten, Eyre & Spottiswoode 1966
Assault from the Sea, Rear Admiral Maund, Methuen
Campaign in Northern Norway, E. Ziemke, German Report Series US
   Army

Chapter 26 Bjerkvik to the Capture of Narvik
With the Foreign Legion at Narvik, P. Lapie, John Murray 1941
Cinq Années d'Experience, General A. Bethouart,
Assault from the Sea, Rear Admiral Maund, Methuen 1949
The Campaign in Norway, T.K. Derry, HMSO 1952
Campaign in Northern Norway, Col O. Munthe-Kaas, US Publications 1946
Norway Campaign 1940, General Molten, Eyre & Spottiswoode 1966
Campaign in Northern Norway, E. Ziemke, German Report Series US Army

Chapter 27 The Beginning of the End
The Campaign in Norway, T.K. Derry, HMSO 1952
Norway 1940, Francois Kersaudy, Wm Collins 1987
I was one of them, Z. Lityinski, Jonathan Cape
The Scots Guards, D. Erskine, Wm. Clowes 1965
The Irish Guards, Major D. Fitzgerald, Gale & Poland 1949
The South Wales Borderers, J. Adams, Leo Cooper 1968
Narvik, D. Macintyre, Evans Bros 1959

Chapter 28 Operation Juno
Narvik, D. Macintyre, Evans Bros 1959
The Campaign in Norway, T.K. Derry, HMSO 1952
Hitler's Naval War, C. Bekker, MacDonald
Carrier Glorious, John Winton, Leo Cooper 1986
Naval Ops for Campaign in Norway, D. Brown, Frank Cass 2000

Chapter 29 A Leader to Match a Leader
The Campaign in Norway, T.K. Derry, HMSO 1952
The German Occupation of Denmark and Norway 1940, Dr W. Hubatsch, Musterschmidt
    1952

Primary documents from National Archives - Kew

Cabinet War Office and Foreign Office Papers
WP (39) 162 German and Russian designs on Scandinavia
CAB 65 Vol. 2 paper 16 Abuse of Norwegian Waters
CAB 65 Vol. 2 paper III (39) Attitude of USA
CAB No. 120 (39) 20/12/39 War Cabinet conclusions and FO 371/23667
CAB 65/11 WM (40) Policy to stop export of Swedish ore
WP (39) 179 Chiefs of Staff conclude opportunity a great one
Fo 419/34 Telegram from King Haakon VII
WO/1858 Cabinet Papers Norwegian Op. Chiefs of Staff Committee
WO 106/204 Stratford
CAB 65/12 War Cabinet 14 March 1940

Supplements published by HMSO in *The London Gazette*

Operations in Central Norway 1940
Dispatches by Lieutenant General H.R.S. Massy 1940
Supplements No. 37584 29 May 1946
The First and Second Battles of Narvik
Dispatches by Rear Admiral R.H.C. Halifax and Vice Admiral W.J. Whitworth
    25 April 1946
Supplement to No. 38005 3 July 1947
Dispatches by Major General P.J. Mackesy 15 May 1940
The Norway Campaign 1940
Dispatches by Admiral of the Fleet the Earl of Cork and Orrery 17 July 1940
Dispatches by Lieutenant General C.J.E. Auchinleck 19 June 1940
Supplements to No. 38011 10 July 1947

Bibliography By Author

Armstrong G, *The Sparks Fly Upwards*
Amery L, *The Amery Diaries*
Auphon P, *La Marine Francaise*
Air Ministry, *Rise and Fall of German Air Force*
Ash B, *Norway 1940*
Adams J, *The Doomed Expedition*
Adams J, *The South Wales Borderers*

Brown D, *Naval Ops Norway 1940*

Butler J, *Grand Strategy*
Bekker C, *Hitler's Naval War*
Barnett C, *Engage the Enemy more Closely*
Broch T, *The Mountains Wait*
Barclay C, *History of Sherwood Foresters*
Butler R, *The Art of the Possible*
Bethouart A, *Cinq Annees d'Experience*

Colville J, *The Downing Street Diaries*
Churchill W, *The Gathering Storm*
Curtis M, *Norway War Documents*
Carton de Wiart A, *Happy Odyssey*
Clarke D, *Seven Assignments*
Chapman G, *Why France Fell*

Dilks D, *Diaries of Sir Alex Cadogan*
Derry T K, *The Campaign in Norway*
Doenitz Adml. K, *Memoirs*

Elting J, *Battles for Scandinavia*
Eden A, *The Reckoning*
Erskine D, *The Scots Guards 1919/55*
Fieling K, *Life of Chamberlain*
Fraser D, *And we shall shock them*
Fitzgerald, *Irish Guards Rgt History*

Gilbert M, *W S Churchill*
Getz O, *Fre Krigen I Nord Trondelag*

Hansard, *House of Commons Debate*
Hinsley, *British Intelligence*
Hambro C, *I saw it happen in Norway*
Hingston, *KOYLI Regt. History*
Haarr G, *German Invasion of Norway*
Hubatsch W, *Problems of Norwegian Campaign*
Hauge A, *Valdres 1940*

Insight Guides, Denmark, Norway, Sweden, Finland
Ironside W, *Ironside Diaries*

Jensen J, *Krigen paa Hedmark*
Janes, *Fighting Ships*

Kennedy J, *The Business of War*
Kersaudy F, *Norway 1940*
Koht H, *Norway Neutral & Invaded*
Keegan J, *Encyclopaedia of WWII*
Kynoch J, *Norway 1940*

Lukacs J, *Five Days in London 1940*
Lapie Capt. P, *With the Foreign Legion in Narvik*
Lityanski, *I was one of them*

Mowat C L, *Britain Between the Wars*
Murphy D, *Britain 1895-1951*
MacMillan H, *The Blast of War*
Medlicott W, *Economic Blockade*
Moulton J, *The Norwegian Campaign*
Maund Admiral, *Assault from the Sea*
Munthe Kaas Col. V, *The Campaign in Northern Norway*
Macintyre Capt. D , *Narvik*

Nicolson H, *Diaries and Letters*

Quisling V, *Russland og vi*

Rauschning H, *Hitler m'a dit*
Roskill Captain S, *The War at Sea*
Ruge O, *Field Diary*
Roberts A, *The Holy Fox*
Richards & Saunders, *The Royal Air Force 1989/45*
Rhys-Jones G, *Churchill and the Norway Campaign*

Salmon P, *Britain and Norway*
Scheidt, *H Scheidt to Admiral Boehm*
Sheffield V, *York and Lancaster Regt.*
Synge W, *The Green Howards 1939/45*

Terraine J, *The Right of the Line*
Thompson W, *Sixty Minutes with W Churchill*

Underhill W, *The Royal Leicestershire Regt.*

Woodward L, *British Foreign Policy*
Wegener W, *Sea Strategy of World War*
Waage J, *The Narvik Campaign*
Williams C, *The Last Great Frenchman*
Winton J, *The Carrier Glorious*

Ziemke E, *The German Northern Theatre of Ops*
Zbyszewski K, *The Fight for Narvik*

Index

240

Poseidon, submarine, 77
Pound, Adml Sir Dudley, 10, 12, 32, 211, 222
Price, Petty Officer, 65
Prien, Lt Günther, 75–6
Primrose, Operation, 82
Profumo, John, 151
Prunella, Q-ship, 197
Prytz, Bjorn, 31
Puffers, 165, 168, 171, 177, 191, 195, 224
Punjabi, destroyer, 66

Quisling, Vidkun, 38–9, 52, 91, 208

R17 and R21 minesweepers, 50
R4 operation, 36, 82–3
Raeder, Grand Adml E., 37–9, 43, 74, 197, 203, 209, 212
Ramsden, Capt, 111
Rana river, 126, 167
Randsfjord, 96–7, 99, 161
Rauenfels, supply ship, 63
Rauschning, Hermann, 38
Raven, Sir Geoffrey, 192
Ravenhill, Cmdr, 127
Rawalpindi, armed merchantman, 12
Rawson, Lieut, 124
Rena, 97, 99, 113
Renown, battle-cruiser, 36, 44, 47, 198, 202
Repulse, battle-cruiser, 45, 47, 69, 198, 202
Resolution, battleship, 183, 205
Ribbentrop, Joachim von, 8, 19, 91
Rieve, Capt, 53
Roa, 99
Roberts, Maj, 104
Robinson, Lt Col, 123
Rognan, 168–71, 191
Rommel, Gen Erwin, 156, 168, 210
Roosevelt, Franklin D., 4, 14
Roros, 113
Rosenberg, Alfred, 38, 91
Rosti Gorge, 139
Rosvik, 191–3
Rosyth, 36, 39, 45, 88
Rovaniemi, 22
Rowan, Sgt, 119
Rowlinson, Sgt, 106
Royal Artillery, 174, 180, 185–6
Royal Leicestershire Regt, 100–101
Royal Marine, Operation, 36
Royal Oak, battleship, 11, 74–5
Ruge, Gen Otto, xiv, xvii, 90, 97–8, 100, 103–104, 119, 138–9, 143, 148, 194, 209–10
Rundfjell, 193–4
Rundstedt, Gen von, 154, 156, 159
Rupert, Operation, 82–3, 86–7

Ryan, Private, 122

Saalwachter, Adml, 197
Salangenfjord, 173
Saltdalfjord, 168–9, 171, 191–2
Salter, Lt Col, 85
Saltern River, 169
Saumur, transport ship, 146
Scapa Flow, 11, 43–4, 69, 72–3, 75, 86, 115, 146, 196–8, 200, 202, 205, 222
Scharnhorst, battleship, 12, 43, 47–8, 59–60, 72, 197, 199–203, 207, 222
Schillig Roads, 43
Schmund, Adml Hubert, 53
Scissorforce, Operation, 82, 87, 125, 163
Scotland, xviii, 68–9, 75, 140, 146, 161, 175, 202, 209, 218
Scots Guards, 83, 88, 164–70, 172–4, 182, 191–2, 205, 212
Seal, submarine, 80
Sealion, submarine, 80
Sheffield, cruiser, 121, 125, 142
Sherwood Foresters, 89, 100–101, 108–109, 140
Shurbeck, armed merchantman, 79–80
Sickle, Operation, 82
Sickleforce, 114
Siilasvuo, Col H., 22
Simon, Sir John, 1, 5–6, 9, 32, 149, 151, 215
Simpson, Lt Col, 103
Sinclair, Sir Archibald, 7, 34, 150, 153, 159
Skaanland, 164, 175, 180, 193, 227
Skaansund, 135
Skaw, 47
Skua, 69, 71, 139, 196, 203, 205, 227
Slaughter, Lt Cmdr, 77
Smith, F.E., 215
Snapper, submarine, 80
Sola airfield, 53, 67–8, 71
Somali, destroyer, 126
Sorkedal Ski Co., 98
South Wales Borderers, 83, 164–5, 175, 185, 191–2,
Southampton, cruiser, 70, 172–3, 195
Sparbu, 135–6
Spearfish, submarine, 78–9
Spiller, Capt, 90
St Magnus, troopship, 89
Stack, R.S.M., 164
Stammers, Surgeon Lt, 201
Stannard, Lieut Cmdr, 146
Stanning, G., 62
Stavanger, 30, 35–6, 39, 42–3, 47, 51, 53, 67–8, 71, 75, 77, 81, 84, 87–8, 95–6, 101, 125, 139, 204
Steffens, Maj Gen, 92, 96